BEING A TEACHER

BEING A TEACHER

A Positive Approach to Change and Stress

Guy Claxton

CASSELL

Cassell Educational Limited
Artillery House
Artillery Row
London SW1P 1RT

First published 1989

British Library Cataloguing in Publication Data
Claxton, Guy
  Being a teacher: a positive approach to change and
  stress.
  1. Teachers. Stress
  I. Title
  371.1'04

ISBN 0-304-31822-1 (hardback)
      0-304-31824-8 (paperback)

Typeset by Input Typesetting Ltd, London
Printed and bound in Great Britain by
Biddles Ltd, Guildford and King's Lynn

Contents

Acknowledgements		vi
1	On knowing where to tap	1
2	So what's it like, then, being a teacher?	16
3	Getting like that	42
4	Back into shape	72
5	From balance to personal power	91
6	Changing teaching	116
7	A change of climate: a climate of change	131
8	The articulate critic	154
9	Good learning	175
Appendix		203
Notes		207
Name index		211
Subject index		213

Acknowledgements

I would like to record my thanks to some of the people who have contributed to this book. Many of the PGCE workshops have been co-led with Sheila King Lassman and Renee Heatherington, two counsellors from whom I have learnt a lot, especially about listening to feelings. Terry Davis, Peter Mitchell and Michael Naish, successive PGCE Course Tutors at the Institute of Education, were kind enough to keep asking us back. Then there are the people who formed the 'core-group' of the Education Network: Terry Barker, Chris Base, Joe Burlington, Douglas Dunn, Peter Gray, Michelle Hochland, Paddy Mellor, Jacek Opienski, Jenny Paul, Barry Peters, Fiona Prain and Rashida Punja. Special thanks to Joe, for being wise, kind and clear, and to Chris, who by her example reminded me what base values were, and who reassured me that the vision of this book is realizable, not least through her delightful ability to find it . . . and lose it . . . and find it again. Thanks to the generations of students who talked to me and told me what they thought of my 'stories': especially Jackie Brown, Mike Foley, Jenny James, and Dirk Johns, but dozens of others too. And to the two people whose thoughtful comments on the first draft of the book have helped me to improve it no end: Mark Cohen and Judith Ryder. And lastly the Carrs, Malcolm (Director of the Science and Mathematics Education Research Centre, University of Waikato, New Zealand) especially, and Polly, Merophie and Margaret as well for their friendship and for making it possible for me to look up from writing this book and see, not London sleet, but the sun on the Tasman Sea.

Extracts from *The Challenge for the Comprehensive School* (Routledge & Kegan Paul, 1982) are cited by permission of David Hargreaves and International Thomson.

The extract from 'The end of schools as we know them' (*SET: Research Information for Teachers*, 1984, 1, pp. 6–11) is cited by permission of Professor Richard T. White.

The Appendix is adapted from *Stress in Teaching* (Croom Helm, 1984) by permission of Jack Dunham.

The cartoon on p. 77 is reproduced from *Wicked Willie's Guide to Women* (Pan, 1986) by permission of Gray Jolliffe.

To Chris and Joe, for their example

Lord, give me the courage to do those things that I can;
The serenity to accept those things I cannot;
And the wisdom to tell the difference.

Chapter 1

On knowing where to tap

Nobody made a greater mistake than he who did nothing because
he could only do a little.

Edmund Burke[1]

This book is about how to be a successful schoolteacher in a
time of uncertainty, change, increased pressures and conflicting
demands. The majority – I would conjecture the *vast* majority –
of teachers, particularly in secondary schools, are feeling overloaded, pushed around, confused, fed up and unappreciated. They
would like to be feeling more cheerful, enthusiastic and powerful,
but don't know how. I want to explore what room for manoeuvre
individual teachers have, in the middle of all the very real difficulties, for staying positive, and for dealing with the pressures in
the most effective way possible. I believe that this is absolutely
vital, not only for teachers' sanity, but also for the health of the
education system as a whole.

Of course there do exist many positive individuals, schools and
authorities. Perhaps the most obvious characteristic of the school
system at the moment is how different schools can be. Some of
these differences are in the structure and organization of the
school – differences that will persist despite the National Curriculum. But more striking (and more important) are the differences
in ethos and atmosphere. When teachers from different schools
get together and chat, they are often stunned by how different
the working lives of others – even those who work close by and
in similar schools – can be. Teachers who enjoy their work, feel
supported by colleagues and can speak frankly about their ideas
and difficulties in the staffroom and in meetings may find it hard
to believe (unless they have recently worked in such a school
themselves) the stories that other teachers tell about suspicion,

1

isolation and backbiting in the school down the road. While to the latter the former seem to be living either in paradise or cloud-cuckoo-land.

The question that this variability raises is whether the decline in morale is an *inevitable* consequence of the increase in pressure and uncertainty. The evidence suggests not. If this diversity in ethos cuts across any diversity in the objective conditions in which teachers find themselves, as it seems to, then there is reason to doubt the idea that decline in these conditions is the cause of teacher demoralization. It may be *harder* to keep seeing change as 'challenge' rather than 'threat' when the going gets tough, but whether you can or not may say more about the way difficulties are met and the emotional repercussions they generate than about their very existence.

There is a story about an old man who was called in by a factory to fix their ancient boiler, which had ground to a halt. He wandered around for fifteen minutes examining the piping, whistling quietly to himself, stopping occasionally to put his ear to a joint, and then pulled a hammer out of his tool-bag and tapped smartly on one particular valve. Slowly the boiler began to rattle and, sure enough, it lumbered into life. Two days later the company received a bill for £500. They thought that was a bit steep for a quarter of an hour's work and sent back the bill with a request to itemize it. Two days later, back it came itemized.

For tapping with hammer: 50p
For knowing where to tap: £499.50

For all those who think that we are still stuck with a form of schooling that is frustrating to teachers and that fails to deliver a satisfactory start in life to at least a sizeable proportion of its clientele, the question is: Where to tap? Legislation? Curriculum development? In-service training? Selection? Teacher training? Better management? Better salaries for teachers? Revised forms of assessment? They all have their proponents. But my guess is that the place to tap is the state of mind of teachers themselves. The success of any reform, whether to curriculum, teaching method, school organization or administration depends upon teachers being 'in-play', willing to participate in the search for a more powerful and enabling form of schooling, and to give proposed reforms (to quote the Americans) 'their best shot'. In sufficient numbers innovation-weary teachers can make any change a change for the worse if they implement it in a resentful, half-hearted or half-baked fashion, and under these conditions even the brightest and the best schemes are going to flop. The recent history of educational innovation, from Nuffield and mixed ability onwards, shows that unless change is generated and/or who-leheartedly appropriated by teachers it will end up on the mount-ing scrap-heap of 'good ideas that never quite took off'. And the cumulative effect on teachers – as we are seeing now – is to fill them with a sense of weary déjà vu when another good idea comes along, so that resistance to change becomes a reflex action, even when the teachers themselves, in their own quiet moments, know that some non-tinkering kind of change is needed, and, if they were in a different, less harassed, state, would likely welcome it.

In such a mood it is inevitable that the Government's attempts to bring about change through legislation and increased prescrip-tion will be generally felt to be yet another attack on autonomy and yet another indication of a lack of trust in teachers' judgement and their ability to do a good job. These signals from above, coupled with the day-to-day lack of respect that many experience in the classroom, combine to produce an atmosphere of personal stress and institutional cynicism that serves further to undermine teachers' confidence and competence. From a position of stress, change – *any* change – feels like more 'problem', not like possible 'solution'. It follows that a critical mass of teachers who see their job as not just delivering education but as re-creating it, in how-ever small a way, is the absolute pre-condition for change that is purposeful and cumulative.

It is my contention that entrenchment and cynicism both reflect and serve to heighten an atmosphere of demoralization; that they arise as a result of a semi-conscious decision by teachers about how to cope with doubts and demands; that while this stance often seems the only possible option it is a mistake to adopt it; and that through insight into the dynamics of the decision-making process, a better stance can be found, even in very trying circumstances, that offers a greater opportunity for personal satisfaction and institutional success. This, in a nutshell, is the argument of this book. In the present climate it is not just a matter of professional duty to stay engaged with the possibility of change: it makes better sense. And this applies *particularly* when the actual freedom for manoeuvre that a teacher has is limited. Let me repeat Edmund Burke's remark: 'Nobody made a greater mistake than he who did nothing because he could only do a little.' In this book I want to explain *why* this is such a big mistake, and *how* one can avoid making it, or rectify the situation if one has already opted out.

About three years ago I was running a workshop for students training to be secondary teachers at the Institute of Education in London, something I and colleagues have been doing annually for the last ten years or so. These so-called 'Less Stress Workshops' are designed to allow students who choose to do so to explore the coping strategies that they use to deal with the emotional issues that arise in school. For obvious reasons this workshop is usually scheduled for just before their second block of full-time teaching practice. (The first block has given them enough experience to pinpoint their anxieties more accurately, but not enough to overcome them.) This particular year, however, due to popular demand, we had to run a 'second sitting' during the summer term, after teaching practice had been completed. As usual, after some warm-up exercises, we got to the point in the workshop when we ask participants to help us create an agenda for the rest of the day by sharing the particular concerns that were on their minds.

We had come to know what to expect: worries about keeping control, not being liked, being judged and evaluated, feeling lonely in the staffroom, being caught between the conflicting advice of Institute and school tutors. But we wondered what we would get from the students at this later stage in their training year. All of them were now looking forward to starting their careers as 'real' teachers – but with a particular, and strong, shared anxiety. For more than thirty out of the forty students, the biggest fear was that they might, as one of them put it, 'end up like that'. They all knew without much discussion what 'like that' meant: cynical, bored, boring, burnt-out. They had all met teachers 'like that' on teaching practice: the ones who told them they needed their heads looking at for wanting to go into teaching, who were sarcastic to the pupils and disparaging about almost everything. We were surprised by the degree of unanimity in this concern, but also in a way by its maturity. For the worry that they themselves might go down the same road meant that they could see that teachers who were now 'like that' had once been enthusiastic, committed students like themselves. Whether it is true or not that good teachers are born, not made, they accurately perceived that bad teachers, at least in many cases, are made, not born. And they wanted to know how they could immunize themselves, so that they would not succumb in their turn.

One of the answers which this book suggests is that it pays to keep taking stock of how you are coping. Time spent reflecting on the predicament is time well spent. For example, in the workshop we asked the students to compile a list of the *benefits* of becoming 'like that'. It was easy. You don't have to think or worry so much. You don't have to update your lesson notes. You don't get so tired. You don't have to try out new, risky things in the classroom. You don't have to stick your neck out in meetings. You don't have to jeopardize your standing in the staffroom. Then we asked the students to sit quietly with their eyes closed and think about the *costs*. When they gave their replies there was a powerful feeling in the room. The costs they came up with included satisfaction (other than simply getting by without trouble); real communication with colleagues; idealism; and self-respect (can you really like yourself?). On reflection the students agreed that, however attractive the benefits might become, the costs would always be too high. The only problem was to keep remembering that.

There are two types of innovation that we shall look at. The first is change that individuals would *like* to see, whether in their own teaching or in the running of their school. To attempt such change you need an accurate sense of what opportunities and risks are involved. The second type of demand is that which originates elsewhere. There are two positive ways to respond to changes that are being pushed your way: to implement them whole-heartedly, and to resist them intelligently. Whatever type of change you are dealing with, you need your wits about you. You need to see the situation clearly, evaluate the pros and cons of possible courses of action accurately, and to behave firmly and astutely. But it is these very qualities of perception and judgement that are reduced by stress. In a stressed frame of mind, things look blacker, opportunities smaller, risks greater and burdens heavier, than they really are. As demands crowd in on you it becomes increasingly difficult to keep things in perspective. In Hemingway's famous expression, what teachers need at the present time is 'grace under pressure', and my intention is that the discussions in this book should be very practical aids to the development of this valuable commodity.

I need to state clearly what the book is *not*. First, it should be clear, from what I have said already, that Grace Under Pressure does not mean accepting the situation with 'good grace'. My message is not that teachers ought to quit complaining and make the best of a bad job. I am not going to give you a list of Reasons to Be Cheerful. I hope to show you that there are things you can do to improve your frame of mind; and that this is a necessary preliminary to engaging with change, whether by promoting, implementing or opposing it, in an intelligent and powerful way.

Second, the book is not primarily a *programme* for change. At the end I will lay out some rough ideas about the direction in which I, and a whole lot of other people, would like to see schools move; and some suggestions about how to get started. But my principal aim is to help to create a mood in which individual teachers are more keen to push for their own changes, and to become more effective in doing so.

Third, the book does not contain a compendium of specific advice about how to deal with the realities of classroom life. It is not about how to achieve better discipline, or make maths more interesting, or organize the filing cabinet in which you try to keep track of the GCSE coursework. There are many other books that offer that useful kind of advice and information, and I don't intend to duplicate it. Of course the attempt to overcome problems by changing the way you do things – by altering the curriculum, the timetabling, the provision for special educational needs, the conduct of meetings, the school rules – is sensible and vital. My aim is to start further 'up-stream' than that, by helping teachers who wish it, to get in a frame of mind where they can be *interested* in that kind of advice. Being 'moralized' (as opposed to demoralized) is a necessary condition for being ingenious, committed and enthusiastic.

And fourth, this is not going to be a close scrutiny of the current wave of educational issues and innovations. We will talk about the National Curriculum, appraisal, opting out and the 7, 11 and 14 tests, as well as GCSE, TVEI, Records of Achievement, Personal and Social Education and the rest. But I will do no more than offer a few remarks about their rights and wrongs, focusing instead on the most productive ways in which teachers can develop and promote their own positions. I believe that what is needed today is the creation of a climate in which teachers themselves feel interested and able to contribute, through their own practice as well as through discussion, to the crucial deep debate about where education should be going. The most damaging effect of the Education Reform Act would be if it snuffed out teachers' belief that it is worthwhile thinking and talking about what they are doing. Teachers do not have a monopoly on educational debate. They are not the only people who know what they are talking about when it comes to children and education. Everyone, even the much maligned administrators, politicians and academics, have a right to throw their views into this most important of melting-pots. But teachers (or most of them) clearly care about education because they have decided to earn their living at it. They know about it, not just in rhetoric but in reality, and they have the opportunity to get to know a wider range of young people than parents or any other professional group.

My own opinion is that the terms of reference of the public debate about education that have been established on the one hand by the political parties, and on the other by the teaching unions, are stupefyingly narrow. If teachers in substantial numbers are not going to be ready, willing and able to speak their minds, complete with all their doubts and uncertainties, who else is going to give the debate the greater depth and breadth that it so urgently needs? But more than that, as I have said already, a demoralized teaching force that feels disenfranchised from the process of educational change will be resistant to the changes that are thrown at them by outsiders. When teachers feel put upon and pushed around, hectored, lectured and badgered, their confidence and enthusiasm are undermined and their willingness and ability to contribute to the development of young people, as well as each other, suffers.

Who exactly is the book for? Clearly not all teachers are in a position to make significant contributions to national debate. Nor, for that matter, are they all able to make first-hand experiments with teaching style, some of them having been promoted out of contact with the pupils. But all teachers are concerned about their own level of stress, and how to lead a satisfying working life. And all of them are having to deal with innovation in some way or other. So I imagine the theme of the book will be of relevance to everyone in schools. And there will be specific discussions in later chapters concerning the different kinds of change that teachers are commonly involved with: change in classroom practice, change in school policy and change that is being imposed from outside the school. If however I had to single out one particular group of teachers to whom I hope the book will appeal, it is those who have been in the profession for about five to ten years. They are the ones who – as one such teacher put it to me – are over the hump but not over the hill. They have got the platform of competence and confidence to look beyond the day-to-day realities of school and classroom life and ask themselves hard questions about it. They can do it, and they are wondering why they *are* doing it. It is this group who will be the senior teachers, heads and inspectors at the beginning of the second millennium, and it will be they who will therefore have the opportunity, if they choose to take it, to play a crucial role in educational reform.

I hope, in addition, that the book will be of interest to people who are concerned with education, or about it: administrators, educationalists, journalists, politicians in local and central government, and of course parents. It might appeal to such people for two reasons. First, some of the analyses of the interrelation of stress, change and power, and some of the practical guidance, might be relevant to them personally, Second, they may be interested to get a more accurate and detailed view of the teachers' world than is commonly provided by the media and the various pundits, each with some axe or other to grind. Anyone who is interested in the human side of innovation, and who suspects that the management of change is a subtle business, about which there is always more to be learned, might find something useful here.

People who are concerned to preserve their own well-being, and also to strive to do a better job, need to look in two directions for help: they must look inwards, to gain insight into the dynamics of their own stress; and they must look outwards, to understand better the social forces that surround them. Self-awareness, as I am going to show, enables people to handle their emotions more skilfully. And social awareness enables them to create opportunities and neutralize opposition more skilfully. So we need both a psychological and a sociological perspective. The book starts with the personal, and then shifts as it progresses to more interpersonal and organizational perspectives. Chapter 2 reviews the predicament in which teachers currently find themselves, and gives a feel for their working lives.

In Chapter 3 we will lift up the stone, so to speak, and look at the private anxieties and insecurities that are triggered, for many teachers, by their situations. We shall see how stress arises as people attempt to cope with the undermining of self-confidence and self-esteem that ensues. Perfectly normal, kind, well-intentioned people will behave oddly, becoming upset, withdrawn or even vicious, if you put them in certain kinds of unusual situations. There is much research which shows how ordinary people are prone to behave 'out of character' when they are subjected to extreme conditions.[2] Being a teacher today constitutes for many just such an intense set of pressures, stresses, conflicts and uncertainties which often leads people to behave in ways which they do not like, but seem powerless to control. One of the most troublesome symptoms of 'stress' that teachers report, for example, is an increasing punitiveness towards both pupils, colleagues and family. They feel guilty about getting so ratty, can see that it only serves to make things worse by souring relationships, yet they are unable to stop themselves.[3] What I shall be arguing is that this is not simply because the kids are so difficult, nor because teachers are intrinsically powder-kegs of suppressed rage, but because the way most decent people view the world – their implicit personal philosophy if you like – breaks down when pushed to the limit and delivers misguided answers to difficult questions.

Chapter 4 gives a review of things which teachers can do, in the face of difficult circumstances, to preserve their equanimity, and to try to keep on good form. Chapter 5 focuses particularly on the thorny question of idealism. In the present climate it appears that for teachers to be thinking about their own educational ideals is at the very least a waste of time, and more than likely an additional source of upset. With such a mass of demands something has got to go, and it seems as if 'vision' is expendable. I shall argue that this reasonable conclusion is actually a big mistake, and that loss of vision makes things even worse.

However, it is also a big mistake to underestimate the strength of opposition that enthusiasm for, and participation in, change may encounter – and it is in Chapters 6 and 7 that we begin to turn our attention outwards to the social context. Many of the dynamics that attend times of doubt and change are collective ones: they are sociological rather than psychological. There are in staffrooms (as there are in every institution) tacit rules that define what is collectively thought of as normal, acceptable, odd or inept and which therefore influence the kind of reputation and influence an individual has. Those social pressures are real, and transgression or rejection of them will be accompanied by transient or even permanent loss of respect, status or goodwill.

But forewarned is forearmed, and we shall explore the power that is wielded especially by two important groups: the 'management' and the cynics. Let me say a preliminary word about each of these now. Senior staff are strong influences on the implicit staffroom rules. But they also possess much more obvious power. If 'higher authorities' are prohibiting the changes you want, or starving you of resources to carry them out, then life is made even more difficult and frustrating, and energy has to be put into challenging these constraints and/or finding ways round them. Being smart and persistent are vital qualities in pursuing change, because whatever you want, you can be sure that someone, usually someone higher up the tree, is going to be against it, and is going to try to force their solution on you instead. This is as true for headteachers as anyone else, by the way. It was, ironically enough, at a conference of headteachers about five years ago that I first heard this now familiar piece of Machiavellian wisdom quoted by an HMI.

> There is nothing more difficult to take in hand, more perilous to conduct, or more uncertain in its success, than to take the lead in the introduction of a new order of things. Because the innovator has for enemies all those who have done well under the old conditions . . . and lukewarm defenders in those who may do well under the new. This coolness arises in part from fear of the opponents, who have the laws on their side, and partly from the incredulity of men, who do not readily believe in new things until they have had a long experience of them.[4]

And what of the cynics? From their point of view talk of enthusiasm is merely symptomatic of naivety and talk of possibility and individual responsibility merely shows how out of touch with the harsh realities one is. (They will already have curled their lip at a book such as this and moved on.) They use their criticism not to refine plans for change but to block them. Cynicism achieves some of its power by masquerading as maturity. At a recent conference of educational psychologists in Scotland I was foolish enough (again) to be arguing for the practical importance of such grand-sounding notions as idealism and commitment. I quoted examples showing that significant changes in organizations can be catalysed by the presence of even a single individual who is willing to engage with the problem deeply, persistently and openly. And I instanced Bob Geldof as someone whose commitment to the problem of hunger had certainly got things done, and inspired millions of people to see (even if only transiently) that they could make a contribution to a problem that they had previously held in their minds, albeit not very consciously, as 'not mine' and 'hopeless'.

I was followed on the platform by a self-confessed cynic who poked clever fun at my talk and finished by saying '. . . and anyway, Bob Geldof is naff', as if the *only* relevant criterion for judging his contribution was one of personal taste and style. The speaker got his laugh. And it is the same attitude of world-weariness and sophistication that socializes each generation of students and new teachers into believing that their own blends of ill-formed idealism, intermittent enthusiasm and nagging doubt about the true value of what they are doing are merely the embarrassing stigmata of the beginner, to be covered up as much as possible, and grown out of as soon as possible. Chapter 7 gives some advice about creating a school climate within which it is the people who are bitter and negative who are on the back foot, and where ideas and adventures can prosper. It talks about the role of the headteacher, and how to mount effective campaigns for changes in school policy.

In fact I have not met a single teacher who does not want to be their best and do their best for young people, even though what this means in practice is very different for different teachers. I have come to suspect that the underlying motive to help younger people grow up to be confident, competent adults, and to derive pleasure from doing so, is something that a person can bury, ignore or conceal, but not amputate. And I think this is true of the cynics too. Caught off guard, in a mellow mood, away from the pressures that the stance has been developed to shield them from, they too will admit to being disappointed and confused, not as hard-bitten as they make out, and as having found only a very inadequate solution to what seems to be an insoluble problem: how to do a good enough job. Very few teachers are irredeemable, however hard-bitten they may appear.

One of the major pitfalls that people face if they are willingly embarking on change – in their teaching, for example – is their own unrealistic or inaccurate expectations. In Chapter 6 we shall look at what some of these common misapprehensions are, so that people can avoid creating unnecessary disappointment and frustration for themselves. Again insight is an invaluable accompaniment to effective action.

In the last two chapters, Chapters 8 and 9, we will finally come to the question of the *directions* in which teacher-supported change to schools might proceed. First, in Chapter 8, we will review the most fundamental misgivings that teachers, and many others, have about education. It emerges that one of the foci around which these criticisms gather is that schools do not reliably, nor for all pupils, inculcate the habits and attitudes of 'good learning'. What this means, and what schools would look like if they were *truly* dedicated to helping young people become good learners, is explored in Chapter 9. I am going to offer, more as a case-study than a prescription, my own thoughts about what education ought to be, and what kind of 'schooling' would be an appropriate channel for its delivery. The argument is simple and reflexive: if the body of this book has been about helping teachers to be more able to deal with uncertainty, conflict and change – in a word, to become better learners – then the tail asserts that the core of their job should be to help young people to become good learners in their turn. I believe this must be the heart of education, not just because every human being will have to cope with the unexpected, with disruption to routine and the loss of what is dear, but because it is singularly appropriate to the current generation of young people who find themselves growing up in a world that is characterized by instability. They are born under the ancient Chinese curse, 'May you live in an interesting time', a time in which values, lifestyles, relationships, employment are up for grabs, and in which traditional answers to the question 'How to live?' are weak and conflicting. In such a time anyone who lacks the courage to be curious and questioning, the capacity to grow into new competencies, and the confidence to communicate and collaborate with others, is severely handicapped, and his or her educators are guilty of gross dereliction of duty. (I am reminded of a passage in a book by Doris Lessing, where she says: 'I want this court to condemn Volyen utterly, root and branch, for failing to instruct its young in the rules that its own psychologists and anthropologists have extracted from research and study: for failing to arm its youth with information that would enable it – the youth – to resist being swept away with any system of ideas that happens to be available'.[5])

I dare to present this point of view because I believe it is not just my little pipe-dream. Whenever I talk to groups of teachers who are willing for a moment to lay aside the grim realities and talk and think big, I hear them saying exactly the same. They want young people to be empowered and enabled, confident and resourceful, articulate and sociable, with self-respect and self-esteem. My hope is that with the aid of a little psychology, I might be able (without becoming abstruse) to clarify what these fine ideals mean, and thus to contribute to the debate about how they might be best promoted. If you find such dreaming unacceptably romantic, just skip it. I have no illusions about the likelihood of its transforming schools in the next ten years. Nevertheless, I find it useful to play at imagining what kind of school system could provide a congenial conduit for my educational ideals. It helps to refine the vision, to keep me in touch with the eventual need to 'realize' any ideals, to sort the conceivable from the fantastic, and to have some interesting conversations.

I should perhaps say a little about how I came to think this way: that the key to educational change is in the stance that teachers individually and collectively adopt towards change. The argument does not rely on research in the conventional sense, certainly not my own and only occasionally other people's, which I shall mention in any case more to illustrate points than to prove them. Nor does it rely principally on my experience in classrooms, though I have been, briefly, a secondary schoolteacher and have been visiting schools and working with young people in a variety of ways on and off for the last sixteen years. My research, if I can call it that, has involved (over the same period) a cyclical process of listening to teachers, tidying up what I think I've heard into some more-or-less coherent story, and then telling it to other teachers to see if it makes sense to them, and captures in an interesting, plausible and fruitful way something significant of their experience. Their comments and suggestions are incorporated into the next version, and so the process goes on. To the extent that they are spontaneously enthusiastic about the story, can easily make it their own and see implications for their own practice, and ask me back, I reckon I have been successful.

I see this book as another stage in the process. If you are a teacher I do not ask you to believe or take on trust anything I say. The questions to ask yourself are: Does this ring any bells? Does it ring true? Is my school like that? Am I ever like that? Do I know any people who are like that? Is he talking about my life or not? And if he is, does he add anything to my understanding? Does it help me to make sense of the atmosphere in my school, or my own feelings? Especially: Can I see any possibilities that I could not see before? If you make it to the end of Chapter 7 and have registered a significant number of Yeses, I shall have done pretty well.

Most of the listening has been done in workshops of one sort or another. For more than a decade I have been running workshops for Postgraduate Certificate in Education (PGCE) students at the University of London, first at the Institute of Education and later at Chelsea College and King's College. Over the last five years I have moved into working with practising teachers and other members of the education service. These, mostly one-day, workshops have occasionally been with a whole school staff (primary, secondary and special schools) and more often with teachers of particular types – probationers, English teachers, science teachers, senior teachers in charge of probationers, deputies and heads on DES management courses, primary heads in one county and one LEA's entire Inspectorate.

In addition I have learnt an enormous amount from the monthly meetings of the Education Network in London, of which I was Coordinator from 1983 to 1987. This diverse group of teachers at all levels of education from primary to university was unusual in one particular way: all its members tried their best to be open. Time and again their commitment to doing a good job proved stronger than their commitment to looking good and it was out of this honesty that many of the insights (if such they be) in this book arose. It was also through the Education Network that I was able to develop and mount a freelance course called The

Education Workshop which has attracted teachers from throughout England, in numbers ranging from thirty to eighty, during the last three years. Experiences seem to be much the same in New Zealand and Australia, where teachers will be reaching the same point of uncertainty that we have reached in England in, I estimate, about ten and five years respectively.

Much of the talking and checking-out has been achieved through seminars and lectures, principally at the Chelsea College Centre for Science and Mathematics Education and its more multifaceted successor, the King's College London Centre for Educational Studies.

This chapter has been a 'trailer' for the rest of the book, introducing the general point of view and some of the key ideas, and indicating the scope and priorities. I have also disclosed my intention for the effect that the book will have. I want it to be teacher-friendly enough so that something of their own experience will be reflected accurately to them. This does not mean that I am not going to suggest some home truths: only that I think they *are* truths, and not another uncomprehending outsider's attempt to cajole, belittle or malign people who are struggling to do their best in a complex and stressful situation, and who know better than anyone else that their best sometimes isn't very good. And then, if I have achieved the aim of helping teachers understand their predicament, I hope that they may *feel* more purposeful, both individually and collectively, and thereby *become* a more powerful source of ideas and projects for the improvement of schooling, which are grounded simultaneously in a clear sense of educational values and an equally clear-sighted, hard-headed sense of what is possible and appropriate. The short-sighted, narrow-minded Education Reform Act should not be seen as ringing the death-knell of teacher reflection and autonomy, but rather as signalling its increasing urgency.

Chapter 2

So what's it like, then, being a teacher?

> .... neglect of the occupational culture of teachers. . . . has led us
> to underestimate the significance of the teachers' culture as a medium
> through which many innovations and reforms must pass; yet in that
> passage they frequently become shaped, transformed or resisted in
> ways that were unintended and unanticipated.
>
> David Hargreaves[1]

We need to start with the question: what is it like being a school-teacher today? If we can get a clear idea about the situation in which teachers find themselves at present, and how they experience it, then we shall be in a better position to see what the most productive way forward is. I shall base my account largely on what secondary schoolteachers have to say, though I have found that the picture is easily recognizable, with some modification to the details, by those working in both primary and further and higher education as well. Indeed I have found that the emotional heart of the matter makes equal sense to school pupils, nurses, people in business, and to other professional groups.

Of course not all teachers will recognize themselves, and probably no one person's experience will match point for point with the sketch that I shall give. I shall describe what seems to be common, though in the knowledge that any picture of such a complex and varied profession must necessarily be somewhat of a caricature. If the description seems an overly gloomy one, it is perhaps because teachers themselves often tend to focus on aspects of the job that they would wish to minimize or remove. In fact it is a characteristic of teachers that their spirits vary quite markedly. They have good days and bad days: days when things seem relatively easy, they are on the ball, and a lot gets done, and days when they just can't face it and phone in sick – only to feel much perkier half-an-hour after putting down the phone, and a little guilty that 'I could have gone in if I'd really had to'. Resilience is highest at the beginning of the new school year and hits rock bottom in February. A good lesson or a little break-through with an awkward pupil can light up the rest of the day, while an unresolved clash with a colleague during morning break can equally knock the stuffing out of you. And the available reservoirs of good sense and good humour vary too with the class to be taught, and the short-term or long-term history the teacher has had with it. When teachers are 'at their best' or 'on good form' they not only *feel* better but *are* better teachers and better colleagues: more straightforward, trustworthy, capable and with greater equanimity. Thus the question, to sharpen up the one we posed in the first chapter, is not: 'How can I stop myself getting "like that"?', as if 'like that' were a chronic condition into which one slowly but permanently sank. Rather it should be: 'How can I help myself to be as little "like that" as much of the time as possible?'

This chapter is divided into three sections. First we need to review the national predicament in which teachers find them-selves. Although the main emphasis of the book is, as I have said, on the process of coping, rather than on the content of what needs to be coped with, nonetheless the discussion will look somewhat abstract if we do not place it within the context of the Education Reform Act and the other present or imminent changes that are around. Second I shall venture to sketch a picture of how teachers are feeling. And third, because this picture will necessarily have to be very general, I shall consider some particular groups of teachers, and the way things look to them.

THE SITUATION

Teaching has always been a demanding and shifting job. Periods of relative stability have alternated regularly with periods of change – and quite rightly, for the business of equipping young people for successful adult life must track the changing demands that adults face. In addition education is as subject as anything else to changes in intellectual or political fashion. But at the present time the pressures seem to be particularly intense. The rate of change is very fast. New skills and awarenesses – of assessment, management, counselling, computing, pedagogy and the rest – are being defined and promulgated at high speed. At the same time teachers are being treated more and more like workers and less and less like professionals, so that their sense of power and freedom to evaluate and select among these opportunities feels diminished. Most of the legislative changes over the last twenty years, for example, have had the effect of increasingly making teachers the implementors of a job description that has been concocted elsewhere. The recently created Conditions of Service, and the enforcement of compulsory redeployment in some parts of the country, let alone the National Curriculum, illustrate this trend.

Even if teachers were given the time and opportunity to develop their professional lives in the ways they felt most suitable, the questions and dilemmas that face them are so many and so deep that it is indeed a daunting task. Within each teacher's subject area there are competing approaches that conflict in educational philosophy as well as in teaching style. Each approach seems to have its merits, yet to be irreconcilable with others. Within science, mathematics, languages and every other subject the 'experts' disagree about what we are trying to achieve and how best to achieve it; so how can we harassed classroom teachers hope to sort it out? We want people to be able to follow their own interests – but the syllabus doesn't allow us enough time. We still have doubts about the effects of GCSE – but if we didn't teach for it we would be handicapping unforgivably the pupils in our charge. We don't like the orthodox approach – but what right do we have to try out our home-grown experiments on other people's children?

We cannot tell in advance in what directions a specific lesson or block of work might lead – but we have to act as if we can. We like mixed-ability teaching in principle – but it's such hard work (if you're not going to cop out and use worksheets all the time) that we find ourselves longing for the good old days of streaming. We hate the constant struggle to keep order – but the alternative is worse. We have to persuade the pupils that what they are doing is worthwhile – even when we doubt it ourselves. We want to settle in one school for a good period of time, because we have discovered how important are relationships, with both colleagues and classes, that have been built up and stood the test of time. Yet we hanker after wider experience and a fresh start.

And perhaps most fundamental of all, we have to try to live and teach according to our ideals, and to promote them, whilst at the same time trying to make a good career within a system that seems at many points to be based on quite antagonistic values.

The problem is compounded by the lack of clear consensus about the purpose or even the nature of education. Back in the bad old days of the 'tripartite system' and the 11-plus, when it was more acceptable to know your place, and upward mobility was not such an unquestionably good idea, life was easier and less personal for teachers because to a much greater extent their values were stably enshrined in the organization and structures of the schools for which they worked. To the extent that these values *were* questioned, by young people, their parents, or society at large, teachers could see themselves as representatives or custodians of what was in effect 'company policy'. They were not themselves in the dock. Today the questioning from all sides is much fiercer, whilst company policy has got thinner and more nebulous, retreating into the traditional notions of 'standards' and 'testing', technocratic concern with 'vocationalism', or humanistic waffle about 'fostering the development of the whole person'. The combined effect is to leave individual teachers feeling more accountable, but more confused and less supported. Even to the now routine enquiries from pupils about 'What's the point?' most teachers I know feel both that they ought to have a good answer, and that they all too frequently don't. 'Because it's on the syllabus' may keep the kids quiet, but it no longer satisfies the teachers. For them the twin notions of 'education' and 'schooling', which are still locked together in everyday parlance, are beginning to tear apart, and there is an uncomfortable sense that the latter may no longer be the best vehicle for the delivery of the former. Thus the pressure, both inner and outer, on teachers to have a clear, articulate rationale for what they are doing is high at the same time as the exploration of the values from which such a rationale must derive is conspicuously out of style.

So what *are* some of the particular issues and demands that teachers today are facing? First and foremost there are all the uncertainties of the Education Reform Act. Exactly how, and how much, the new legislation in England and Wales will cramp teachers' style remains to be seen. Certainly the intention of the Education Reform Act is to increase uniformity, particularly in secondary schools, by reducing the scope that teachers have to decide what they shall teach. The syllabuses for GCE and CSE always prescribed quite clearly what was to be taught to pupils from the age of fourteen upwards. Even when there was freedom to choose between various options, set books and so on, the menu itself was not open to negotiation, except in the special case of 'Mode 3', or through the protracted process of making representations to the Examination Boards. Now we have GCSE, which devolves somewhat the choice of topics and the manner and timing of assessment to individual schools, and shifts the balance of that assessment from the retention of content to the mastery of certain identifiable skills – though in practice how extensive a shift this has been remains open to question.

Teachers are still testing out what the change to GCSE means in practice. but testing at 7, 11 and 14, together with the National Curriculum, seems to many teachers to be taking a significant step in the wrong direction, imposing on younger and younger children a model of education about which they, the teachers, have increasing misgivings. It seems to inhibit the attention that can be paid to the needs and natures of different young people living in different communities. It reinforces the ascendancy that the traditional academic subjects have, in both time and status, over the expressive arts and crafts, physical skill, and the concern with personal well-being that is shared between personal and social, religious and health education. The clock has been turned back, a tide of educational change stemmed, and it is hard for many teachers not to feel despondent. And while one would like to think that opting out might allow schools greater freedom to develop their own distinctive philosophy, it seems probable that the vetting of proposals for opting-out will allow only those schools that are choosing to be more, not less, traditional, to do so.

Nevertheless, all hangs on how those educational reforms are actually implemented: how tightly the National Curriculum is specified, what exactly the 7, 11 and 14 tests are going to look like, the way opting-out proposals are evaluated and precisely how opted-out schools are to be financed, and what their relationship to central Government and local authorities is to be. The most pessimistic view is that the process of 'deprofessionalization' of teachers will become almost complete, leaving them with virtually no autonomy, no scope for exercising their judgement and expressing their interests through their teaching. Their status will be reduced to that of assembly-line workers, required to bolt their prescribed parts on to the pupils that pass before them on the conveyor belt.

There is an alternative, more optimistic view that some people in education are expressing, which sees the current changes as somewhere between an irrelevance and a minor irritation in terms of their own aims and practices. The learning that can be prescribed, they say, can only at the most be a framework within which a vast amount of day-to-day scope for creativity and choice must remain. Peter Mann, principal educational adviser to Dorset County Council, is clearly one of the optimists. *The Times* for 24 September 1988 quotes him as saying that the Education Reform Act, far from signalling a return to traditional teaching, offers plenty of opportunities for continuing experimentation. He claimed that under the National Curriculum there would be sufficient flexibility, for example, for schools to merge the teaching of traditional subjects, or to abolish classes based primarily on age. Schools which were not thinking in such adventurous terms should easily be able to avoid 'a narrow and unproductive concentration' on the three core subjects of English, maths and science. Other people are hoping that the standards that can be set for the 7, 11 and 14 tests must necessarily be so low that they need hardly be attended to. For the optimists, anything that can be insisted upon will be so basic that it will almost inevitably be mastered incidentally, while the class is actually engaged in pursuits that are far more demanding, interesting, varied and relevant.

Depending on the procedural details, as they emerge, I suspect of course that the truth for most teachers will be somewhere between these two extremes. The tests may indeed produce something of a learning-for-the-test mentality, and the extent to which the tests pose a problem will depend a lot on the kinds of pupils: how well the values implicit in the school ethos match and are supported by those of their home, and how far advanced is *their* disaffection with school. But much will hang also on the extent to which teachers succumb to the temptation to *teach* for the test, and thereby create a classroom atmosphere that focuses narrowly on learning the content and the skills that will be tested, and is therefore less lively, less varied, more repetitive and more anxiety-provoking for the pupils.

I can remember once being told by a karate teacher that the trick of breaking planks of wood with the edge of your hand was to aim your blow not at the planks but about six inches below them. You hit through them, not at them. I never got good enough (or brave enough) to test her advice out, but, being by inclination an optimist, I would like to think that something of the same logic would apply to the National Curriculum and its tests. The extent to which they are felt to be a big deal for the pupils will mirror the extent to which they are felt to be a big deal by their teachers. Just because 'levering up standards' appears to be the be-all and end-all of the government's educational philosophy there is no reason why teachers, in their daily interactions with pupils should fall for the poverty and rigidity of this tunnel vision. There are not going to be agents of the DES disguised as pupils planted in every classroom, and teachers, renowned for their creativity, can exercise some of it on discovering creative interpretations of the law. It is after all axiomatic of legislation that the more tightly you try to define and prescribe, the more points of ambiguity, the more potential loopholes you bring into being. Provided the pupils are passing the tests, who is going to care, or even know, what else teachers are getting up to?

For headteachers there are opportunities, but also considerable anxieties, involved in taking on greater financial control of the school budget, and these are bound to radiate throughout the school. Likewise the increased accountability of heads to governors, created by the 1986 Education Act and expanded again in the Reform Act, means not only extra work but extra tensions both for the heads themselves and for their staffs. To have a clear philosophy, and a staff who back it, is not enough: it has to be sold to representatives of the community who have considerable power to make life difficult if they are not convinced. The operation of Market Forces in a time of falling roles, coupled with the possibility of opting-out, and competition from, for example, the City Technology Colleges (if they finally take off) means that schools may face hard choices between promoting a philosophy to which they are committed, and pulling in the punters.

Relations with the LEAs are also a fruitful source of tensions and confusions at the moment. Some LEAs are in the process of major reorganization themselves, so that heads can be on the receiving end of a stream of directives and initiatives that contradict and countermand each other quicker than they can be assimilated. While the Government's campaign to depower, or prescribe the activities of, the LEAs also creates friction in their relationships with individual schools. What, for example, will be the exact financial status of opted-out schools with respect to the LEA? We are told that such schools will be given funds with which to buy back LEA services – if they choose. But will LEAs be able to refuse to be used in this support role? And will we see a booming demand for private-practice educational psychologists and the like? On the level of fact rather than speculation, many schools have experienced or are experiencing the stresses of amalgamations of various sorts, both whole school and for instance in the creation of sixth form consortia. Staff have to go through the undignified and anxiety-provoking process of applying for their own jobs. And schools are required to co-operate with each other in some respects, whilst below the surface competing like mad for pupils.

Within the school, demands arise from a number of sources. In a number of schools there remain underlying – and sometimes still overt – conflicts that were provoked by the Teachers' Action of 1986–7. Resentments may persist between members of staff who belonged to different unions, and in particular the goodwill between headteacher and staff seems in some places to have been almost irreparably damaged. The question of covering the lessons for absent colleagues, for instance, remains in some staffrooms a contentious one. This relationship has also been inevitably altered by the introduction of the Conditions of Service, which require heads to play, whether they like it or not, a much more managerial role, and by the impending introduction of teacher appraisal. These issues will create more or less tension depending on the attitude and skill of the head, and on the existing ethos of the staff. But some degree of uncertainty must ensue.

In addition to the changes in teaching required by the introduction of GCSE there are many other changes in the air that impinge directly on the working lives of all teachers. There are those that relate directly to particular teaching subjects – new teaching packages and teaching methods in history or French or integrated science. Not to mention the ingenuity required to teach chemistry without chemicals, CDT without steel sheet and French without tapes when the consumables budget runs out half-way through the year. More problematic for the school as a whole are those initiatives that are designed to be cross-curricular and pervasive: language across the curriculum, maths across the curriculum, computing across the curriculum. And more broadly still, dealing with pupils with 'special educational needs' in the ordinary classroom; doing one's best to combat racism and sexism in pupils' attitudes; taking account of personal and social education in one's teaching style; paying attention to the deliberate coaching of study skills; providing worthwhile vocational courses for the greatly increased cohort of non-academic pupils who stay on at school beyond the age of sixteen. It requires considerable commitment by already hard-pressed teachers, and considerable organizational skill by the management team, to ensure that such issues are truly taken on board, and do not somehow fall down the cracks between more clearly defined and familiar roles.

There are the demands created by GCSE and by other actual or projected changes in the area of assessment. It takes a lot of time, space and organization to keep track of pupils' GCSE coursework. And more extensive forms of record-keeping are required in order to build up fashionable supplements to GCSE such as profiles, and records or certificates of achievement. Not only are these changes demanding to implement, they are sources of doubt and concern in teachers' minds. However well intentioned, are records of achievement such a good idea? Should we really be making judgements about pupils' ability to relate to each other, and to adults, or even about their skill on the telephone? Can we honestly assume that the way they are in school will be the way they relate to an employer, or to younger children in an adventure playground? We shall return to the issue of assessment in Chapter 8.

Finally in this short resumé of the teachers' predicament, we should mention the more personal factors to which we shall return later in the book: their aspirations, ambitions, values and concerns. Teachers have family pressures, young children of their own to cope with – about whose education they worry at least as much as other parents. They have financial problems, like many people – and more than most if they are trying to bring up a family in London without 'private means'. They are attempting to chart a career path through the foggy waters of appraisal, Special Responsibilities and the radically changed scenario of personal and school-based staff development. And so on.

WHAT WOULD TEACHERS LIKE?

Leaving aside for the moment the nature of teachers' particular educational philosophy, I now wish to move from describing the predicament from the outside, so to speak, to looking at it through the eyes and feelings of teachers themselves. The first important facet of this inside story is teachers' own view of what they would wish the job to be like. Understandably they have high hopes. They want to be *effective* in helping children to learn and develop, and they want to be able to feel *pleasure* in doing so, and *pleased with themselves* (though often they find this a not-quite-nice thing to admit to) for having done a good job. They don't want to be praised and stroked for every little thing, but they do want their work to be noticed and *acknowledged* every so often – and not just when they screwed something up or forgot it. They know the job is challenging and from time to time frustrating: they probably wouldn't have it any other way. But they want the ratio of *satisfaction* to frustration to balance out in their favour. They want most of the time to feel *confident* about what they are tackling, even if they make a few mistakes, and basically *optimistic* about their own future and the future of education.

They want to be *relaxed* and *businesslike* in the classroom and above all for the pupils to be willingly engaged in the process of *learning*. They love it when the pupils spontaneously show affection or appreciation. They would like to be able to be *caring* within limits, and without the fear that they might get overwhelmed or taken for a ride. They want to feel that they are making a *reasonable living*, though they wouldn't be teachers if they wanted to be rich. They want to feel *responsible* so that they are given jobs to do by seniors that are appropriate to their status and skills – and trusted to get on with them. But they also want to feel that they can ask for *support* or advice if they need it without feeling that they are being judged badly for doing so. They want to be *consulted* and their views listened to in meetings even if the decision doesn't go their way. When that happens they will tend to implement the decision without rancour or subversion. They want an atmosphere of *goodwill* amongst colleagues and to have harmonious working relationships even with people with whom they disagree. They want to be able to discuss and collaborate, and to feel part of a team. In both classroom and staffroom they want to be *authentic* and *energetic*: to be able to display their enthusiasm and true beliefs without being disparaged. They want scope for their own professional *development* and personal growth.

Some of these hopes are illustrated in this letter, which was written by an English teacher in one of the Education Workshops. Participants were asked to write a letter to themselves as if from an imaginary – or real – ex-pupil, expressing their appreciation for the contribution that they, the teachers, had made to the pupil's life. Participants were asked to write the letter so that, if they had really received it, they would have been delighted at how many of their own aspirations as a teacher had been fulfilled – at least for this one pupil. Peter's letter went:

Dear Mr White,
   I don't know if you remember me, but I was in your English class many years ago. I have thought from time to time that I would like to write and let you know how much those lessons meant to me – and now I am! I found your lessons lively and humorous. I was aware of your love of language and literature and the involvement which you obviously felt was contagious, and came over to me as being very real. You aroused an interest for me in literature which has been a resource to me for the rest of my life and a source of real enjoyment. I feel that, apart from this, you showed an interest in me and my development which enabled me to grow both in the exercise of my talents and in the confidence that I had such talents. This whole process gave my life an additional fullness which has gone on gathering momentum since I left school. I don't think I would have gone on with my own writing if you hadn't shown such interest and liking for my work (which I must admit I was a bit suspicious of at first!).
   I liked the way you did not conceal your feelings but revealed yourself to us as a real and vulnerable person who had feelings you were not ashamed to share with us. This openness was a terrific lesson to me, and something I have emulated (often with electrifying effect!) on those around me. You encouraged me to think for myself – not just to absorb your opinions but to consider those of others and develop my own. This on reflection is what I think education is all about: not the mere acquisition of knowledge and passing of exams – though I thank you for your help in that area too – but the ability to stand on my own two feet intellectually.

With best wishes
Sylvester Alleyne

It is an interesting reflection of the diversity of views and values in school that one of the readers of the first draft of this book commented on this letter: 'How sentimental! This will confirm all maths teachers' worst fears about English teachers!' If it strikes *you* this way, let me remind you that Peter's particular values are not the point at issue, and invite you to sit down quietly and compose your own, very different equivalent. What I am trying to illustrate is the fact that teachers will mostly admit, if they are feeling bold enough, that they want to feel that they are doing something important, that other people think so too, that a fair bit of the time they are doing it well, and that they are getting better at it.

WHAT'S THE REALITY?

The reality is now, as it has always been, that teaching is a demanding, and at times frustrating profession. What is new is the intensity of demand and the degree of frustration. As we review the way teachers are feeling about their job at the present time, many of the experiences will be common enough. But it is their cumulative weight that has brought about an unprecedented, and critical, situation.

Glimmers

The reality is that teachers *do* feel good about what they are doing, but that the occasions on which they do so are often conspicuous more by their rarity than their regularity. In a taped interview with Jill Jones, Head of Science in a comprehensive, which I shall quote from several times, I asked her, after she had been talking for a while about the frustrations, what made it all worthwhile. She replied:

> A couple of things. When a kid really learns something. It may not be very much but for him or her it's a remarkable achievement. And when they are really involved in finding things out – even though

they aren't doing it right, or getting the right answer. And when I've done a good lesson – whatever that means – when it's gone down well. Something just happens . . . it's not very often . . . once in every three weeks about. . . . At times like that I feel I'm doing a good job. I feel happy, I suppose. It's worthwhile after all!

What keeps most teachers going are these intermittent flashes of light, which they often hoard, like interesting shells found on a beach, and can proudly display if asked. This is the complement of many people's memories of being in school as a pupil: one or two teachers, and a handful of 'high spots', stand out against a background that was, for many, at best unmemorable and at worst something to be deliberately forgotten.

Hard work

Teachers work very hard, most of them. Their working day is a succession of lessons for which they have either prepared something interesting, dug out last year's notes, decided to just do the next bit in 'the book', or are unprepared. Whatever their state of readiness and interest, each lesson is a constant stream of decision-making, and of matters of judgement, both large and small, about situations that are unprecedented, and for which there is insufficient time and usually not enough available information to be sure of getting it right. Shall I let Robert go to the toilet this time? What am I going to do with Balwinder, who has finished already? Have I got time to fit this next chunk in before the bell? Should I try to split Mark and Kevin up and risk the confrontation that might result? How can I carry on when the bulb in the overhead projector has blown? And so on and so on. However well prepared teachers are, their lives are ones of constantly living on their wits. And in between the lessons, and before and after school, in discussions with colleagues and with pupils, the content may change, but the endless round of what the psychologists call 'decision-making under uncertainty' is likely at any moment to disrupt the cup of coffee and the quick look at the newspaper. Teachers have constantly to buttonhole each other as they pass in the staffroom and tack extra things to do on to the bottom of each other's already overlong agendas. 'You won't forget to let me have that note about Artemis Kostika, will you?' 'Did you know there is an extra Language Group meeting tomorrow?' 'Has anyone heard anything about Tracey Griffiths?'

Rush

Teachers do not have enough time to do the job that they feel they ought to do and want to do. There is not enough time to meet even short-term demands for preparation, marking, report-writing, sorting out pupils' disputes and clearing up heat-of-the-moment misunderstandings with colleagues, let alone to invest in the longer-term necessities of clearing the backlog of paperwork, replying to letters, ordering supplies, planning schemes of work, reorganizing last year's course, thinking about what your tutor group can contribute to the fourth year assembly, setting up a meeting with the educational psychologist about Jessica, and spending some time with the word processor manual. Miraculously much of this *does* get done, but there are few teachers, if any, who can walk out the gates at four o'clock, knowing they are up-to-date,

Stopgaps

When there isn't enough time to do what must be done, you find yourself papering over the cracks and making stopgap decisions. Issues that should take at least an hour of discussion with colleagues, as well as with the pupil concerned, have to be dealt with in two minutes at the staffroom door during break. You were late getting in your order for the film (though you swear the office forgot to send it on) so on the appointed day, when it isn't there, you have to cobble something else together – and then show the film, when it arrives four weeks later, in the middle of a block of work to which it does not relate.

Priority decisions

As well as making quick botch jobs of things that need careful repair if they are not to fall apart again next week, teachers, when they confront the impossibility of doing everything they ought to do head on, are faced with making some very tough priority decisions. If I can't do it all, which of those things that I really need or want to do am I going to have to leave undone? The working party on Equal Opportunities that I said I would convene? The meeting I ought to set up with Samuel's parents? Getting my brains round that new, interesting-looking book on personal, social and health education? Or (how many years have I been promising myself this?) sorting out the stock cupboard/prep room? When they don't have enough time, teachers know, even if they are fairly successful at not thinking about it, that in some way or other they are letting down their pupils, their colleagues or themselves.

Pragmatism

Teachers do not, as a breed, read or talk much about education and this presumably reflects the general feeling that 'something's got to go', and that concern with ideas and ideals seems to be one of the areas that is dispensable. They are often distrustful of any kind of technical or academic thinking about education, and for the most part their experience of the social sciences during their teacher training has compounded the problem. As David Hargreaves notes,

> The social sciences studied during training have entirely failed to provide teachers with a new working vocabulary. Because it is seen to be of little direct help to teaching, that knowledge and vocabulary is abandoned and left at the college gates as soon as the BEd exams are over. I sometimes think that the principal function of professional training in education is to inoculate teachers against books on education.[2]

Jill Jones is slightly less hard on her college days, but the message is similar. I asked her if her work at college had forced or stimulated her to think about school in general, and what it is for. She said:

> Not much. Not much if I'm honest. What I really learnt about teaching was when I actually started the stuff. When I look back at what I learnt in college I'm disappointed to think that they didn't teach me more. What we had was basically method things where we

were given lots of experimental things we would do in the laboratory, but no real philosophy behind it, no sort of follow through. It was just all snippets of things.

John Holt (one of the few authors whose books still seem able to appeal to students despite their inoculation) writes of a common experience that mirrors mine with the Scottish educational psychologists.

In 1965, soon after *How Children Fail* appeared, a teacher wrote me saying, in effect, 'I have just read your book, and like it. But there is something you don't know that you should know. For over thirty years I have been teaching in the public schools of New York City. For over thirty years, along with my fellow teachers, I have been going to educational conferences, and training sessions, and workshops, to hear countless leaders in education talk, as you do, about the dignity of the child, and the importance of individual differences, and of fostering positive self-concepts, and building on the interests of the child, and letting the child learn from curiosity rather than fear. And for thirty years I and my fellow teachers, as we went back to our classrooms, have said to ourselves, "Well, back to reality", and had gone on doing just what we had been doing all along, which was to try to bribe, scare or shame children into learning what someone else had decided they ought to know. What makes you think you can change all this?' A few years later, while I was talking at a meeting on educational reform, a local superintendent of schools rose from his seat in the back of the room and, moving to the door, said scornfully, so that many could hear, 'Well, back to reality'.[3]

Given their experience of the remote jargon of their teacher training, and of the demonstrable lack of impact of the pundits on education, as well as their weariness and preoccupation, it is entirely understandable that teachers should be turned off ideas at least as much in 1989 as they were twenty-five years ago: understandable but a mistake, as I am trying to argue. What we and they have witnessed is certain *types* of ideas *mishandled* in certain characteristic ways, not the impotence of reflection and cognition themselves. On the contrary, for teachers to be grappling individually and collectively with the deepest and knottiest problems in education provides the only hope they have of recapturing their equanimity and satisfaction.

Dissatisfaction

I do not know any (secondary) school teachers who, in private, are not willing to say that they are substantially dissatisfied with the job that schools are doing, for at least a substantial proportion of pupils. Even student teachers, who might reasonably be expected to be the least jaundiced and most optimistic informants, aren't happy. On the spur of the moment the other day I asked a seminar group of sixteen PGCE students (a third of whom were over the age of thirty) after a three-week preliminary block of school experience, whether they thought that schools were (a) fine as they were; (b) in need of some modifications; (c) failing a sizeable proportion of young people; (d) seriously failing all young people. I was shocked when the voting was nine for (c) and seven for (d). What it is that teachers are dissatisfied about we will return to later.

Unappreciated

Time and again, when I ask people in workshops what it is like being a teacher, they say they feel unappreciated: unappreciated within the school by seniors, colleagues and pupils, and unappreciated by the world at large – parents, politicians, pundits, the media. At parents' meetings they must be prepared to be blamed by mothers and fathers with unrealistic expectations of their, the teachers', and the children's abilities. (One teacher, Karen Armstrong, writing recently in *The Guardian* quoted the following encounter. ' "What do you mean, she finds modern poetry difficult?", one father bellowed after I had tried to explain why his not very able daughter had failed her mock exams. "She *is* a modern poet!" '[4] While from the Secretary of State for Education downwards, they feel themselves to be on the receiving end of all kinds of unfair accusations.

Within the classroom too teachers have to live with an active or passive resistance to their best efforts. Subjects that they care about are fended off by the pupils with the familiar complaints that they are 'boring' or 'stupid'. And frequently decent adults and pleasant youngsters seem to forget that others have normal human feelings. A kind of casual cruelty abounds in which, almost as a matter of routine, teachers say to pupils, and pupils to teachers, things that are wounding or upsetting. But because it is part of the school ethos (for teachers and pupils alike) that it is embarrassing to show that you have been hurt, people remain mostly unaware of the pain that these mundane disparagements cause. Many teachers, I have found, can remember from their own schooldays the shock and guilt they felt when a teacher finally broke down in the face of what, to the class, had seemed to be 'just having a bit of fun'. And equally they can recall the lasting resentment caused by a teacher's blatant unfairness, or by a public humiliation.

Acting

It is a prevalent source of distress to teachers that they are unable to 'be themselves' in school, and this is the reason that they often give for leaving, or wanting to leave, the profession. It is as if they can find no other way of being in school than one which feels phoney and uncongenial. They feel they are being sucked inexorably and against their will into the adoption of a rather ugly or artificial persona, though there are various expressions that this mask can take. An anonymous teacher writing in *Time Out* said: 'I decided that I had to get out of teaching when, walking down the corridor, I heard myself screaming "Tie!" at some kid I didn't even know. I suddenly realized that I wasn't myself any more: *I* didn't give a damn whether he was wearing a tie or not.'[5] And Karen Armstrong, in the article from which I have just quoted, explained why *she* left teaching.

> As the years passed I discovered that I had developed a special school 'personality' which was a distortion of myself. I had built it up, at first quite unconsciously, but later it became a deliberately assumed mask. The 'personality' had to conceal my natural impatience, my moods, my fatigue and make me appear endlessly dynamic and reassuring. With it I wooed the children to learn by setting out to entertain them. It became increasingly difficult to switch off, without my crumbling into a disintegrated heap. I discovered that I had become a 'character' and was fast becoming a caricature of myself.

Here is a third example:

I was talking recently with a group of fourth-year boys – the girls were at a talk on sex education. The boys were bemoaning that they were not there, too. 'Trouble is, Miss,' said one of the boys, 'school doesn't teach us anything we really want to know.' Pursuing the notion of building sex education into the curriculum, I asked whether they would not be embarrassed to talk about sex with a teacher they saw around all the time. 'Well, yes, maybe,' said the same boy, 'but perhaps we need not have a teacher – perhaps we could have a proper person.' I am beginning to believe that it is almost impossible to be both teacher and 'a proper person'. It has taken me twelve years to be as sure as I am now, and it might take a few more to be absolutely sure. However, given the choice, if that is a choice, there is no question as to which I would rather be. That is why I think I shall probably give up teaching in two or three years. I shall not really want to.[6]

Isolated

It is still much more common than not for teachers to do their teaching behind closed doors, unobserved by another adult, and to feel somewhat threatened on the odd occasion when they are being watched. Perhaps as a result of their experiences during teaching practice and their probationary year, observation has come to connote judgement rather than support. This tends to leave their perception of their own teaching – both how they do it and how well they are doing – in a rather uncomfortable vacuum, especially if the staffroom ethos prohibits any kind of discussion other than crisis-management and grumbles about individual or whole-class 'personalities'. Even if the ethos does permit them to check out *how* they are doing, it remains unlikely that it will encourage anything more than a superficial sharing of doubts about *what* they are doing: about the disparity between their hopes for teaching and the effects, or lack of them, that they and their colleagues seem to be achieving.

These are some of the characterizations that one will find both on and below the surface of teachers' lives. They are, in brief, hard-working and somewhat stressed; feel dissatisfied with the job they are doing (or at least bits of it); confused about what they should be doing but wanting to change in the direction of greater impact and relevance of what they do; have no clear idea how to go about it; do not feel optimistic about things getting better; are worried about the amount of emotional energy the job takes up; and mostly do the best they can, try not to think about it all too much, and hang on till the holidays.

SUB-SPECIES

Within the teaching profession there are obviously subgroups which have their own particular concerns, and their own preferred strategies for coping. At the most junior level there are the students, about whom we have spoken already. They have the problem of learning the basic skills of teaching, of keeping order, of creating varied and interesting lessons, of the kind of language that is suitable to different ages and levels of achievement, of pacing and of developing the vital intuitive sense of how much you can get done in forty or seventy minutes. On top of this, inevitably but it seems rather unfairly, they have to deal with the problem that faces every teacher in a new school: the fact that they do not know its geography, its structure and its rules, both explicit and unwritten, nor do they have a chance to get to know the personalities and quirks of more than a handful of either pupils or teachers. And they may be torn three ways, between the practical direction they are getting in the school, the advice they are being given in college and by their teaching practice tutor, and their own developing sense of the kind of teacher they would or would not like to become. The unlucky ones find themselves pig-in-the-middle between college and school tutors, each of whom is convinced of the rightness of their own particular way of teaching and the wrongness (hopelessly impractical, hopelessly out-of-date) of the other.

Students are more than likely having to cope, perhaps for the first time in their lives, with a threateningly high level of conspicuous and recurrent failure, and the way they cope with anxiety will play a large part in determining what kind of a fist they make of it. And buying into this self-doubt will be the old lags in the staffroom who are telling them they must be daft. As one teacher trainer put it not long ago, 'I have been in education for 25 years and I have never known morale so low. Many, many of our students are coming back from teaching practice reporting that teachers are urging them not to enter the profession'.[7]

Secondary teacher trainees, being graduates, are uniquely ill-equipped to understand the vast majority of the school population who are not like them, and have no intention of becoming so. Only a few of them have any idea what it is like for school to be a persistent diet of boredom, incomprehension and failure. Only a few will have had, as close schoolfriends, those for whom this is the reality. Instead they enter college wedded through their own experience to an implicit theory of schooling and teaching that will serve as a working template for some groups of pupils they teach, but which will be wildly inappropriate for others. They go into school wearing comfortable old clothes and rapidly discover they need to tailor for themselves, and quickly, a substantial wardrobe, not only of ways of operating but of ways of thinking, feeling and perceiving as well. It is the skills of tailoring they will need throughout their careers (until promoted out of the classroom) to fabricate and negotiate again and again, with each new class, an effective and hardwearing working habit. The process of supplanting their initial unconscious caricature of school with a kaleidoscope of skills and attitudes that can be shaken into a host of new shapes to meet new needs is an unprecedented and, for most students, a painful one.

New teachers in their first year or so are still very much in the process of finding their feet. Most of the problems of the student will also be theirs: they are still on trial. Depending on their flair and the quality of their training they will need differing degrees of support, and depending on the school and the LEA they will either get it or not. Their main priority during the year will be to learn enough and develop good enough relationships in both staffroom and classroom to survive. For most of them it will be without doubt the most taxing year they can remember. And as well as learning the job of teaching, they are learning its culture as well: how it is 'acceptable' and 'normal' to act, think, feel and talk as a teacher. They will observe in the staffroom an array of different stances to the business of teaching, and, measuring these against their own developing and conflicting set of aspirations, begin to make some intuitive decisions about the track they are going to follow. Can I find a way of being a teacher – can I see any role models – which allows a satisfactory compromise between my career ambitions, my wish to be a good *subject* teacher, my desire to promote my broader educational ideals, my intention to be a 'real person' as much as I can, and my commitment to improving the status and conditions of teaching as a profession? And if I can't, can I begin to entertain the thought that teaching may not be for me (as a substantial number of new teachers do) without feeling guilty or a failure?

As Colin Lacey says:

> The new teacher is preoccupied with the basic problems of survival and acceptance. The strain of being 'new' is in itself considerable. As the newness wears off, that is, as many of the appropriate behaviour patterns are learnt and habitualized, these strains are reduced. The energies released enable the young teacher to 'try again' on some of the preferred but unsuccessful teaching strategies of the first year. But once again there are competing pressures and choices to be made. As the pattern of career advancement becomes clearer and the expectations of the established senior staff are communicated, these expectations become pressures that must be taken into account . . .
>
> The school now appears as an arena in which teachers strive for two goals. The first is . . . acceptance into and promotion within the existing structure of the school . . . The second goal is to make the school resemble more closely the sort of place within which the teacher would like to teach . . . this second goal can become of considerable importance, and in some situations of conflict it can become more important than the first. That is, teachers will take a stance that they know will damage their careers in order to uphold a principle about how the school should run.[8]

Many teachers would like to be more adventurous, creative and experimental than they feel it is possible or safe to be. To make a gross oversimplification, the younger teachers are the most inclined to be adventurous, but are the most at risk if they try it. Their ability to control and to recover control of a class is more tenuous, and their reputations are more vulnerable. The more experienced teachers, on the other hand, are generally more secure both in their competence and their status, but may have lost their fire. Perhaps one of the most important groups for the stimulation of change is that which falls between these two poles: those teachers who I would see as belonging to the 25 to 35 year-old age group, or perhaps those who have not been teaching for more than six, or less than three, years. They are the ones who have been long enough in the profession to have lost some of their naivety and to have mastered the art of teaching, whilst they have not been teachers long enough to have become demoralized and cynical.

Jill Jones seems to fall into that category (she has been teaching for seven years). She says:

> I'm prepared to give things more of a go now, and I don't mind if they fail. I don't care if someone comes into my room and it's a mess. I can say 'It was a failure but it was worth a go'. Whereas before the insecurity would have been there, I suppose, that might have stopped me trying things. Of course sometimes when it doesn't work that depresses me because it's not because it doesn't work, it's because of the constraints of the system that you cannot make it work. That gets me down. I sometimes wish I *didn't* think so much about what I do, and just pottered along doing it the way it's always been done (like the bloke in the next-door room does!).

I asked her, 'What is it that gives you the confidence to try things out?'. She said:

> It's partly the status I have within the department. I know there are people around who think I'm an OK teacher, so if I screw up occasionally that's not going to sink my reputation. If the Headmaster walks in and there's a bit of chaos I can tell him why it's a mess and it doesn't bother me. I know he could walk in the next lesson and things would be perfectly OK. It would have bothered me though a few years ago. I'd probably been teaching for about four years before I began to have that confidence. If it doesn't work I know now I can re-establish things with myself and with the kids. I think it's more difficult now to get that basis of status and confidence for new teachers coming in to the profession, if only because there aren't the promotions or the movement of new jobs. And the status *is* important. You need to have someone to say 'You're good. . . . you're worth this'. But if you're stuck on Scale 1 for years you don't feel in a position to try anything new.

As I said in Chapter 1, if this book is directed at any particular group of teachers it is probably these. From their ranks today will come the senior teachers of AD 2000, so it is crucial for education, as well as for their own well-being, that this group is preserved from the fates of burn-out and cynicism. It is also members of this group who have the strongest personal motivation for thinking about and working on the educational system, for they in the main are the teachers with young children of their own, at the beginning of their school careers. They are engaged with the issues not only as professionals, but as parents as well.

As the student or the new teacher scans the staffroom, he or she will find some of the more senior teachers who have kept their sparkle, who have a developing educational philosophy of their own, and who enjoy educational debate. But unless she is lucky she will also meet others who have opted for different solutions to the problem of how to be a teacher. There are the careerists amongst the senior management of the school, some of whom will seem to have 'sold out to the system': to affect a philosophy in so far as it looks in their own interests to do so, to have become executives and to have lost touch with the pupils. They may have their private regrets that they could not find a way of solving the equation of conflicting interests that offered deeper satisfaction as well as personal advancement, but it is unlikely that they will reveal these.

She will see those who have committed themselves to the traditional model of education, some as a matter of principle, but others because to question it opens up too big a can of worms. They like their subject, and want nothing more than to be left alone to teach it to groups of pupils who want to learn it. For some of these people the time is past when they could reappraise their stance. The kind of teaching that they enjoy, value, and entered the teaching profession to do may no longer be appropriate for many of the classes that they have to take. For good or ill, they may not agree with the way things have turned out, or are developing at the moment. Rightly or wrongly they may feel unwilling or unable to adapt. Because education has become more and more of a depersonalized commodity that can be delivered in principle by anyone, their technique as teachers is thought of as paramount and their preferences as incidental. This 'technological' view of education and teaching also prevents teachers from deliberately gravitating to schools whose ideology they like, and in which they will feel comfortable. Schools where the staff are aligned with a practical philosophy which is more than the usual 'whole person' rhetoric do exist, but to find your way, as a teacher, to the one that suits is, in these egalitarian and bureaucratic days, often a hit and miss affair. It is also hard to move without being promoted, so if you do not want more administrative responsibility, or are not promotion material, again you are inhibited from searching for a more congenial workplace.

Many of the teachers who fall into this category are those who have given up hoping that there will be any room for their beliefs in debate or in classroom practice. Unable to reconcile their view of education with the form of schooling they are now required to deliver, they have regretfully had to turn off the tap, and substitute instead a tape-loop of the sound of running water. Teachers who find themselves in this position are of course free in principle to leave. Many of the younger ones do, and many of the older ones would like to, but are trapped by financial commitments, pension prospects and the fear, accurate or not, of being unqualified for or unable to find an alternative job.

It may indeed be that for some teachers there really is no possibility of working with real integrity, and consequently no possibility of deriving any deep satisfaction from what they do. If they stay they must deliver an emasculated version of their own educational vision, and in such a position it is easier to deny the ideals than to stay open, day after day, to the disappointment and the sense of inauthenticity. The choice that is left is to go through the motions either with counterfeit conviction, or with subversion and disdain. There are, to point to two easily identifiable groups, the old grammar school teachers who do not like and have not mastered mixed-ability teaching; and the old secondary modern teachers who still feel second-class citizens in the staffroom.

Somewhat in the same boat may be groups of younger teachers who see education in personal/emotional, or in political terms, and who are feeling their values particularly heavily trodden on by the current educational reforms. The commitment of such teachers is to the emotional and personal well-being of the pupils, and they may be openly critical of the content-based, exam-passing philosophy of more traditional colleagues. But despite the current popularity of Personal, Social and Health Education, Active Tutorial Work, and so on,[9] and whatever the rhetoric of the school, they can see that their prime concern is only incidental to the formal scheme of things, and they know that the national tide is not running in their direction. Nevertheless in many schools their lobby is a strong one, and even those who have no real sympathy with their priorities find it unfashionable to say so.

Then there are the 'activists'. Some people go into teaching with the intention of becoming active in the union, either out of genuine commitment to teaching as a profession, or because it offers a political platform. Many others join the unions, but with considerable misgivings. They find them overly concerned to engage with 'management' in an adversarial relationship, in ways that seem harsh, legalistic and materialistic. Of course teachers want a reasonable salary and decent career prospects. But more than that most want the satisfaction of feeling they are doing a worthwhile job well – and here the unions don't seem to offer much help. They are as traditional, narrow-minded and uncreative in their approach to educational debate as the Government. They seem only capable of being negatively reactive to other people's suggestions, and disappointingly preoccupied with status and regard, to the almost total exclusion of serious educational debate. Yet despite these misgivings in teachers' minds, the unions offer (witness the strength of feeling in the 'action' of 1986–7) a channel of expression for the frustration and confusion that they feel. The agenda of that action was reasonable, but its impetus was provided, in considerable measure, by the need to channel private doubt and uncertainty into some form of public declaration. Given that nobody (except the academics, who don't count) was talking *education*, the dispute about pay and conditions provided an alternative hoarding on which to display their disquiet.

This chapter has offered a summary of what is more or less evident when one looks at teachers' lives today. Despite some simplification and the occasional caricature, I doubt there is much in what I have said so far with which to argue. But in order to see the seriousness and urgency of things, we need now to invade teachers' privacy, and to explore the effects that these trying conditions are having on their emotional lives. In doing so we shall begin to explore the ways people respond to and cope with high levels of uncertainty and demand, and to open up the question of whether some of these ways are misguided.

Chapter 3

Getting like that

The educational system has always displayed great inertia, a built-in resistance to change, which is contributed to by both teachers and parents alike. Teachers, enjoying tenure, will resist any radical departure from the attitudes and practices they acquired in initial training and, more particularly, during probation: nobody wants their own established expertise threatened. Parents, on the other hand, however much they have suffered at school, or even if they left it with a sense of failure, usually attribute the shortcomings to themselves rather than to the system, and thus find it difficult to envisage school in any form other than the one that they themselves experienced.

John Watts[1]

The last chapter attempted to paint a recognizable picture of teachers' current predicament and how they are feeling. We watched a new entrant to the profession looking around at her colleagues for clues as to how to resolve the tensions, whilst doing as little damage to her integrity (and her career prospects) as possible. What we offered her was a range of 'types' to choose from, ranging from the idealistic and dynamic to the cynical and incompetent. But these caricatures do not tell us much about what is going on with real, complex individuals behind the scenes. Now I want to look at teachers' lives from a particular point of view: that what our hypothetical observer is actually witnessing is people coping, in a great variety of ways, with stress. This chapter is about the way in which the existing predicament of teachers leads them to become stressed, and it is also about whether stress is inevitable in such circumstances or not.

The concern with stress reduction is valid in its own right, but it is also a vital prerequisite for successful engagement with educational innovation. Teachers need to be able to understand and manage their own stress, to be able to deal with it effectively and intelligently, before they are going to be able even to think about what changes they would like to make, and to form realistic appraisals of what is possible. Preoccupied with clinging to the remnants of their well-being, there is no time or energy left over for anything grander. How could there be? From a fatalistic point of view, the resigned response, to the expression of any educational idealism, of 'Well, back to reality' is the only sensible, rational reaction there is. It is only from the vantage point of a better framework that previously unforeseen opportunities open up, and the previously unacknowledged *costs* of resignation and entrenchment become visible. I wish now to set out such a framework.

WHAT IS STRESS?

People use the word 'stress' to refer to both the external pressures and demands they are subject to, and the effects that such stressful circumstances have on their performance, feelings and health. The word typically conflates the *causes* of stress with the *phenomenon* of stress. I want first to focus on the latter meaning, and to describe in some detail what teachers are talking about when they say they are stressed, or suffering from stress. I have collected this catalogue from the dozens of workshops and courses I have run for teachers on the subject of stress. So it (the catalogue) does not represent an objective description of a psycho-medical condition; it shows what teachers say when you ask what stress means to them.

First, stress affects people *physically*. For every aspect of physical functioning you can name, there is some kind of aberration or alteration that some people will see as stress-related. Stress affects the circulatory system: heart rate increases, people are aware of their heart pounding; blood pressure increases (some people claim it decreases); they suffer from nose bleeds; they may even have heart attacks, strokes or other serious circulatory problems. Breathing can be affected: people suffer from shortness of breath or panic attacks in which they are unable to catch their breath at all; stress may bring on asthma attacks if people are prone to them. Digestion can be upset: some people have bouts of diarrhoea or need to urinate a lot; others get constipated; people feel sick and sometimes are; more serious conditions like ulcers can develop. Things happen to the skin: people sweat and go clammy; they may be flushed or alternatively may lose their colour; spots, boils, rashes and other irritations can develop; and again more serious conditions like eczema or psoriasis can break out. People blame stress for changes to their hair: greying or balding are sometimes considered to be 'premature'. Stress affects posture: often people look slumped, their shoulders sag and they hunch their back; alternatively they hold themselves very rigid so that the muscles of the shoulders and neck especially are set; their face takes on a fixed expression with perhaps staring eyes or clenched jaw; muscular tics and involuntary twitches can arise; for some people cramp is stress-related.

Sleep is commonly disturbed in one way or another: some people nod off as soon as they get home and sit down; they wake up at midnight with the TV still on – and then can't get back to sleep again till 3am; some people find it impossible to wake up in the morning and getting out of bed is a real struggle; others are awake at half-past four in the morning with their brains buzzing and churning; some people find themselves getting very sleepy when difficult or anxiety-making things happen. Strange things happen to eating: people lose their appetites and pick at their food; or they stuff themselves; cravings for sweets or junk food appear; and again these can develop into clinical obesity, anorexia or bulimia. Consumption of drinks and drugs go up: alcohol consumption can increase – maybe to a second scotch before dinner, maybe to two Special Brews to get through the afternoon and a bottle of wine every evening; smoking can increase, as can the consumption of tea and coffee – even though these are physical stimulants (and can therefore *mimic* anxiety) rather than relaxants. People may start using pills of various sorts: aspirin for the recurrent headaches, tranquillizers, anti-depressants and sleeping pills; and then there are the 'non-prescription' drugs such as marijuana, cocaine and even heroin.

Sex is a sensitive barometer of stress for many people: they lose interest, their bodies stop responding in the ways they are supposed to, or they find themselves feeling unusually (and perhaps embarrassingly) sexual. Women's periods are often affected: they may become very heavy, lose their regularity, or even disappear for a while. People's energy levels vary: they may feel persistently wiped out. Even if there are little windows of time between jobs, teachers often feel that they simply don't have the energy to take advantage of them. By half-term many teachers feel exhausted, and the last thing they feel able to do in their 'free time' is to undertake anything that smacks of yet more effort, uncertainty or challenge. When you spend the days feeling stretched to the limit and end them emotionally drained, it is small wonder that you want to spend the evening dozing in front of the television and half-term skiing instead of preparing lessons. It is as much as you can do to read the job advertisements in the *Times Educational Supplement*, let alone the leader. Or people can feel hyped up, restless and agitated; or in a kind of listless, uninterested state that feels dead and dispirited. Certain kinds of illness and illness-proneness are experienced: people are more likely to catch a cold or flu, for example, and be less able to shake it off; they feel generally run down and may suffer from mysterious but more debilitating viruses, such as ME or glandular fever, that are difficult to diagnose and take a long time to clear up. Finally, in the physical list there are various kinds of aches and pains: headaches, migraines, neck and shoulder pains, back aches, perhaps the recurrence of old injuries.

Then there are *behavioural and social* aspects of 'The Stress Syndrome'. There may be an element of self-neglect: normal standards of personal hygiene are lowered – showers are taken less frequently, clothes unwashed, things not tidied up, meals thrown together. Physical co-ordination can suffer: plates are dropped, and more serious accidents can happen, or nearly happen, as one steps off the kerb or pulls out without looking. Procrastination sets in: jobs that ought to be done are left to pile up; weak excuses made to avoid doing anything difficult. People are avoided if they are likely to be at all stressful; phone-calls go unreturned; even social events that would normally be pleasurable and fun may feel like yet more demands on a person's time. Habits and patterns of work can become more disorganized: people may be unable to focus on one task because all the other things to be done keep crowding in; at the end of a very busy day little seems to have been accomplished. Perhaps also under this heading might come an increase in complaining: people find themselves becoming self-centred and self-justifying in conversations and perhaps feeling that they are becoming boring (and often are).

Next there are the *mental* effects. Below the surface there lies, for many teachers, a nagging sense of doubt and confusion about what they are doing, what they ought to be doing and what they are doing it for. As one teacher put it to me, 'on a bad day I have the feeling that I am struggling hard to do something that may not be worth doing at all'. Their position, one might conjecture, is characterized by what in psychiatric circles would be called a 'double-bind', woven out of these underlying beliefs:

> What I'm doing isn't good enough.
> I don't know (at all clearly) what else to do.
> I don't feel able to do anything significantly different.
> There doesn't seem to be much support for trying or even thinking about it.

Trapped within such propositions there is no satisfying solution to be found, nor even avenues to be explored. Yet at the same time thinking can become obsessional and repetitive for some people. Some teachers have responded to the confusion by simplifying, and therefore being able to live with, the conflicts and demands of the teacher's predicament. Single-minded devotion to one's own advancement, or to better pay, or to just one cause, strengthens one legitimate ingredient of the complex personal equation – but sometimes to the point where it eclipses and pre-empts the others. Confusion is certainly reduced. But if the tentative claims for attention of deep, albeit hazy, personal beliefs are consistently ignored, clarity has been bought at a high price: damage to integrity and the loss of real satisfaction. The discomfort of uncertainty and change is high, so the drive to avoid or resolve it is high too. But any solution that involves disconnecting activity from true values may in the long term take an even greater toll. It is with this fact, semi-consciously, that the new teacher in particular struggles.

Reasoning powers can deteriorate: people may begin to think irrationally (and do so even though they *know* they are doing so); they may begin to get paranoid, feeling that others are slyly poking fun at them, excluding them from discussions, or being condescending or patronizing. They jump to unwarranted conclusions without realizing they have done so, so that 'crossed-wires' and other misunderstandings arise. A sense of balance is lost: one can't tell what is important or what really matters. For many people a prime symptom of stress is loss of their sense of humour: playfulness is replaced by earnestness or snappiness; casual jokes that one would normally return in good spirit are felt to be wounding and hurtful. People say they become imperceptive; they spend hours looking for the car keys that were on the table in front of them all the time; they become preoccupied and inattentive to what other people are saying to them ('But I *told* you the Smiths were coming over *yesterday*. Three times . . .'). And memory seems to deteriorate: people forget promises and appointments and become absent-minded.

And finally there are the *emotional* aspects of stress. As we have noted already, anger and all its varying intensities and hues are a common part of the stress syndrome. One of my friends on an off-day defined school as 'the place where everybody is always cross!'. While 'everybody' and 'always' are exaggerations, there is some truth in this. When you are being spat at for doing your best in difficult circumstances, it is hard not to become spiky and defensive. When your own resources are low, you've forgotten to set homework and you are getting a cold, it requires the forbearance of a saint to keep making allowances for other people's fallibility and forgetfulness. When people are feeling wound up, there are different things that can unleash the barbed remark: another small demand for their attention, a lost key, not being taken seriously enough by the person to whom they are cataloguing the disasters of the day, or TOO MUCH NOISE. Noise is a potent trigger and its constant presence is for many teachers very wearing. Through parental rows, war movies, barking dogs and football crowds, noise comes to be an automatic, unconscious signal of loss of control and of aggression, and there are teachers whose daily lives are an eternal battle to contain the unease that noise calls forth in them. Teachers report themselves becoming punitive and stroppy with pupils, colleagues and their own families. The fact that they can see how counterproductive it is not only doesn't seem to stop them, it makes matters worse. They feel bad about themselves for being so irritable, and bad about themselves for not being able to control it. People may become violent in thought if not in deed.

But not all the feelings of stress are so public. On the contrary, anger is often the external tip of a self-destructive internal iceberg. People become vulnerable: they feel very thin-skinned; over-sensitive and self-pitying; moody and unpredictable, with a cheerfulness that is transparent and brittle; they may become tearful, perhaps breaking down over an item of television news or for no apparent reason at all. Partly as a result of the potent and embarrassing mixture of irritability and vulnerability, people commonly experience feelings of withdrawal: they may feel lonely, hopeless and depressed. Allied to this comes guilt: guilt about being such a wimp; guilt about being so secretive; guilt about having been such a bitch or a bastard; guilt about all the things not done; guilt about mistakes and errors of judgement; guilt, in other words, about Not Being Good Enough.

To complete this bitter emotional brew there is *anxiety*: that feeling of dread or agitation on waking up in the mornings; stammering and blushing; fear of making another fool of yourself, or of your last mistake being uncovered. In conditions of uncertainty and overload anxiety is inevitable, though it may, with some effort, be transmuted into something else, or denied. The 'something else' is often more irritation and anger, as when a driver who has almost had an accident transforms his fear into a prolonged tirade against the other driver. Teachers may be apprehensive about any number of things. The fear of losing control of a class lurks just below the surface even for teachers with 'good discipline', and for many this puts the brake on changes to their own way of teaching that they might otherwise like to try. And allied to this are concerns about 'not getting the results' and about one's reputation with colleagues in general, and especially with the senior staff whose opinion can make or break a career.

This is what teachers call 'stress'. Of course this is a cumulative list and no one teacher (I hope) can put a mental tick against all of these elements. Nevertheless, if you think this catalogue paints an unnecessarily bleak picture of how teachers are feeling, then I can tell you with some confidence that you have been deceived by the cover-up. The moment teachers feel safe enough to tell the truth (which is often anywhere but in their own staffrooms), they rush to unburden themselves of feelings and symptoms such as those which I have described, and are surprised and relieved that other people are feeling the same way. The feelings are no less intense for inspectors and headteachers than they are for students and teachers in their first appointment.

Before we go on to explore in some detail how the Stress Syndrome comes about I want to make a couple of general points. Many of the aspects of stress, especially the physical ones, are examples of psychosomatic disorders. Some years ago the word 'psychosomatic' was often prefaced by the word 'merely' and was used to suggest that an illness was in some way unreal or made up. People who had psychosomatic complaints were probably malingering (if male) and hysterical (if female), and the appropriate treatment was a stiff talking-to, designed to exhort or scare them into 'stopping all this nonsense' and 'pulling themselves together'. It should go without saying these days that to be suffering from something psychosomatic is not to be guilty of lack of moral fibre, but to be exhibiting a condition the cause of which is, at least in part, psychological. As it is now hard to think of any disorder, physical or mental, that does not have some element of the psychological in its origin, we can, I hope, reject the pejorative meaning.

The second point to note is that there is a positive sense of the word 'stress', which refers to a certain level of challenge which is bracing, energizing and focusing. This is how most teachers imagined the job would be: demanding, tiring and requiring a lot of commitment and resourcefulness. But that is mostly not what they mean when they use the word stress. To them stress occurs when that point has been well passed, and tiredness becomes exhaustion, commitment becomes slog, resourcefulness becomes desperation and challenge becomes threat. When they complain about 'stress' they are not saying they want to spend the rest of their lives lazing about in the sun being brought rum bamboozles on a silver tray (though the idea has its appeal). They are saying they want to get back to the point where their hard work brought frequent, real, deep satisfaction. Many other jobs involve 'hard stress' of this latter kind – foreign exchange dealers and nurses work intensely for long hours. But they know what the game is, and they know when they have done a good job: the rewards are tangible and clear. Teachers' stress is different: it is 'fuzzy stress', where the rules and the returns are shadowy and ambiguous, and where debilitation is not regularly punctuated with bursts of exhilaration and satisfaction.

HOW DOES STRESS COME ABOUT?

The fact that the word 'stress' is commonly used to refer both to the situation in which teachers are working *and* the way they are feeling and reacting suggests that many of them subscribe to the 'Hay Fever Theory' as an explanation for how stress comes about. The Hay Fever Theory sees stress as an objective feature of situations. They can be more or less stress-ful. If you are unlucky enough to find yourself working in a heavily stress-laden environment (which schools are) then, inevitably, you will 'catch it' and 'come down with it'. If we were all hay fever prone, then whenever we happened to be in a place where the pollen count was high, our eyes would start streaming and our noses running. There would be no choice in the matter. Likewise, according to this theory, as we are all stress-prone, we are bound to get stressed when we find ourselves working somewhere where there is a high stress-count. We therefore have only three options open to us when we are stressed: move, ameliorate or suffer. Leave teaching, have a good moan and another drink, or shut up and get on with it. ('If you can't stand the heat, get out of the kitchen' versus 'When the going gets tough the tough get going'.) These are in fact the only options that many teachers feel are open to them.

The fact that the position is more complicated, however, should be obvious if we remind ourselves of the point I made at the beginning of Chapter 2: how variable teachers are. This variability applies in the arena of stress as much as anywhere else. Most people vary enormously in the reserves that they have available, so that the things that floor them at the end of term may be the same small irritations that they sailed through at the beginning. And people are sometimes aware that the kind of stress they feel is different depending on what the stressful circumstances are. I have discovered for example that the acute stress of being interviewed makes me sweat a lot, an afternoon of difficult telephone calls leaves me with lower back pain, while the run-down-at-the-end-of-a-long-hard-term kind of stress makes me irritable and forgetful.

We may show the same kind of symptom but with different degrees of severity or persistence. You can imagine, for most types of stress reaction, a scale running from mild/everyday/once-in-a-while/not-much-to-bother-about through to severe/debilitating/chronic/better-do-something-quick. Occasional raised blood pressure is normal; long-term high blood pressure is a killer. A drink or two extra on a Friday night may be OK; a glass of vodka before you can face school in the morning is more worrying.

There are big differences between individuals as well, not only in the amount of pressure they can handle before something begins to crack, but in the way they become stressed and the kinds of things that stress them. Some people get back pain, some get irritable, some withdraw, some become frantic and panicky, some assume a calm, out-of-touch-with-reality veneer, some spend all their time moaning about what's wrong. . . . Everyone has their own variable limits and their own characteristic 'stress portfolio'.

All this variability both within and between people suggests that the story of how the Stress Syndrome comes about cannot be as simple as the Hay Fever Theory would have us believe. Specifically it suggests that something about how we respond, react to or construe the stressful situation has a lot to do with how stressed we feel, and how we feel stressed. It is this 'something' that we need to investigate, because the more we can understand what turns stress on, the more we may be able to devise new and effective ways of turning it off.

HOW DOES STRESS REALLY COME ABOUT?

It will help to see what the personal ingredients are, and at what point in the arising of stress they are added in, if we take the story 'from the top', and look at it as we might the development of a complicated chemical reaction. First we need to start with the 'givens' of the situation – the objective features of the predicament which we reviewed in the first part of the last chapter. We might say roughly that there are two sorts of givens which we could call *duties* and *wishes*. By duties I mean the responsibilities of which teachers' work is composed. It is these duties that are approximately laid down in their conditions of service: to work for so many hours, to teach those classes, to attend these meetings, to undertake these extras. In addition there are the more general, personal responsibilities to pupils and to colleagues, and the implicit expectations that they will keep up with their subject and methods of teaching it.

By wishes I am referring to the internal directions and aspirations that people have for their own professional lives and development: their preferences, their ambitions, their chosen career path, their enthusiasms and above all their values. If duties are what you must or should do, wishes are what you want to do. Duties are specific to each profession or kind of work, whereas wishes are in general a reflection in the working context of the kinds of personal values that people hold. One of the things that distinguish teaching as a profession is the extent to which people's implicit personal philosophies are constantly and necessarily relevant to their professional impact. In most jobs, even, to an extent, in medicine and law, one's professional performance can be divorced from one's values. But in teaching, where the qualities of relationship and self-presentation are vital determinants of how and how well people do their jobs, one's entire professional life is illuminated and coloured by what one, wittingly or unwittingly, believes and values. Furthermore, at a time of indeterminacy and change like the present, where there is frequently no strong institutional ideology to subscribe to, individual values matter all the more. There is no escape for teachers from showing their values. Even the mouse and the cynic are constantly making an exhibition of themselves.

Next into the 'reaction' must go *limitations*, of which there are several kinds. There are limitations of *personal resources*. Every teacher at whatever level of the hierarchy has a certain reservoir of skill, experience, aptitude and common sense, sufficient to enable some jobs to be accomplished swiftly, easily and confidently, but not others. It is not of course an attack to refer to someone's limitations, nor is the acknowledgment of limitations to oneself a cause for shame. New teachers have limitations on their ability to keep classes orderly and interested. New headteachers have limitations on their ability to manipulate the administration in County Hall, or to conduct a delicate personal conversation with a depressed and withdrawn head of department. In any non-routine form of work, professional responsibilities and personal goals will be continually pushing people up against their limitations of personal resource.

Equally importantly there are very real, sometimes crippling limitations of *external resources*, from not enough books and pencils to go round, through a drying up of goodwill between colleagues, to a general reduction in financial and material support for schools as a whole. Limitations are imposed by the fact that you have to wait two months for the educational psychologist, you have to close the biology lab when it rains because it leaks and they haven't sent anyone to repair it yet, you have to apply for a short in-service course rather than the full-time MA that you really wanted to do because there aren't any secondments any more. Not to mention the classes of thirty or more, and all the other sources of frustration that prevent you from delivering the service you should, and doing the job as you would like.

Many of the limitations appear not as abrupt cut-off points, distinguishing what we can do from what we can't, but as limitations of *rate*. Things people have not yet mastered they may nevertheless be able to accomplish given sufficient time, material and support. You may need to ask for advice, or even have one or two dummy runs, but given time you can get there in the end. The trouble is, as we saw in Chapter 2, that time is the one resource *par excellence* that teachers feel short of. Duties are changing and accumulating at a faster rate than they can be successfully discharged. The extra time and support that are necessary (a) to perform jobs that are pressing at the limits of personal and material resources, and (b) to invest in learning how to do them better, or to assemble additional resources, so that the time taken to perform them is reduced, are not available. Opportunities to take *seriously* such issues as girls and science or the merits of negotiated assessment, or to acquire skills in the areas of active tutorial work or special educational needs are few and far between, and often have to be carved out of evenings and weekends.

In addition to rate and resource limitations there are *contradictions* and *conflicts* within the set of jobs and goals that form a teacher's working agenda. Teachers who listen to all the conflicting noises that are made about education by the pundits will inevitably feel (quite apart from their own ideals) that there is no pleasing all of the people all of the time. 'More care and concern, especially for disadvantaged pupils' runs headlong into 'Teachers are not social workers: school is for learning, not for trying to rectify social injustice'. Thinking they were doing the right thing, some schools set out to understand and respond to the particular problems faced by children of West Indian origin – only to discover that their parents, dissatisfied with 'low expectations' and 'lack of discipline', were setting up their own alternative, strict, traditional schools that their children were being sent to on Saturdays. Or schools get very excited by computer-assisted learning, ordering equipment and retraining teachers – only to find that the pupils, so full of enthusiasm three years ago, have totally lost interest, while the 'experts' are once again suggesting that it wasn't such a good idea after all. Any teacher could write their own long list of countermanding pieces of advice that have come their way.

These factors are conflicts and contradictions within the set of duties. As intense are those between duties and wishes, and even within the set of self-selected, personally appropriated goals and ideals. Not all the good ideas that curriculum developers and academics come up with are daft or unrealistic. Some of them align quite well with teachers' own hopes and principles. 'By all means', they may say. 'Just take these other duties off my shoulders and give me a day a week for the next year to attend a decent training course so that I can master it, and I'm yours.' What they often get instead is a pat on the back, a stack of reading matter, an order form and a two-day pep talk. It is hard to know which is more frustrating: having to do what you don't want, don't agree with and haven't been consulted about; or not being able, through lack of time, energy and support, actually to do what you do want. Teachers are very familiar with both, and I do not intend to go any further into a detailed discussion of difference in educational opinions. It would not be difficult for any reader to jot down, at this point, lists of their own frustrated wishes and unwanted duties, and it might indeed be useful to do so, so that you can keep the argument grounded in the realities of your own life. But because I do not want to get led off into a critical discussion of the issues, I want to keep this part of the book as clear as possible of content, and keep focusing on process. Suffice it to say here that teachers today feel themselves to be pulled, both by external forces and by their own internal beliefs, in several incompatible directions. Many of these boil down to the simultaneous call to go back to doing it the way it was, to keep on doing it the way it is, and to move forward to doing it differently.

When the requirements of duties and wishes exceed the limitations that people are working within, we may say that they come to constitute *demands*. The greater the disparity between what teachers want to do, what they are being asked to do, and what they can do, the greater the demands, and the more demanding the situation. Resources are being mobilized to the best of their ability, and that is not enough. We might say:

(DUTIES AND WISHES) + LIMITATIONS → DEMANDS

In a demanding situation, as thus defined, people inevitably begin to experience *overload* and to feel under *pressure*. By overload I mean that their performance of the job begins to break down as their current level of competence is pushed to the limit and beyond. We described overload in Chapter 2. It is part of teachers' daily experience. They begin to make mistakes and errors of judgement. They have to fly increasingly by the seat of their pants, knowing that their trouser-material is sometimes not going to be strong enough to hold them up. They find a backlog of work building up, in which important but less urgent planning and discussing never get to the top of the pile, being submerged by the constant stream of things that have to be dealt with immediately. They find themselves indulging in crisis management and employing stopgap solutions and holding operations. They have increasingly uncomfortable decisions to make, sometimes consciously but frequently by default, about priorities. And, working beyond the limits of confidence and competence, responses to situations have to be produced that are experimental, and the effect of which is uncertain.

Overload describes the inevitable objective consequences of demand. Pressure refers to the subjective corollaries that we have met before: rush, confusion, uncertainty and anxiety. This is the way overload *feels*. Notice that, although I have just summarized some of the teacher's predicament that I described in Chapter 2, we have arrived at the summary by a different route: not by reporting what people say, but by *looking at the inevitable consequences of working in a demanding situation*. When demand and conflict are running high, therefore, the phenomena of overload and pressure are not optional. Given the conditions in which most teachers are working, and given that they are human beings – that is, they have limitations on what they can do, and how well and how fast they can do it – they could not be feeling otherwise than rushed and confused, nor acting otherwise than fallibly. Up to the point of overload and pressure, you might say that the inexorable logic of the Hay Fever Theory does hold.

DEMAND → OVERLOAD AND PRESSURE

There is an additional complication to this picture which is the increasing effect of demand over time. So far I have described the situation in 'steady state' as if constant demand produced constant overload and pressure. But research into the biology of stress[2] suggests there are three phases. If a new demand is short-lived, it may be possible to find a way of meeting it without any overall loss of performance. You can find some extra energy or resources from somewhere. You can stay up late for a few nights to finish that urgent report without getting irritable or asking too much of the people you live with. But if the demand remains intense and protracted, or if new demands keep arriving, then the reserves begin to get drained and overload and pressure start to increase. If continued, you may enter the third phase in which you are having to draw on resources that are actually necessary to support the level of competence that you normally can display. So not only are your jobs consistently exceeding your limitations, but the limitations themselves are getting greater. When time and energy are spread too thinly, even those things that you could do with ease when you were 'on good form' become more trouble-some. Thus if you are in a state of continuous high demand, there may be an inevitable tendency for the situation to deteriorate, and for overload and pressure to build still further.

But notice that stress, as described at the beginning of this chapter, has not *yet* appeared in the equation. The mysterious ingredient X has not yet been added. It is possible to imagine a teacher – and there are a few rare ones – who reacts to this predicament with complete equanimity. 'OK', they say 'I'm not doing a good enough job at the moment. I forgot the departmental meeting and I bawled out the wrong kid yesterday, there's a stack of mail that I haven't even opened in my pigeon-hole, my marking is getting pretty cursory, and I have decided regretfully that I don't have the energy to organize the third-year science field trip this year, nor the time to prepare properly for my A-level group.

But', (said completely non-defensively) 'there's only so many hours in the day and some of them I need to listen to music and to be with my family. If you find me more time, or get an extra teacher in the department, I'd *love* to be doing better. As it is I just can't. And yes, thank you, I'm sleeping fine.'

To take a different example you might imagine an adviser who has left herself just enough time to get to a school for a meeting, bombing down the motorway and getting a puncture. She pulls over on to the hard shoulder, gets out, opens the boot, gets out the spare tyre and the jack, jacks up the car, takes off the old wheel, puts on the new one, lets the jack down, puts it and the wheel back in the boot, closes it, gets back in the car and drives on, knowing that she will be fifteen minutes late. Most of us, however, would stir into the incident rather more than this. We get out of the car, stomp round to the wheel, look at it, kick it, swear, look at our watch, feel guilty about not having left enough time to cope with the unexpected, open the boot, bang our head on it, swear again, wonder whether it wouldn't be better to walk to the phone, decide to change the wheel ourselves, lose one of the nuts and eventually arrive at the meeting half an hour late in a filthy temper, and take up the next five minutes explaining that it must have been a sharp chipping off one of those construction lorries and they overload them to save money and they ought to do something about it. . . .

Now I want to suggest that what makes the difference – what transmutes overload and pressure into full-blown stress – are what I shall call *injunctions*. Injunctions are Ingredient X. They are beliefs, buried in people's personal philosophies, about personal worth. They specify what makes a good person and a good teacher. Despite the fact that these injunctions are buried, and people are often not able to articulate them spontaneously, we are nevertheless very sensitive to occasions on which the injunctions are breached. The injunctions set the standards that we ought to live up to, and their effect is to make people's self-esteem contingent on living up to them. They say, in effect, 'If thou wishest to feel good about thyself, thou shalt be X and Y and Z. And conversely when thou findest thyself being not-X or not-Y or not-Z, thou shalt pay for thy transgression with a loss of self-esteem.' When people fall short of their standards, and are thereby in breach of their injunctions, somewhere inside they start to feel badly about themselves, and to begin to doubt their worth and acceptability. They get rattled.

$$(\text{OVERLOAD AND PRESSURE}) + \text{INJUNCTIONS}$$
$$\rightarrow \text{BAD FEELING}$$

This crude summary of a wealth of understanding is commonplace in the worlds of counselling and psychotherapy. Many of the people who seek these kinds of help are those who, while living and working in (apparently) normal circumstances, find themselves crippled by unusually strong injunctions. Whilst most of us, for example, can cope with having the occasional murderous thought about people we love, or work with, there are other people for whom such thoughts constitute a profound assault on their self-worth, and who must, therefore, either suffer that sense of worthlessness or involve themselves in an intense effort to deny or rationalize the thought. To take a specific and vivid example, it is very common for mothers (and fathers) to feel a violent impulse towards babies who cannot be pacified. For some of these parents the injunction against such feelings is not too strong and they can accept their falls from grace with a certain amount of equanimity. (It is easier to do so if you have friends who can own up to feeling the same way.) But for others such an impulse provides the clearest evidence of their unsuitability for parenthood and their inadequacy as a person. Paradoxically it is the pressure created by the enormous guilt, and by the doomed attempt to deal with it, that builds tension to the point where it is more likely to explode into real physical abuse.

What is less well documented, however, is the effect that injunctions have on people who are normally functioning well, when they find themselves in situations that are abnormally intense or challenging – like teachers in school. If someone's performance is not up to the standards set by the injunctions, *no allowances are made*, even if they are doing their best to cope with severe or even impossible demands. Injunctions do not listen to excuses, no matter how reasonable. They insist that the forfeit of self-esteem must be paid. Unless one is aware of the injunctions and the effect they are having, the penalty is automatically exacted, like a direct debit, and self-worth is threatened. The phenomena of overload and pressure constitute, for many teachers, just such a breach of some basic injunctions so that the situation of working under heavy demands itself leads, via the activation of these injunctions, to an assault on self-esteem.

The nature of these pernicious and self-punitive injunctions is probably already obvious. For X, Y and Z in the basic formula we can substitute *competent, clear, confident, comfortable, in control,* consistent *and coherent.*

A worthwhile person is always competent: he never makes mistakes, slips of the tongue, errors of judgement or loses his thread halfway through a lesson or a meeting. If he does, that means he is not good enough, and ought to feel badly.

A worthwhile person is always clear: she never loses her grasp on what is going on, gets confused, or is at a loss for an explanation, or at the very least a coherent understanding of what is going on. If she does, that means she is not good enough or bright enough, and ought to feel guilty.

A worthwhile person is always confident: he does not feel uncertain about the effects of his actions or doubt his ability to do the right thing. If he does, that means he is not good enough or strong enough, and ought to feel inadequate.

A worthwhile person always feels comfortable: she never gets agitated, apprehensive, shy, embarrassed, tongue-tied, scared or anxious. If she does, it means she is weak and feeble, and ought to feel ashamed.

A worthwhile person is always in control, not only of his classes but of events and feelings. He should not get too emotional, moody, tearful or truculent, especially if he can't explain why to his own and other people's satisfaction, and if he does he should feel concerned.

A worthwhile person is always consistent: she acts within her normal personality and does not surprise herself or other people by behaving oddly or 'out of character'. Everyone has a right to expect her to be predictable (however trying things are) and she ought to be worried and apologetic if she behaves strangely.

Finally, a worthwhile person is always coherent, in the sense of being all of a piece. He never appears wildly different in different contexts – regardless of what those contexts are. So if he finds himself behaving very differently in school to how he behaves at home, one of them has to be 'real' and the other 'phoney'. People should feel as if there is something wrong with this and be upset about what is happening to them.

The net effect of these injunctions (as well as others we shall meet later) is to ensure that the natural inability of human beings to respond 'perfectly' to all situations, however demanding or paradoxical, is construed by those human beings as clear evidence of personal inadequacy: they lack the ability, resilience or ready-made savoir-faire that they somehow ought to have, in limitless supply, if they are to be able to look themselves in the eye in the bathroom mirror each morning.

Injunctions make the effects of demand *personal*. What started out as an objective assessment like 'That lesson didn't go as well as I had expected' gets recast as 'I made a mistake' which leads to 'I'm a poor teacher' and even 'I'm a failure (as a person)'. At each stage the judgement becomes more general, more negative and more personal. After a series of experiences that are construed in those terms, the cumulative effect may be an assault on the core of a person's self-image and self-respect that is lasting and pervasive. Identity itself is damaged and the negative effects of stress in school begin to leak out and contaminate people's confidence and competence in other, perhaps all, aspects of their lives.

When the injunctions are triggered, and their verdicts are accepted without appeal, another crucial demand is added to the already overlong list. It is a demand that begins to override the others, and to require immediate attention. It is the demand to feel better, for one of the most basic injunctions of all is the one that tells us, tautologically, that worthwhile people do not feel worthless. The dis-ease that people feel when things begin to go wrong, and their ability to stay calm and competent frays at the edges, is itself a feeling that OK people do not have, and it becomes yet another cause for concern and an occasion for self-doubt. Thus do the injunctions feed into and exacerbate each other's effects.

BAD FEELING → THREAT

So how are people to satisfy the demand to feel better, especially if they are unable or unwilling to 'get out of the kitchen'? While the jobs and goals continue to exceed people's limitations, overload and pressure will persist. In the heat of the moment it does not usually look as if there is anything to be done about the heat. And while the injunctions are subject to unwitting acceptance, it is impossible to call them into question. Because they are hidden, it looks to people, if they try to analyse why they are getting upset and uptight, as if the cause for the bad feeling *is* the overload and the pressure. 'It's the job that's making me feel bad.' But, as we have just said, it usually doesn't seem possible to do anything about the job. The situation begins to feel like a trap, reminiscent of the song 'There's a Hole in My Bucket'.

Defensiveness

There is one strategy left, and that is to *hide*. First people have to start hiding from themselves, because that is where the hardest and most persistent voice of criticism is coming from. So what is required is a constriction of awareness which will remove some of the bad feeling and/or make the predicament look less severe or less intractable.

THREAT → DEFENSIVENESS

One common kind of strategy, which we have met already, is to *hide the complexity*. This involves reconstruing the situation so that it looks more straightforward and easy to handle, thus allowing sides to be taken or a stance adopted which reduces the confusion and allows at least some action to be taken – a villain to be defeated, a wrong to be righted, a battle to be fought. Doubt and ambivalence are transmuted into clarity and certainty, and any attempt to reintroduce complexity into the debate is rejected as 'mere nitpicking' or 'a deliberate attempt to muddy the issue'. Reflection is pooh-poohed, and understanding is put into a state of suspended animation, so that it has no chance to develop in its complexity, realism or power. Instead the need to do something is channelled into a single stark campaign. This might be something that has a legitimate place in the original complex equation – it might be peace education, anti-racism or teachers' rights – but which is inflated to fill the whole screen. Or it could be something pretty trivial like who smokes where in the staffroom, or colleagues' standards of dress. As strategies go this is not a bad one at all, for at least it leaves the people involved feeling that they have some power, purpose and (usually) some solidarity with others. But it runs the risk of becoming polarizing and divisive. Thoughtful people who are not able to buy the simplistic analysis are written off with contemptuous slogans like 'If you aren't part of the solution you are part of the problem'.

The second way of hiding from oneself is to *hide the feelings*. This is most effectively done using some variant of the 'whistle-a-happy-tune' strategy. Here the skilled operator establishes in her own consciousness a network of alarm signals which go off when the train of thought starts chugging along in a dangerous direction. Immediately the points are switched, so that the specific signals for feeling bad are never actually encountered. This may also involve physically not going to places (e.g. the staffroom) or meeting people (your head of department) who might set off the alarm by mistake. And a collection of routine thoughts and physical distractions are useful for filling up the spaces created by the avoidance. Lots of time spent reading light novels, listening to music, watching the television or talking are helpful, as is the ability (perhaps aided by a drink or a pill) to fall asleep when these more active anodyne activities come to a halt. The ploy of inflating some molehills in order to provide manageable substitutes for the mountains you are busily ignoring also serves as an effective distraction.

The third common way of hiding from oneself is to *hide the responsibility*. This has the advantage over the previous two strategies of allowing people to leave relatively undistorted their awareness of the complexity of the situation and of their own fallibility, but at the expense of construing themselves as partially or completely powerless. There are a number of specific methods of achieving this. Rationalization refers to people's efforts to construct an explanation for their fallibility which allows them to own it without feeling bad about it. This explanation is then offered to others with the intention of getting them to agree that circumstances conspired to prevent you from performing with the excellence and flair that you would, in the normal course of events, have displayed. It is helpful in this context if one's account of the circumstances can be exaggerated in some way, until it becomes clear that nobody, however marvellous, could have coped any better than you did. The teachers' vocabulary for describing individual pupils, colleagues, classes and lessons, as well as events such as meetings, is full of such inflationary terms: awful, dreadful, terrible, animals, bastard. 'I'll *die* if I have to take 3Y on a Friday afternoon again', 'It was an utter *disaster*', and so on. 'I didn't control them' becomes 'They were completely uncontrollable'. (The jargon expression for this ploy is 'awfulizing'.)

There is a rather more dangerous kind of exaggerating, described by Eric Berne in his pop psychology book *Games People Play*[3] as the game of 'Harassed', which involves making things *really* dreadful for yourself. If a person has, say, five jobs to do as part of his professional responsibility, and is beginning to feel inadequate because he isn't doing them all perfectly . . . take on ten more. This guarantees total inadequacy, but the pay-off is (a) the knowledge that nobody could cope with all fifteen, and that therefore the failure does not reflect badly on him personally, and (b) some self-righteousness at how hard he is *trying* to contribute, and resentment at those who are not 'pulling their weight'. This strategy is reminiscent of the poster (visible, interestingly enough, in quite a few staffrooms and offices) saying 'I'm going to have my nervous breakdown. I've worked for it. I've earned it. I deserve it. Now I'm damn well going to have it'.

The last kind of strategy for denying responsibility is to give it away to someone else. If you can find someone else whose *fault* it is, then you can give up worrying that it is your own. It is here that the anger begins, in the form of blame, resentment and self-righteousness. 'If she had done her job properly, I would never have been in this mess in the first place.' 'The head's so out of touch with reality that it's not surprising things are going wrong.' 'My tutor hasn't a clue: he hasn't taught since before the war I don't expect.' And again it helps if one can get a group of other people to agree with you.

The recognition of these strategies, the ones which preserve self-respect by denying opportunity or responsibility, is absolutely vital in the process of moving away from hostility and resignation, and towards a more powerful stance as a teacher. For their side-effect is to confuse us about what is truly possible. It is a fact that many teachers have precious little elbow room, and that often this confinement is created, or exacerbated, by other people's actions. There are real limits, and some people really are to blame. But in a stressed state, and especially if one is playing helpless, one cannot see clearly what the opportunities and risks actually are, and one therefore cannot act with discernment and intelligence. While anger may stimulate the courage to do something, it may at the same time cloud the perception of what to be courageous about. If one cannot feel accurately what the scope and limits of one's own responsibility are, there is an increased chance of behaving either fatalistically or recklessly. Clearsightedness is a prerequisite of effective action. It is important to emphasize this because some people tend to polarize the 'personal' and the 'political', and to confuse the willingness to explore one's responsibility with the oppressive tactic of 'victim-blaming'.

To point out that complaining often functions as a self-defence is *not* to say that the complaint is invalid. Accusations that have some truth to them make the most watertight defences of all. But the purpose of making such an accusation is, if it is made defensively, to cement oneself into a position of self-righteous stasis, and not to bring about change. This state is easily distinguished from the rational and purposeful promotion of a particular philosophy, or the rejection of a demand, by its resistance not only to 'impositions' but to the offer of responsibility and choice. If the 'authorities' which have been 'pushing us around' change their tack and say: 'OK, what would *you* like? Tell us and we'll try to provide or support it', they will suddenly find themselves being attacked for 'not doing their job' and 'abdicating their responsibilities'. They cannot win, for the aim of the stressed work-force is to avoid having to embrace the discomfiting uncertainty by construing itself as victimized and manipulated.

Thus real and objective limitations and risks (of which there are many) may be magnified still further by teachers' projections. Instead of seeking to have what little impact they can, they come to feel completely surrounded by impasses which seal up the potential gaps between the proliferating demands. Compounded by their own unconscious survival strategy, their room for manoeuvre appears to shrink until it vanishes. In the good old days, when we were respected and trusted (so the train of thought might go), we had the freedom to explore opportunities to contribute to education. As the net tightened, though, and those were taken away, so the only possible freedom became to *protect* ourselves and to try to consolidate our position. Then, as things got worse, and our professional rights and status were further eroded, it seemed as if the only freedom left was to *resist*. Given no avenues to think for ourselves, we could at least say 'No' to what others were seeking to foist upon us. And when even this right is removed, and overt opposition becomes too difficult or too risky, we can, as a last resort, lapse into the passive, covert stance of lethargy and resignation. There are many teachers who feel that things are that bad, and for whom, at some tacit level of decision-making, becoming 'like that' has presented itself as the only sensible, or the only possible *modus operandi* that is left. It may indeed be. The only freedoms of the truly enslaved are subtle subversion and private dissent. But it is no disrespect to enquire into the possibility that some teachers may, through no fault of their own, have reached this position prematurely, and that other, more positive options still remain open.

We have so far said little about the way the Stress Syndrome spills over into teachers' personal relationships out of school. One is an increasing conflict about the use of time. A conscientious teacher may feel inclined to take work home (both mentally and physically), yet also feel – perhaps guiltily – that they wish to prevent work from encroaching on their private life. Jill Jones, for example, said:

> I overwork, I know that, and I try to do too much sometimes. One bit of me says well you've got to, you've got to do it like that. And the other bit says, 'You've got a life to lead!' But it's important to me: I want to do it right, even though I'm not sure what doing it right means! I feel as though if I didn't have that drive I would have opted out of teaching long ago. It's that that keeps me going.

A second way in which stress begins to subvert home life is through the *displacement* of feelings of anger. Although these feelings may originally be focused, whether appropriately or not, on colleagues or superiors within education, the targets may be inaccessible or it may be, or seem to be, too dangerous to tackle them directly. Particularly when the ability to be rational about specific issues becomes diverted into a petulant or punitive attitude, and one cannot trust oneself to 'keep one's cool', yet the feelings demand expression, it may be easier to 'blow up' with those who seem less able to hit back effectively. Sometimes this may be unfortunate pupils who happen to be in the wrong place at the wrong time; but often it is the teachers' families who begin to bear the brunt, and whose reserves of tolerance and goodwill may also, after a while, begin to dry up in turn.

In addition to hiding from themselves, teachers also begin to feel the need to *hide from each other*. For the assaults on self-esteem that arise from unwitting acceptance of the injunctions may be mirrored and compounded by assaults on public esteem, if the community in which people work gives its collective assent to the same injunctions. If everyone (or at least those who can mould opinion and wield sanctions) implicitly agrees that it is weak to get upset, and a sign of personal incompetence to make mistakes, then openness entails real risks to staffroom status and even to promotion and other career prospects. (The fear looms that the all-important reference might then contain sentences like 'However Miss Smith is prone to emotional displays, and to occasional lapses of judgement' – as if there were people who weren't.) Thus the overload and pressure that teachers are experiencing must be concealed. Many teachers know of their own cover-up operations, and fear lest a personal Watergate scandal be revealed. Guilty secrets begin to pile up that may be disclosed to no one else at all, not even friends or family.

Although many teachers are genuinely on good form, at least from time to time, others adopt a cheerful and casual manner in the staffroom as a front that bears no relation to how they feel as they drive home, exhausted and depressed, at the end of the day. Putting on a brave face for colleagues may also compound the feeling of inauthenticity or emptiness which they are experiencing in the classroom. There are a lot of people who know of a colleague who appeared to be the *last* person to go under – 'Jim always seemed such a jolly, easygoing chap' – until his absence one day was followed by news of his nervous breakdown, or heart attack, or suicide.

The kinds of conversations that can be held with colleagues may become restricted to those that are safely superficial and impersonal, and the developing staffroom ambience may bind such social conventions ever more tightly. It may become increasingly necessary to avoid contact with certain people as much as possible. These threatening contacts are of two kinds: the difficult and the sympathetic. People with whom one has had personal or professional differences – a row or a clash of principle – are best avoided (albeit sometimes with real regret) because meeting them might demand emotional resources that aren't there, open old wounds, or challenge one's public certainties that in fact feel all too precarious. While people may even find themselves avoiding others who would be understanding, precisely because their concern may threaten to breach fragile defences and bring on the 'crack-up' that feels as if it is only just being fended off, as it is.

The other way of hiding from others is to be absent. Some teachers are continually ill. Some apply for every in-service training course that is going. And senior teachers, especially heads, have the additional option of the flight into bureaucracy, or into the development of a national reputation for something or other, that enables them to spend considerable time away from school at important meetings.

Hiding from self and hiding from others interact in a particularly unfortunate way. The undermining of self-esteem may lead to assumptions about the reactions of others that are unjustified. It is common for us to imagine that others are going to be as critical of us as we are of ourselves. Just as the injunctions may serve to exaggerate the feeling of powerlessness, in the face of a limited (even if substantial) loss of power, so they lead people to exaggerate the imagined risks of being honest. Instead of seeking opportunities to come clean, being realistic and perceptive about when and to whom to make an 'advance', and taking risks that can be recouped, self-doubt floods the whole question with anxiety, and replaces a balanced point of view with crude prejudices and images of disaster. What people have done once (perhaps in a moment of stress themselves) becomes set in cement, evidence of a chronic inability to be understanding or kind. 'I could never talk to Jennifer. Do you remember the time she reduced that poor student to tears in the staffroom?' The fact that there may indeed be real risks attached to opening up and talking from the heart is not in dispute, just as the limitations on teachers' freedom are very real. The point is that when the injunctions are triggered, they serve to increase *apparent* levels of risk or constraint and to damage people's ability to perceive the facts of the matter in an accurate and differentiated way. They lose their nous (and, as they say in some quarters, their 'bottle'). The situation comes to seem increasingly hopeless.

In several ways this loss of hope acts as a self-fulfilling prophecy. If there is nothing one *can* do, then there is clearly no point in thinking about what one *might* do – so the effort to formulate what might be desirable becomes merely wasted and frustrating effort. But on the other hand if one has no vision, no sense of what it might be worthwhile to do, then there is equally clearly no point in trying to do anything. 'Can't do' reinforces 'Don't know' and vice versa. Powerlessness undermines perspicacity. Lack of opportunity breeds indifference to vision. Routine thinking throws up no ideas about how to work on or round or against a seemingly impossible situation – which reaffirms powerlessness.

Toxic waste

Hiding in one or other of these ways may 'work', in that the self-recriminations that the injunctions breed, or rather the awareness of them, is reduced to manageable levels. Many teachers are able to function pretty well and to keep their doubts and feelings under reasonable control. In fact it is hard to imagine anyone working under demanding conditions who does not need to use some such strategies of damage-limitation. The peace of mind that they produce however is won not without some costs. The hiding strategies themselves produce additional effects that are unwanted and unpleasant, and which may add to the net level of discomfort rather than reducing it. Hiding from others may save face, but at the cost of an increased weight of private guilt and doubt. If people cannot speak openly to others about their errors and anxieties, it is easy to feel more and more isolated and inadequate. The disparity between private truth and public convention leaves them feeling that they are the only person having trouble. Spurious comparisons with the overt confidence of colleagues make the inability to cope seem an ever more clear indication of personal inadequacy – which in its turn makes openness about problems appear yet more risky and impossible.

Alternatively people whose predominant coping strategy is to blame, project and rationalize may find themselves drifting towards isolation as well, as other people's patience and tolerance wear thin. Friends may start making excuses: after all who wants to spend the evening with someone who is becoming so surly and boring? In addition it is hard for people who are becoming bitter and negative to see what is happening to themselves without incurring further guilt or self-dislike. So they either have to accept this noxious side-effect of their coping strategy, or to project it outwards with increasingly strident, dogmatic and simplistic vigour.

At some point, if the side-effects cannot be contained, and bad feeling continues to mount, people begin to resort to another mechanism of self-defence. Instead of working psychologically on their own awareness, they may now, involuntarily, try to hold down their discomfort by physical means. By exercising muscular control, certain kinds of feeling can be inhibited. The impulse to cry can be controlled by setting the muscles of the face firmly (adopting literally a stiff upper lip). The impulse to shout can be inhibited by clamping the upper chest so that breathing becomes shallow and energy is dampened. The impulse to hit is curbed by hunching the shoulders. The feeling of fear is restrained by tensing the muscles that surround the stomach and the anus. And so on. One might protest that such primitive devices would not be relevant to the civilized conduct of staffroom and classroom, but it is surprising how thin the veneer of civilization turns out to be. And adults do not need to be on the verge of shouting or crying for these mechanisms to be involved. For many people, particularly those brought up under the sway of the Judeo-Christian religions, physical control of emotional expression is learnt at an early age, and by adulthood can be practised to a high level of subtlety and skill. (Children who are beginners in the art can sometimes be seen 'overdoing it' when they go completely rigid, stop breathing, and rapidly turn a variety of interesting colours.)

By becoming 'tense', 'wound up' and 'uptight', a measure of emotional control can be established – but again at the price of creating further toxic waste. To the unwanted social and psychological fall-out produced by the earlier hiding strategies are now added various kinds of physical discomfort: the 'psychosomatic' conditions we reviewed at the start of this chapter. Depending on which muscles are involuntarily clenched to suppress which feeling, for how long, and with what force, so people lay themselves open to the range of stress symptoms, from staring eyes to constipation; from tics to migraines; from vomiting to lower back pain; from insomnia to nosebleeds. If the tension is sufficient it will contain some part of the problem, whilst also ensuring that it will balloon out somewhere else. A chronic illness increases isolation. Soldiering on with lower back pain makes it hard not to be preoccupied. Inability to sleep drains resources. Turning to pills and/or alcohol can take its toll in hangovers, reduced awareness and the risk of growing dependency.

In whichever direction the Stress Syndrome develops, if it does, one can be sure that two effects will occur. The first is the breaching of further injunctions, such as 'Worthwhile people don't get so tired, need a drink before school, smoke so much, eat so much, behave so badly to their friends, feel so bottled up, become so forgetful' or whatever. As people adopt wilder and wilder attempts to keep the bad feelings down, so it is ever more likely that these feelings will bounce up and hit them even harder in return. And the second effect is a further reduction in real competence, so that jobs take longer to do, require more resources to do them, and are done increasingly shoddily. Thus limitations

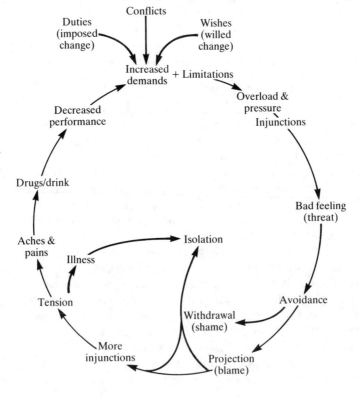

Figure 1   The stress cycle

grow, the weight of demand goes up, and overload and pressure expand still further: which is where we came in. A simplified version of the vicious cycle – at its worst – is shown in Figure 1. This is the story of the Stress Syndrome. It is the condition in which the attempts to avoid, cover up or evade responsibility for bad feeling – bad feeling generated by the impossible need to live up to inflexible standards – themselves create yet more bad feeling. Coping strategies are unthinkingly deployed which tend at the least to be ineffective, and which often produce unintended, unwanted side-effects that breach the same or other injunctions. If the process persists too intensely and for too long, ever more desperate and damaging controls need to be applied, controls which may involve abuses of the body, of food, drink and drugs, and of other people. All of these controls are, however misguided, attempts to cope and to preserve self-respect that make sense within the person's framework of assumptions and values. From inside that belief system the responses that are made to overload and pressure will seem, in so far as they are considered consciously, to be sensible, vital or even inevitable.

Chapter 4

Back into shape

Here's a two-step formula for handling stress.
Step 1: Don't sweat the small stuff.
Step 2: Remember, it's all small stuff.

Anthony Robbins[1]

When people are within the vicious cycle of stress, their top priority becomes limiting the damage that is being done to their self-esteem. Some of the ways of doing this are more effective, and create less toxic waste, than others, but many of them share a concern with maintenance at the cost of growth. The conclusion therefore is that the recapturing of a sense of well-being is a necessary pre-condition for creating a climate within which teachers are willing to think about, and to become involved in, the development of schooling and teaching. If we are to move towards transforming schools so that they deliver to young people a more appropriate and empowering kind of education than many of them currently receive, and if, as I have argued, this must happen with the committed participation of substantial numbers of teachers, then it follows that the promotion of integrity and self-respect amongst teachers is the most urgent challenge that education currently faces. The concern with personal well-being is not, as we have said before, an individualistic alternative to practical action, but its *sine qua non*. There is all the difference in the world between encouraging people to feel good, and encouraging them to feel good *about the situation*.

The challenge is to help create a climate within which it is not just acceptable but *normal* for teachers to talk openly about their feelings, their perceptions, their misgivings, their ideals and their experiments, whether large or small, successful or unsuccessful. The only possible form that climate can take is one which acknowledges as legitimate and appropriate expressions of doubt, uncertainty, confusion and anxiety. Unless people are free to say 'I don't think it's good enough', 'I don't feel as if I'm doing a good enough job', and 'I don't have a clear idea of how to do it better', teacher-generated and teacher-appropriated change will not happen. If you have to be *sure* before you dare open your mouth, most people are going to stay quiet. This type of open learning environment is after all standard for social workers and counsellors, and there is no reason why it should not be equally standard for teachers.

The first step is to start talking about stress, not as something shameful but as an interesting, understandable and, up to a point, an inevitable accompaniment to high levels of demand and uncertainty. Stress needs to be dealt with not just through one-day workshops that some teachers are brave enough or desperate enough to attend. (I have been told many times by participants in such workshops that they have felt it necessary to conceal from their colleagues where they were going!) It needs to be on the agenda, both formal and informal, of most if not all staffrooms. We need to build an atmosphere which reverses the dominant value systems of those staffrooms in which it is seen as silly to be open, to want to have real conversations about education, and mature to be flip and dismissive. It should be the people who are 'like that' (and also 'beyond hope') who are on the defensive: those who stamp on students' enthusiasm (however naive it may be) who get the funny looks – not the students.

Some schools have such an ethos already. Some have it sporadically or partially. And some are in disarray. We need to encourage as many schools as possible to shift from the third to the second, and from the second to the first category. That shift will take place as a result of three forces. The first is ordinary teachers, in increasing numbers, becoming more perceptive about their own predicament and more effective at dealing with their own stress. The second, smaller but also growing band, will be teachers who are strong enough and courageous enough to stick their necks out publicly. They will be secure enough about their own capabilities and limitations to take the lead in talking in ways which the old lags will continue to denigrate for a while as 'weak' or 'idealistic'. They will not be martyrs, for most of them will be astute as well as honest. And their effect will be considerable, for they will merely be modelling the kind of attitude and commitment that most teachers have buried but not lost. They will at first be assailed after meetings by colleagues saying 'Good for you' and 'I wish I'd had the courage to say that' and 'That's just what I think. I'm glad someone else thinks the same way'. Rapidly they will find themselves supported *in* the meetings as well.

The third force is the headteachers, for it is they who have the most decisive influence on what it is or is not safe to do or say in a school. Some teachers will have been saying, as they have followed the argument up to this point: 'All very well. But you come and try saying how stressed you are in my school and see how long you last. Nobody participates in meetings for a very good reason: anything at all important is all sewn up before it ever gets on the agenda'. I shall focus on the role of headteachers and how to deal with them in Chapter 7. First though I want to see what help and advice it is possible to give to teachers in the first two groups: we will focus on the 'destressers' in this chapter, and on the 'change agents' in the next.

COPING WITH STRESS

There are some common pieces of advice that people swap when they are asked how to deal with stress. They include the exhortations to Stay Calm, Keep Things in Proportion, Don't Think About It, and Don't Let It/Them Get To You (the last one of which includes the more specific Avoid Confrontations). These are extremely sensible. The only problem with them is that they do not tell you *how*. They describe desired states, not how to achieve them. What seems to be of more use to people are specific things they can do to help them achieve these states. Fortunately teachers know of a great many such techniques. In this section I shall describe some of these, again culled from the wide range of suggestions that have been offered during the course of workshops. I will indicate, as I go through them, the way in which they work: that is, how they fit into the diagnostic story that we developed in the last chapter.

Relax

As we saw, a large part of the Stress Syndrome, once it is in full swing, arises from sustained physical tension. People may tense their bodies in a variety of ways to cope with the threat of strong feelings, but then as it were forget to relax the muscles after the immediate threat has passed. To start unravelling stress 'from the bottom' they may invent or seek a range of tension-reducing activities, which we might group into two categories, those that relax softly and gently, and those that involve a more vigorous release. Into the first category fall the following. *Resting, sleeping* and generally *vegetating* are obvious ways of unwinding. Teachers often report that they completely switch off at the beginning of the holidays, or sleep for abnormally long periods of time for several days. If there remains an insistent voice that keeps telling you there is something 'wrong' with sleeping twelve hours a day, or reminding you of how much there is to do, turning into a vegetable may not be an effective technique, and something more explosive or cathartic may be required. Any kind of physical *stroking* can aid relaxation. Having your neck and shoulders rubbed, or better still a full body massage, is a good investment. And people report that time spent stroking pets, particularly cats, is very therapeutic. Cuddles and hugs, the longer the better, and preferably accompanied by deep sighs, are highly recommended – although they can be risky in staffrooms. (Trying to promote hugging in the staffroom would be a suitable project for the more courageous change-agent.) Some people learn particular techniques such as *meditation* or *relaxation exercises*. Most of these are basically simple, involving sitting or lying down comfortably and focusing awareness on a pleasing thought ('Still and calm. . . . still and calm' or whatever; or invent your own); a soft 'nonsense sound' (a *mantra*) that you repeat under your breath; on the rise and fall of your chest as you breath; or successively on different parts of the body, starting at the toes and working upwards. For the latter it is better to buy a tape, or to make your own, and listen to that, rather than to try to do it yourself as you go along. (The Appendix to this book gives you the basis for making a tape. It is adapted from Jack Dunham's book *Stress in Teaching*:[21] you can adapt it further as you like.) Either way you are bound to drift off into unconnected chains of thought, which doesn't matter a bit. But this can be irritating, and the opposite of relaxing, if you are trying to keep track of the sequence yourself. If you still find that you are getting more tense with the effort to concentrate (which is possible: some people find relaxation exercises absolute torture) stop doing it. An effective stress-reduction technique is one that works, not one that someone else says *ought* to work.

Incidentally a trap here is to feel guilty when you find that you have given up doing the exercises that you so fervently swore you were going to do every day. Many people find that they drop their meditation practice or whatever it is at precisely the time when they think they need it most – i.e. when they are feeling most stressed. This is entirely normal and may even in the long run be healthy: who knows? The important thing is to view these lapses with indulgence. If you make it a chore or a conflict you are already back on the vicious cycle.

Release

As well as, or instead of, relaxing gently, people find ways of exploding the tension. Physical *exercise* is good if you enjoy it – jogging, playing squash, working out or whatever. The trap to be avoided here is to turn the exercise into another source of demand by forcing yourself to go faster every day, swearing that you are going to beat your partner next time, or overdoing it with the weights. Many techniques for stress reduction can be appropriated by the same injunctions to *succeed* that got you stressed in the first place, and should be discontinued if you spot that they have been subverted in this way (unless your goal has also changed along the way from stress reduction to record-breaking).

Provided sexual energies have not been drained by the stress itself *orgasm* is a great form of tension release, whether achieved through making love or masturbation. (Far from diminishing, some people find that their libido during periods of stress reaches embarrassingly high levels.) And there are various forms of emotional release. 'Having a good cry', especially while being held by someone who is not trying to talk you out of it, is good, provided doing so does not seriously breach further injunctions about being 'feeble' and 'out of control'. It is often startling how people's faces soften and their bodies relax after crying. Screaming

Figure 2

and shouting are a help, though stress may be transferred to neighbours or family unless they are prepared for it. Finding lonely bits of countryside or the middle of a large field to do your shouting is a way out of this problem, as is going to a football match or a rock concert. Beating up cushions releases the feelings pent up in the shoulders – but such forms of catharsis are sometimes thought to be all right for Californians but not for the rest of us.

Something a little milder like *ranting and raving* about colleagues and pupils, preferably in a self-consciously irrational and exaggerated way, can release feelings and help to restore balance and humour. Some teachers say it is useful to have a pact with someone else, preferably another teacher, which allows you to complain in the most dreadful and unreasonable way to each other, in turn, for a fixed period of time like ten minutes. During your turn you can be as bitchy, whiny or self-righteous as you like – but when time's up, that's it. It is surprising how therapeutic, as well as creative and entertaining, such sessions can be. In the course of such a process you may find either that the resentment or anger goes away (and you realize that you had 'got all steamed up over nothing'), or it doesn't, and remains as a clear, persistent and legitimate grievance. We will come back to dealing with these in a moment.

Relax the rules

Part of the Stress Syndrome is the likelihood that whatever you do to cope will only result in yet more self-criticism. Typical of stress is this feeling of being for ever 'on the run', unable to stop and be at peace with yourself. Yet being able to step off the treadmill and stop judging yourself for a while is the only way to begin to take stock and to start to unwind from the stress spiral. It is useful, therefore, to be able to adopt an attitude of temporary self-indulgence towards habits or feelings that, in the normal course of events, you may struggle with or be trying to change. Teachers report a common range of such self-indulgences: allowing yourself (in the middle of a bad patch) to give in to temptations like cream cakes, cigarettes, a bottle of your favourite booze or a spending spree. As with the other strategies, though, there will be some people for whom this advice is inappropriate: for example if they are unable to avoid feeling guilty, or if the risks involved feel just too great. People with members of their family who are or have been alcoholic may, very understandably, be too scared of 'hitting the bottle' themselves to allow even a temporary licence in that area. People who are under medical direction to lose weight or quit smoking may likewise be quite rightly unwilling to give in to their impulses. But it is a matter of realistically weighing up the pros and cons.

At some times, for some people, a binge may be just what is required to break through the wall of Dos and Don'ts within which one has become imprisoned. There is also some satisfaction to be gained from being deliberately rebellious or doing something outrageous and saying 'F*** you!' to your own conventions for a night. In some cultures such safety valves are explicitly provided. In Japan, for example, you can get away with saying and doing things when you are drunk that would be unthinkable when sober. The key to the success of such releases, though, is always that you do *not* have to pay for them with significant amounts of guilt or regret the next morning.

Re-create

In stress the undermining of self-confidence and self-esteem begins to overflow from its original forum and adulterate other areas of life. One's sense of oneself as a worthwhile person is in jeopardy. To counteract the spread of this blight, and to keep it contained, people often report on the importance of having another life outside school. If school is becoming a place that you do not enjoy, where you doubt your competence, and whose value you are questioning – then find an alternative activity that you enjoy, value and are good at. Through this 'recreation' people can re-create their self-esteem. Some people literally develop another life in which they display a side of themselves that would shock their pupils as much as their colleagues if they were to find out. An ex-student of mine, a white woman who looked pretty 'straight' in her school clothes, used to frizz her hair and play bass in an otherwise all-black, all-male band in the evenings. A primary headteacher in Kent is an enthusiastic hang-glider at weekends.

In quite a different vein, one teacher in a workshop described how she spent part of each weekend visiting old people in her community. And of course teachers' own families, and having fun with their own children, can be an enormous source of satisfaction. For these teachers the time taken up by their extra activities more than repays itself in renewed zest and self-confidence in school.

There is a general point here of some importance. Teachers commonly believe that the reason they are so tired is that they have so much to do. Yet they equally commonly affirm the observation that by taking on additional 'jobs' from which they derive real enjoyment and satisfaction, their energy and resources seem, paradoxically, to be replenished rather than further drained. It begins to look as if *what is exhausting is not the amount of work per se, but the lack of clear values to underpin it* and the consequent lack of regular enjoyment and true satisfaction that arise from it. Doing extra things that help you get back to feeling good about yourself tends to recharge the batteries for school itself. 'Hobbies', doing crossword puzzles, gardening or whatever can have this restorative effect if the challenge they present is self-chosen, and enjoyable.

Communicate

One of the linchpins that holds the Stress Syndrome in place is isolation. Isolation creates a social vacuum, an absence of intimacy which removes both comfort and knowledge. One is deprived of information about how others are feeling and managing, and of feedback about one's own coping strategies and their public face. And this vacuum is the perfect breeding ground for the inflation of self-doubt and self-criticism, and increasingly unfounded imaginings about other people's competence, or about their disdain towards oneself. Ungrounded in social realities, fuzzy anxieties become magnified and fixed into unpleasant certainties. To begin to decrease this isolation is therefore a vital part of the stress-reduction programme.

To take the initiative yourself, however is often too difficult: your mind may have convinced you that your confusion is so much greater than other people's, your backlog of work so much longer, your reputation so much lower, that to open yourself to the social confirmation of these frightful facts would be a pointless and self-sacrificing thing to do. The likelihood of social *dis*confirmation seems too slim and too implausible to make the risk worthwhile. Alongside this there may be another internal voice that is piling on further self-criticism for being so feeble, for having lost touch with friends, for being an outcast, or whatever. Within this frame of mind exhortations from well-intentioned others to 'tell me what's wrong' or 'to seek some help' may be heard as another confirmation of one's own inadequacy. It is important to remember that there are risks attached to being kind to people in this state, and important also not to underestimate how difficult it may be for such people to reach out on their own. But that said, the efforts to peck oneself out of the shell of isolation, and to knock politely on other people's, are perhaps the two most essential strategies for the general reduction of stress. For one's frailties to be known by someone else, someone who does not add their voice to the clamour of internal judgement, is the first step back towards being able to view one's predicament simultaneously with accuracy and equanimity.

The most vital resource for stressed professionals is at least one other person, preferably but not necessarily a colleague, to whom they can tell the truth. This kind of *heart-to-heart* conversation is quite different from a form of interaction where solidarity is established around common causes, or against common enemies or threats. These are not without value: they do give a sense of belonging which combats superficial isolation. But they do not bring air to the underlying issues. They do not provide the safety within which individuals can clarify and express their own feelings, perceptions and inchoate beliefs, for the staffroom cliques are based on certainty, and function to hold at bay doubt and anxiety. My experience in workshops is that people are dying for more honest forms of communication. When they are asked to share their true thoughts or feelings with an unfamiliar partner or in a small group, I have never known anyone to object, or complain that the exercise is an invasion of privacy. Teachers *want* to have their privacy invaded, provided they are given a little nudge and they feel sure that there isn't going to be any 'comeback' in their school. (It is not surprising that workshops with large numbers of staff from a single school are much more ticklish in this respect, though the long-term gains can also be more dramatic.)

Teacher *support groups* are increasingly being set up to provide the opportunity for greater honesty, and it can be less threatening for people who feel isolated to join one of these than it is to make individual overtures within their own staffroom. Such support may be available for groups of teachers who share a common predicament – such as women, ethnic minority teachers, new teachers or headteachers. But when their focus is on personal experience rather than the discussion of issues, the parallels between the emerging agendas will often be striking. There will be more practical advice about how to run a successful support group in Chapter 7.

For teachers who feel more comfortable with one-to-one meetings than with groups, various kinds of *counselling* can be sought, and again it may be possible to organize this so that unsympathetic colleagues or superiors do not find out. Unfortunately people who could benefit from some counselling are often prevented from doing so by their own injunctions. 'I ought to be able to sort this out on my own.' 'It is a sign of weakness to ask for help.' 'You must have to be pretty sick to see a shrink.' And so on. There is still a lingering feeling around that if you need this sort of help there has to be something 'wrong' with you, and this admission may further attack self-esteem and seem therefore to exact too high a price.

Wake up

The injunctions that are undermining self-esteem can only do so when they are unobserved and unquestioned. They derive their power from being taken for granted, so that they can do their destructive work without themselves being checked for validity or reality. A worthwhile longer-term project, which gets closer to the heart of the matter, is therefore to begin to unearth these injunctions, to bring them to light, and to put them to the test of rational and empirical scrutiny. This can form part of the deeper work of a support group or a counselling relationship. To the extent that these arenas support and acknowledge people's feelings and their search for greater clarity, they must presuppose a set of values that is different from the one which underlies the common staffroom ethos; and after a while this clash of values may become explicit. As it does so, individuals are able to become more conscious of the assumptions about personal worth and 'correct conduct' that they themselves had been tacitly making, and to see that an alternative personal philosophy could generate greater inner strength, and decrease their dependency on other people's approval.

This is a long-term project because the injunctions, though often easy to describe, are buried deeply inside the way people spontaneously think and act. Detecting them is just the beginning of a process in which only slowly, and with considerable backsliding, one becomes aware of the multiple ways in which they manifest themselves as evasiveness, defensiveness, spikiness, apprehensiveness and so on.

Support and feedback from others is very helpful. One way in which other people can help in daily life is by giving us feedback when we have unconsciously lapsed into our familiar stressed pattern. Such *alarm calls* can help us to wake up sooner, before we have been swept too far into the groove of sulkiness, paranoia or self-pity. However, it is important that alarm calls have been requested from and agreed with the other person when we are in our right minds. If others offer us alarm calls without their having been previously ordered, they usually feel like an intrusion and a criticism, and will be fended off. When someone says 'Hey, you're whining again', you have to be able to say 'Thank you', rather than 'Who the hell are you to talk?' Alarm calls are best requested from people who you like and trust – such as family and good friends – because they can place some strain on a relationship. And it is better if you have something you are allowed to wake *them* up about as well, so that you are not always on the receiving end.

What people can do for themselves is to set up the equivalent of alarm calls: *trip wires*. For most teachers I have worked with, their particular stress portfolio unfolds unconsciously up to a certain point, after which they become aware of the fact that they are getting seriously stressed and need to take care of themselves in some way. The things that act as signals are their intuitively created trip wires. They include, to give just a few examples, realizing that they have re-read the same page of a book three times without taking any of it in; nearly getting knocked over crossing the road; yelling 'Tie!' at a pupil they don't know; noticing that they are both reading a magazine *and* watching the television while having their evening meal; spotting the line of empty wine bottles that has accrued since the weekend. It is a useful (though again slow and very fallible) personal project to try to identify the symptoms of one's personal stress earlier and earlier in its course, so that remedial action can be taken before things have got too bad.

Affirmations are an additional technique for decreasing the power that the injunctions wield in making people's lives a misery. They are deliberate attempts which people can make to counteract their injunctions by asserting their opposites. Such affirmations can be written down and left in places where a person knows he or she will regularly come across them. They can be as immodest and as positive as you like – although the risk of being embarrassed if other people find them has to be taken into account. It would be a brave character who pinned a large notice with the words 'Here sits a wonderful teacher' above her chair in the staffroom, for example. Among the affirming reminders that people have generated for themselves in workshops are:

- I do a good job *and* I make mistakes. (Note the crucial word here is the *and* rather than a *but* in the middle.)
- Relax! You deserve it.
- To be not good enough is good enough.
- To feel good about myself is my top professional responsibility.
- What's wrong with being 'only human'?

The point behind many of these affirmations is to keep reminding oneself of the obvious fact that in a situation where it is clearly impossible to be perfect, to be less than perfect is the best one can be.

Organize

Stress undermines efficiency and increases the level of demand by making people disorganized. Time spent in *taking stock* is time well spent, even in the middle of a hectic day. One very common technique that people use is making lists of things to be done, and physically crossing them off as and when they are completed. One embellishment to list-making which I have found keeps my spirits up is to include in the list (a) one or two things I have done already; (b) a few things that are easy and unproblematic; (c) the item 'Make List'. As soon as the list is complete, therefore, there are already several items that you can cross off, which gives you a flying start with the rest. The fact that I am conning myself, and know it, does not, strange to say, seem to render the technique ineffective. Another trick that I have learnt is for increasing the likelihood that I will actually get down to a job which is becoming urgent but which I don't want to do. Simply add to the To Do list other tasks that are less urgent, and which are even more unappealing. I hate writing letters, for example, so if I lard my list with 'Write to Eddy', 'Write to Mary', 'Write to Aidan' and so on, the item 'Do Psychology Booklists' becomes relatively more attractive. (Of course, for my friends to stand a chance of receiving any correspondence from me means that I either have to wait for the guilt level to rise sufficiently (which is a slow process), or to unearth other things to put on my list like 'Install central heating' and 'Decorate bathroom'.) Other people, more strong-minded than me, use the reverse tactics of promising themselves a reward when they have done something difficult. I suspect these are people who, as children, were able to make their sweets last longer than anyone else's and to keep the best bit till last. Given these various personal ploys, it always seems to make sense to prioritize the list at the time of making it, and to number the items in the order in which you are going to do them. Having done this coolly and rationally there is less chance of wasting time between each job on deciding which to do next. It is also important to give yourself a realistic – even generous – and flexible budget of time, so that further self-punishment does not accrue if you fail to complete everything in a day.

Other aspects of taking stock include *realistic goal-setting* (jargon borrowed from behavioural psychologists for making sensible decisions about what, given your talents and your time, you can hope to get done) and *delegating*. When people get into a stress-induced panic about their workload they may (a) begin to load more and more on to their own shoulders, and (b) feel so overwhelmed that they can't seem to get started. The trick is to give away what you reasonably can, to put straight into the waste-paper basket everything which it is not absolutely necessary to do anything about, or which it is now too late to do anything about, and then to begin to nibble away at the rest.

The remaining strategies are designed to decrease the overload and pressure themselves. As you will have noticed, the strategies we have reviewed have been operating back along the stress cycle (as shown in Figure 1 on page 70) at points nearer and nearer the source. If you imagine stress as being in 'hot water' then there are roughly three stages in its creation. First the tap is turned on (demand rises); then the water gets hot (injunctions activated); finally stress occurs (withdrawal, anger and tension arise). Our coping strategies have been listed in reverse order. If you can't do anything better, keep mopping up. The next thing is to reduce the heat so that the water doesn't get so hot. And best of all is to turn the tap down so that the flow of demands decreases. These are the last group of techniques we are going to consider.

Leave

The simplest solution to the problem of stress is to leave the demanding situation. People take early retirement, move to a new school, get a job out of teaching, get seconded on to courses or research projects, or just wait for the holidays. Many teachers, however, either feel trapped in the job or, like Jill Jones, actually want to stay in teaching, stresses and all, and do the best job they can. What alternatives do they have for reducing the demands?

Learn

Remember that demand, leading to overload and pressure, is a function of the disparity between duties and wishes on the one hand and limitations on the other. Recall too that limitations are of different kinds: internal resources, external resources, rate, and conflict. Demand can thus be lessened either by reducing the number and variety of jobs or the importance of self-chosen goals; or by reducing the limitations that are being experienced. We shall look at the reduction of limitations first. How can people increase their personal resources? In a general sense that is what many of the strategies which we have already discussed are aiming to do. Stress directs resources away from dealing with the job to dealing with the emotional discomfort and personal threat. Reduce threat and discomfort, and resources of commons sense, energy and resilience become available again for doing the job. The more permanent way to reduce limitation, however, is to increase capacity – that is to invest time and effort in learning the skills that the job requires so that it can be done more smoothly, more confidently and more speedily. There are training days at teachers' centres for new teachers, LEATGS courses for in-service development, management courses for deputies and new head-teachers, and of course the Baker days for whole-staff development. All of these are useful, and collectively they offer nothing like enough. Most of these courses are too short, merely providing the beginnings of a new competence or a new viewpoint that is often swept away when people return to their hectic routines. As we noted before, one of the prime concerns of teachers is that they do not have enough time to carry out the day-to-day tasks and responsibilities of their jobs to their own satisfaction, let alone to invest in enhancing their own skills, or reflecting on their roles and priorities, to anything like the extent which they would like. Learning is a strategy that is potentially available, but its use is often prohibited by lack of time and money. And the informal learning that teachers could so usefully acquire from each other, through talking about their teaching and watching each other teach, is often prevented by overcrowded timetables (and, of course, the vexed issue of 'cover') and/or by a staff ethos that discourages such activities.

Assert

Unreasonable or excessive demands can sometimes be removed or reduced by a forceful and rational challenge, preferably one that commands widespread support and which can be backed up, if necessary, with an effective threat. This is the main *modus operandi* of the teachers' professional associations (unions): to work to decrease demands by fending them off, whilst campaigning for more (external) resources. Recent years have made teachers familiar with this strategy, and with the costs that are associated with it, especially when one is trying to negotiate with a fairly implacable demander. Much more can, has been and should be written about teachers' collective action, and I am not going to pursue it here. The main point I want to make is that, looked at from the perspective of an individual teacher's working life, this kind of action constitutes one very important strategy within a whole repertoire of ways of improving their pleasure and satisfaction in the job. As I said before, the risk of collective action of this sort, which is regretted by many teachers (as reflected in the rise and fall of the memberships of the different unions over the last few years), is that it tends to reduce to the lowest common denominators of more pay on the one hand and a narrow-minded, knee-jerk resistance to change on the other.

Within the more immediate sphere of a teacher's own school, there are also demands to be met, sought or resisted; resources of time, material, money and responsibility to be fought for. I shall return to this when we look at staffroom ethos and the promotion of change in more detail in Chapter 7.

Clarify

As an adjunct to assertion and challenge it is vital for teachers, both individually and collectively, within the school and externally, to be able to clarify the whole structure of the demand/limitation framework within which they are working. This involves a number of areas, such as costing jobs as accurately as possible in terms of time and resources, and identifying any inherent contradictions and incompatibilities within the set of demands. For each member of staff a clear role specification is important if the grey areas of responsibility within which guilt and resentment breed are to be avoided. Pastoral and other cross-curricular involvements can form domains of confusion where such stress-enhancing feelings are rife. By combining these two exercises, teachers are in a much better position to be able to say to the demanders, whether parents, government or somewhere in between: 'Given the resources of time, material, support and expertise, we are able to do A, B and C or C, D and E, but not A, B and E, let alone all five. Which would you like us to do?' Most teachers want to work hard, and they will not generally use this exercise to con people into giving them an easy life. But they also know, through recent, extensive and bitter experience, the difference between a sane and an insane workload, or rate of change. It is as stupid for a government to try to whip and cajole an entrenched profession into changing as it is to try to pull a fed-up donkey along the road by its ears. It is not only more kind, but more intelligent, to give it a rest or let it slow down. Likewise it is smarter of the donkey to explain calmly that it can only go so fast, than to keep trying to bite its owner. Yet what we have heard more of, in the recent discussions of the Conditions of Service, the introduction of GCSE, or of the 7, 11 and 14 tests, is precisely this ineffective cacophony of haranguing and braying.

It also repays the effort to clarify one's own strengths and weaknesses, for an objective inventory of what one is good and bad at, finds easy and difficult, is attracted to and repelled by, helps in two ways. It helps one bid rationally, and more coherently, for congenial responsibilities, and therefore to feel more powerful and less resigned about the way these are distributed. At the very least a clear case is owed a clear explanation if it is rejected. And secondly it helps to combat the unconscious drift from inevitable professional limitation to guilt-inducing personal inadequacy which the injunctions, like unseen magnets, are trying to bring about.

Lastly it is most important of all that teachers apply the process of clarification to their own values and their own vision of education, and it is to this issue that we will turn in the next chapter. Before we move on, however, a few cautionary words are necessary regarding stress.

'Coping with stress' books often offer people a prescription: lots of techniques and good advice that are claimed to have been tried and tested and of proven value to all. But the ways people can best deal with their own stress are as varied as the ways in which they express it. What I have tried to do here, therefore, is to present a flexible and varied menu of approaches from which people can perhaps derive ideas that seem congenial, or at least find some support for their own home-made kit of idiosyncratic but effective methods. As you will see from my strategies – all of which, let me repeat, are derived not from my own beliefs but from what teachers say they actually *do* – what works for one person may seem quite bizarre to another, and serve only to increase the distress of a third. Remember the not uncommon example of the person who gets progressively tense and more frantic as she struggles to relax bits of her body to order. None of these methods will ease all of the people all of the time.

The most appropriate way to reverse the stress cycle depends not only on who you are but on how bad the stress is. If people try to apply a 'turning off the tap' strategy when they are hopping up and down in scalding water they may merely make themselves feel worse. For example, trying to get organized or to clarify your situation when you are at your wits' end may not work. You are likely to make a mess of it, lose your To Do list or confront people in an attacking rather than a rational way. What may be more appropriate in this case is to relax, release or have a heart-to-heart: getting drunk and crying on somebody's shoulder, perhaps. Only when you have unwound somewhat and are back in balance are you able to progress to a more powerful strategy that involves insight, persistence or talking to the headteacher. The recovery of a certain amount of poise, perspective and power has to come first.

The second theme I have tried to illustrate throughout this chapter is the distinction between good coping strategies and bad coping strategies. Bad coping strategies are those that have hidden costs: they produce toxic waste which makes things worse, not better, in the long run. Good strategies cope with the focal problem without exacerbating the overall problem. Joining an effective support group is a good strategy. Avoiding everybody in the staffroom is likely in the long term to be a bad strategy because its result is isolation. Going for a long walk in the country on a Sunday afternoon when you've got a lot of marking still to do, or having an affair with a colleague – they could go either way.

The particular case which I want to develop in the next chapter is that those strategies that involve sustained denial of or inattention to personal ideas, values, philosophy and vision, are bad strategies.

Chapter 5

From balance to personal power

How can I go forward when I don't know which way I'm facing?
John Lennon[1]

So far we have been looking at teachers' well-being, and how to enhance it. But as I have been emphasizing as we have gone along, we have to locate this concern within the wider perspective of *change*. First of all it is the great rate of change in education at the moment that is making it increasingly difficult – and therefore increasingly vital – to hold on to one's senses of balance, proportion and humour. And secondly the nature of the changes being imposed not only creates more pressure and uncertainty but, for many teachers, raises serious questions about the educational values involved. An investigation of stress leads inevitably to a concern with the practicalities and the philosophy of change.

Rehabilitation and consolidation of well-being are necessary conditions for successful engagement with change, whether self-chosen or imposed. You need to be on good form and to have your wits about you if you are to make a go of either promoting your own ideas or opposing someone else's. You need to be astute and perceptive about what opportunities and risks the situation holds. But as well as enthusiasm one needs clarity – clarity in one's own values and wishes – so that one knows why one is embarking on this campaign or resisting that directive. If the last chapter was about increasing one's energy, commitment and perspicacity, this chapter is concerned with developing one's sense of direction.

Throughout the country there are thousands of teachers and schools that are involved in principled change, or thoughtful criticism, and yet cumulatively it does not seem to be enough. Despite

91

the considerable energy and ingenuity that teachers have retained, an observer of the educational scene could be forgiven for supposing that teachers, by and large, have little desire for change. As far as the grass roots are concerned, it looks more like winter than spring. Such change as there is, it seems, is being imposed on dormant teachers by insensitive and interfering outsiders. Yet this situation reflects not so much a lack of interest by teachers in education, as a relatively weak sense of ideological clarity, in addition to the relatively high sense of stress, on the part of large numbers of individuals.

We immediately encounter a big problem here, because as we saw in Chapter 3, a prevalent constituent of the stress reaction to overload and pressure is a turning-away from a concern with values, wishes and principles towards what seems like a more manageable and less depressing pragmatism. When life is becoming so full of pressure and conflict, it can look as if reflection on one's own philosophy is an indulgence, a pointless waste of precious time, that can be safely dispensed with. Part of the work of this chapter will be to examine this reasonable-sounding conclusion and to look for hidden premises on which it may be based, and unacknowledged costs that it may exact.

WHAT PERSONAL QUALITIES ARE NECESSARY FOR CHANGE TO HAPPEN?

Before we embark on that enquiry, however, it will be useful to lay out more generally the direction in which the discussion is moving by summarizing the personal qualities that people need if they are to be effective and sane participants in a complex process of change. Some of these qualities are those which we were concerned with in Chapter 4, but others will lead us on to the issues that we will need to think about next.

Honesty

If people are not able to be honest with themselves about the situations they are in, and about their personal perceptions, misgivings and dissatisfactions, they will not admit the desirability of change. The willingness to say 'It's not good enough' is an important contextual condition for change to be possible.

Responsibility

As well as seeing that something needs to be improved, self-motivated change requires the ability to take responsibility for doing something about it which in turn demands the willingness to say 'My performance is not good enough'. It's not just the system, or the headteacher, or the kids that need to be different: I need to be different.

Tolerance for fallibility

Honesty and responsibility are unlikely to emerge as personal qualities unless people are able to face the fact that they might not be perfect. This quality is also necessary in order to act experimentally in an uncertain situation, where there is an inevitable risk of unexpected or unsuccessful outcomes of action.

Lack of blame

Honesty and responsibility are also inhibited by the tendency to lay blame. Blaming others is an attempt to put responsibility (and culpability) on them, thereby shifting it away from oneself. Blaming oneself tends to reinforce feelings of guilt and shame which undermine self-esteem and thereby lessen effectiveness. Blaming is a backward-looking stance, whereas change requires a forward-looking outlook. The confusion between accepting responsibility and feeling at fault tends to work against change.

Tolerance for ignorance

In many circumstances where people feel dissatisfied with their situation, or their current level or style of competence, they also start from a position of not knowing clearly what to do about it.

To be able to admit to oneself that one does not yet have a good programme for change is a prerequisite for developing such a programme. If one cannot say 'I don't know', then one is unable to do what it takes to find out.

A sense of possibility

This quality is the sense that circumstances will permit some change, even if only gradually or in small amounts. If people's perception of their situation is that no change is possible, then they feel trapped and hopeless.

Power

This quality refers to the sense that an individual – I – can make a difference, even if it is only a small one. It indicates a belief that one possesses the personal resources to change as and when the circumstances allow. The sense does not have to be very great but it must be present at least minimally. If it is not, one feels powerless and helpless, and change cannot be initiated.

Courage

Courage is a vital ingredient of change. It means the ability to go ahead and try out new things even though one feels apprehensive or nervous about the outcome. Courage is not the absence of anxiety but the ability to act on one's vision despite that anxiety. (I read a magazine interview with Erica Jong a few years ago in which she said: 'I have not ceased being fearful, but I have ceased to let fear control me. I have accepted fear as part of life – especially fear of change and fear of the unknown – and I have gone ahead despite the pounding in the heart . . .'.) People who are completely inhibited by their injunctions not to be anxious or uncertain may become completely stuck.

Vision

Now we come to the two qualities with which this chapter will be mostly concerned. Unless there is some goal in mind, albeit only dimly specified, it will not be possible to organize one's change, or to discriminate between change that is successful and unsuccessful, or to evaluate proposals. To be concerned with one's 'vision' does not necessarily mean anything very grand. It merely means giving some attention to formulating how one would like one's practice to be different or better. Of course, vision must be held in mind tentatively rather than dogmatically, and must be constantly open to modification in the light of experience. Vision and action constantly interact during the course of change in order to guide and modify each other.

Insight

The more insight one has into the aspects of one's own character and conditioning that impinge on change, the greater the chance that one will not be unconsciously controlled by one's injunctions and habits, but will instead be able to appraise the personal risks of change on their merits. For example, if one is familiar with one's own tendencies to cop out or give up in the face of possible failure, or of other people's disapproval, then one has the possibility of reevaluating those tendencies in the light of one's commitment to change. One may realize that 'the worst that can happen' is actually not so bad, and is a risk that one is willing to take. Taking the risk often discloses that one's expectations of censure have been exaggerated; that the risk was there, but the results of the experiment made it worthwhile; or that unexpected sources of support and validation reveal themselves. When one reacts to the personal threat of rejection without insight, one sacrifices not only an opportunity to experiment and change, but also one's commitment to changing. The discomfort of being strongly committed to change while being even more strongly afraid to do so is reduced by tactically diminishing, or even denying, the commitment. Insight is thus a quality that contributes significantly to the avoidance of, or recuperation from, deflation.

Realism

Courage and insight need to be balanced with a realistic assessment of the actual costs and risks of changing. It is as counterproductive to underestimate the risk of the headteacher's condemnation (resulting in loss of promotion, a poor reference etc.) as it is to overestimate the social cost of sticking your neck out in a staff meeting. Likewise there are the real and unwanted effects of startling classes who have got used to your style, and who may initially be as apprehensive about doing things differently as you are. One needs to be judicious as well as courageous. Overdoing the freedom, and having to retreat into an authoritarian position to recoup the situation, may necessitate a step backwards.

Open self-image

This means being able to tolerate feeling 'strange' or as if one is 'behaving out of character' for a while. Self-image is largely an internal summary of how one has seen oneself in the past, and to allow this to limit future behaviour is to create a trap for oneself that blocks change. If, however, self-image is seen as descriptive rather than prescriptive, then one is more able to bear the interim feeling of being something of a stranger to oneself.

Self-indulgence

As we argued earlier, change, even self-imposed change, is stressful in that it throws one into opposition with some deep-seated injunctions that make self-esteem contingent on certain forms of conduct and feeling. In such circumstances the ability to 'be kind to oneself' is very helpful. More than usually, people need time for relaxation, lazing about, play, sleep, and for friendship, support and tolerance from those around them. To ask for support without feeling 'weak' in doing so is an important element of this self-indulgence. It may also be expanded by the deliberate acquisition of techniques for relaxation and 'unwinding'.

Resourcefulness

This is the quality of being able to think up things to try out. It may not be absolutely necessary as, particularly in the early stages of change, one's own sense of what is appropriate and potentially successful is likely to be rather ill-formed, and one will need suggestions, ideas, advice and demonstrations from colleagues, tutors or books to get started. In order to become more autonomous, however, it is very useful to develop an intuitive sense of what are reasonable things to try. Without this sense (and especially in the absence of good advice) one runs the risk of being over- (or under-) ambitious, and of setting oneself up to have disheartening experiences.

Flexibility

Knowing when to change one's tack is as important as knowing when to persevere. This is different from backsliding: it is a matter of being open to the acceptance that what one is doing is not going to work, and being resourceful enough to think of another way of achieving the goal. If class discussion consistently gets out of control, for example, organizing small discussion groups with a clear agenda and definite tasks to be accomplished might work better.

Diplomacy

It is very helpful if people changing within an institutional context are able to help themselves by maximizing the support and minimizing the antagonism or incomprehension that their efforts to change are eliciting among colleagues and superiors. In particular it is helpful to keep the issue of change separate from any tendency towards subversion, self-righteousness or any unresolved personal issues that may lead to undue deference or unwarranted hostility to authority. It seems counterproductive, albeit common and understandable, for a small group of teachers in an institution to form a close-knit group that supports its own members but which becomes increasingly isolated from the rest of the staff. In such circumstances perceptions may become polarized and positions struck, so that the in-group sees the out-group as stuck in their ways, indifferent to change and defensive while the out-group sees the in-group as self-righteous, snooty, arrogant and defensive. To allow such a position to develop is tactically inept on the part of the in-group, as it alienates potential sources of support, closes down opportunities to communicate about their ideas within a context of goodwill, and can render the group relatively impotent within the institution as a whole.

These qualities represent some of the most important aspects of the frame of mind that meets change confidently and intelligently. The question is: how are these qualities to be fostered and enhanced? In particular the crucial issue is the extent to which people are able to hold on to, or to recapture, this frame of mind even in conditions that are trying and confusing. What I wish to argue is that teachers *can* expand their elbow room, and increase their equanimity into the bargain, by gaining insight into their own underlying value systems – both what they truly care about, and also the ways in which they may unwittingly sabotage their commitment to these basic values. Let me repeat at this point that to emphasize the psychological ingredient in teachers' perceptions of their current situation is neither to make a subtle attack on their honesty or intelligence, nor to deny the objective realities and demands of that situation. It is, on the contrary, to explore the possibility that teachers actually possess more power than they think, and to indicate the ways in which that power may be repossessed.

BASE VALUES AND FACE VALUES

Let us suppose for the moment that teachers' jobs do allow them some room for manoeuvre, even if it is not very much: that there are some degrees of freedom and some choices that are open to them as to how they operate, both in the classroom and in the company of their colleagues. If this is so, then those choices have somehow to be made. They can be made unconsciously, inadvertently, by default; but at some level the choosers are responsible for the directions they take. Whatever they do will be a reflection of some decision-making process, even if it is only tacit. And in that decision certain values and attitudes will necessarily be embedded. At one end of the spectrum, the stance that teachers adopt will be guided by considerations of what is least trouble, what will require least conscious uncertainty, what is most acceptable to the people whose reactions will affect their reputation or social position: in short, what makes for a quiet life. At the other end, there are considerations of principle, those that constitute people's deeper philosophies about how it is right to be: how, at their best, they would like to be, both as teachers and as human beings.

These two sets of values, which we might call *face values* and *base values* respectively, are to a large extent in opposition. What from one side looks like a pro, from the other feels like a con. The benefits of acting on base values may well feel like costs or risks in terms of face values, and vice versa. If I truly do what I think is right, then the class may be disconcerted and go out of control, and, if the word gets out, I may have to endure the sneers of the cynics in the staffroom. I may get some hostile letters from the parents, and the raised eyebrow of disapproval from the headteacher when I am asked to explain my actions. Acting on base values may well incur risks to stability, status and even career. But the denial of these base values, and the decision to go for the quiet life, also takes its toll. The costs of this choice may be less evident, but no less heavy, than of the other.

For example, giving up one's ideals can have exactly the reverse effect from the one one wants, in terms of *stress*. Research has shown that teachers who have a greater internal locus of control feel less stressed.[2] Internal locus of control refers to a sense of being able to have some influence on one's own life – of having some opportunity and responsibility, whereas external locus of control means placing the power to determine things in your life outside yourself – either in the system or in others who are calling all the shots. The research showed that the more opportunity teachers *perceived* to influence their work situation the less exhaustion, the less anxiety, the less irritation and the more satisfaction they experienced. Notice that 'locus of control' is a *psychological* measure. It is not a direct indication of how much power people actually have. Two people in exactly the same predicament will feel differently depending on how they construe it. This clearly illustrates the interaction between powerlessness and stress. Loss of autonomy coupled with high demand creates a situation within which stress becomes more likely. One of the common aspects of stress, however, is to exaggerate perceived powerlessness, so that one no longer perceives accurately what is feasible, nor even what is important.

The loss of base values results literally in a loss of *vision*. The word 'vision' for idealism is well chosen, for it points to the self-validating nature of the stance we adopt. Perception is set, and attention directed, by the goals that people are currently in the business of achieving. If one is aiming for face-saving and quiet-living, then what one *sees* are opportunities and threats that are relevant to and defined by those aims. What people notice, from this stance, are potential hassles and other people's reactions. What one does not see are opportunities to try out new ways of teaching or to promote causes in which one believes. Conversely a firm commitment to ideals leads to a greater perspicacity and ingenuity about how and when they might be pursued. Thus a commitment to face values creates a real blindness to the possibilities that may arise, or be manufactured, to act on base values. The perceived 'impossibility' and 'hopelessness' of the situations then serves as yet further justification for a lack of concern with ideals: 'Why bother? I'd only be banging my head against a brick wall.'

Without base values one may even be jeopardizing one of the main things that one is after: *stability*. If one feels somewhat directionless it is easier for one's equanimity to be upset by the inevitable disturbances to routine. Each new demand that arises during the working day – conflicts with pupils, requests from colleagues, reminders of jobs not completed – threatens insta-bility. To use an image produced by a workshop participant, imagine the teacher on a yacht in a choppy sea with cross-currents, on a blustery day. If it is the captain's intention to stay still, the yacht will pitch and yaw and roll about with flapping sails and much uncertainty. On the other hand if the boat is under way, then stability is greater, and the forces of wind and sea can, with skill, be harnessed to the motion of the boat, and be used to contribute to the achievement of its goal. With one aim the wind is destructive; with the other it is a resource. Thus a lesson you are unexpectedly asked to cover becomes an opportunity to try out – on a class you do not normally meet – a developing idea. The student who attaches herself to you becomes a source of information about what the people at College are up to. And so on.

The absence of base values may unintentionally create a greater loss of *energy*. The yacht-master may well get more worn out trying to keep his boat still than by sailing it. There is a world of difference between being tired and exhilarated, and tired and depressed – remember the distinction between 'hard stress' and 'fuzzy stress' that we used in Chapter 3. Even if one's sense of freedom to choose is minimal, teachers sometimes emphasize how important it is, for their own well-being, to retain it. In fact the smaller the opportunity, the more vital it is not to lose sight of it. As one teacher said in a meeting of the Education Network: 'The difference between 1 per cent possibility and 0 per cent possibility is 100 per cent, in terms of how you feel'.

Losing sight of base values means that one sacrifices *clarity*, especially about priorities. As we saw in Chapter 2, one of the hallmarks of overloaded teachers is that they have more to do than the time allows, and they are constantly faced with the problem of how best to apportion their scarce time. An underlying set of personal principles is a valuable resource for helping to make such difficult decisions: without them one is more at a loss as to how to decide what matters most, and less able to give a principled explanation if called to account. So there may be costs in terms of a loss of depth or groundedness to one's professional life. One's activities and choices may be felt, however vaguely, to be somewhat aimless or rootless.

One may be sacrificing a sense of personal *coherence*. Decisions that are controlled by face values may be subject to short-term considerations of fashion or expediency, so that the stands one takes (overtly or covertly) on different issues may be quite different, depending on what seems, in the heat of the moment, to be the line of least resistance. One's working life ceases to add up. Such changes as occur do not amount to anything.

One sacrifices some *integrity*, and while this does not necessarily cause another drain on self-respect, it may do so if one feels somehow pusillanimous or guilty for selling oneself short. There is the more likely danger of losing what real satisfaction might otherwise have been on offer. Certainly most teachers cannot expect, in the present climate, to be doing what they feel is profoundly worthwhile every minute of the day. But if they have sacrificed the sense of going somewhere, then there is no possibility of arriving, so that *progress* and *direction* are lost, and work takes on an even more repetitive quality than before.

Finally the loss of base values can have a deleterious effect on the quality of *conversation* and *community*. The inner sense of superficiality becomes mirrored socially, so that the staffroom chat also becomes repetitive and ritualized, used as much to keep people at a distance as it is to welcome them in. While in meetings, because people have not really got to know each other, there can arise the additional uncertainties caused by posturing and by not knowing what people really think.

For the sake of presentation I have been guilty of exaggerating the contrast between face and base values in two ways. First they do not fall so neatly into two distinct areas. The ends of the scale are fairly clear. At one, the Simon Peter end, people sit on their hands, keep their heads down and fail to stand up and be counted when they know they should. At the other end there is the martyrdom of acting on principle even though they know it will very probably cost them dearly. It is not always clear, however, at which end it is better to be: it can be as much a cause of ineffectiveness and regret to be a reckless hero, as it is of guilt to be a coward. In addition there are perfectly valid goals that themselves fall somewhere between the two poles: to make money, have a successful career and achieve a measure of security, for example. And there are also many jobs to be done that neither promote nor conflict with people's private agendas. They are merely routine.

The second oversimplification was to imply that people tend to consistently inhabit one or other end of the scale. Of course there are inveterate idealists, just as there are dyed-in-the-wool pleasers, cynics and seekers of the soft option. But most people vacillate: sometimes they stick their necks out and sometimes they are chicken. For those who want to keep their friends and their jobs, as well as some integrity, the matter is one of juggling their different and conflicting aims, all of which deserve a hearing. The trick is to stay alert to all these voices, so that opportunities can be seen and seized as they come along. If a stance has been adopted too firmly which denies a place to the base values, then the costs I have just reviewed will become more acute. My sense is that most teachers would like to be more adventurous and open than they are. Their regret is more often that they have been too reticent, rather than not reticent enough; or that they seem to have misjudged the risks and pitfalls of a course of action. Why does this happen?

WHAT'S WRONG WITH IDEALISM?

Overcautiousness is due in part to some further mistaken beliefs that teachers commonly possess, often without realizing it. Like the injunctions which we discussed in Chapter 3, they may be loaded unwittingly on to the decision-making scales so that the balance is tipped, more often than necessary, in the direction of safety and self-preservation. Thus even when people are not stressed and are on good form they may still be less effective, especially as agents for change, than they could, or would like to be. For example there is a set of beliefs which people sometimes hold that concern the nature and the effects of idealism. 'Idealistic' is a term that has come to be used pejoratively, and people react to 'idealism' as if it were ineffective or dangerous. When these conclusions are accepted unconsciously, without their rationale being subject to critical inspection, then people become biased against idealism in general, and their own in particular. So we need to clarify exactly what idealism is not.

Idealism is not frustrating

Behind people's suspicion of idealism there may lurk a view such as the following. Here we are, down in some ordinary, unsatisfactory situation called A, let us say; and way up high there are our ideals, at B, representing The Way It Ought To Be. To be idealistic, so this view goes, is to periodically suffer the pain of looking down from B to A, and to feel bad about how lowly our situation, inadequate our performance, and slow our progress, are. Idealism creates more frustration, and often guilt, which make bad things look even worse. So it makes sense not to think about how it might, could, or should be – because you'll only upset yourself unnecessarily.

Now it is true that idealism can be misused in this way, as a rod to beat oneself with. But that need not be the case. Idealism involves not 'dwelling in' B and therefore ignoring, scorning or doing violence to A, but on the contrary remaining firmly rooted within an accurate and, in a way, tolerant sense of the way things actually are. There is no need to lose touch with A, and it is stupid to do so. It is after all the only home you have. In this case B functions to provide a sense of *direction* to activities, especially those that involve an element of choice. It provides orientation and pull. Vision is a way to face, and it therefore defines 'forward'. There is no more need to feel fed up or angry because 'I'm not there yet' than there is to be upset by the fact that the train is going to take another five hours to get to Glasgow. (Sometimes people *do* get upset by such facts, especially when they are caused by unexpected delays or diversions, but this is neither necessary, useful nor pleasant. The upset arises from the attitude people take to the disparity between 'here' and 'there', not by its existence.)

Idealism is not naive or escapist

Some people think that by creating a vision of B, you automatically get blinded by the light to the 'harsh realities' of A. B is cloud-cuckoo-land, mere castles in the air, they say, inhabited only by the fey, who have no impact on the real world. Not only are idealists muddle-headed dreamers, but they need to be, being for some reason unable to 'cope' with reality. They build their castles in the air and then live in them, cocooned in a pleasant fantasy and insulated from issues which they are not only too stupid to understand but too inadequate to confront. Idealists are imagination junkies, on the run from the real world. Again, although it is evident that such people exist, the fault is not in the espousing of values, but in the defensive use to which they are put.

Idealism is not fanatical

Next there is the view that idealists are dangerous and disruptive people, pursuing their private goals with a ruthless disregard for other people or for social order. The vision is so bright that it blinds people in this case to ordinary human values of kindness and co-operation. Idealism generates cruelty, divisiveness and discord. To have such people in a school would tear it apart. Community would be sacrificed on the altar of the One True Way. Prime examples would be Ignatius Loyola and Adolf Hitler. Again we can happily concede that there are these types of people without being forced to the conclusion that concern with base values is in itself a bad thing. What people are condemning is the abuse of idealism, and when vision is kept free of these optional errors, it confers the benefits that I described in the first part of the chapter without generating any unwarranted side-effects. Idealism and realism are not antagonistic but complementary.

Idealism is not martyrdom

It is of course an equally thoughtless fallacy to suppose that awareness of your own ideals leads inexorably to sacrificing everything for the cause. Meeting opposition head-on and throwing caution to the winds is often an inept way of proceeding – though it may also be the only thing that will get an entrenched power-structure to move at all. There may often be alternative courses of action to be found that are more intelligent and which allow one to minimize the risk whilst maximizing the chance to do good. In school, as we shall see in Chapters 6 and 7, it is at least as important to be astute as it is to be brave, if you want to have a real impact on ethos or policy. Once you get branded a fanatic, people stop taking you seriously and you lose your influence.

Idealism is not grandiose

It is true that the words 'idealism' and 'vision' do sound rather grand: people may be inclined to feel that what is being asked of them is a programme for change that is far-reaching and profound.

But one can be concerned with the implications of one's base values in very local areas, as well as for education as a whole. Vision is as relevant to a shift in someone's way of teaching a single class as it is to the promotion of change on a larger scale, and it operates with the same positive effects. A greater adherence to base values can be manifest as much in the way teachers greet their classes as in their willingness to voice an unpopular point of view at the staff meeting.

Idealism is not definitive

There is a feeling in some quarters that vision has to be definitive before one dares expose it to the light of other people's reactions, or to act upon it. People sometimes feel that ideals are fatally flawed if they do not generate an instant, wholly satisfactory answer to any question, however hypothetical or far-fetched. 'How would your theories cope with X? And what if Y?' they ask. They then retire with the smug 'Well, there you are then' of a demolition job well done if you are forced (note, *forced*) to admit that you don't yet know. Of course there is going to be uncertainty in how things turn out in any proposal for change, however well thought out. But when people are resistant to change, there is a strong suggestion of 'Better the devil you know' in their reactions. It is hard not to feel despondent in the face of this attitude, or to adopt the attitude oneself that there is something wrong in being 'half-baked' or suggesting something experimental.

The impossible demand that any alternative can be perfect and foolproof is also used to undermine people's right to speak out about the imperfections they see in the present system. It sometimes feels as if it is against an unwritten rule to say, in the same breath, 'I don't feel happy with the way it is' and 'I don't know what to do instead'. The implication is that people have no right to criticize unless they could do better – the kind of counter-attack that is sometimes used on reviewers by wounded authors and directors. This ploy is very effective at inhibiting individuals from speaking their minds and making suggestions, and it also nips the possibility of any honest debate in the bud if people fear that their tentative but heartfelt contributions are going to be 'shot down'.

The request for vision to be definitive is also a misconception of its essentially provisional nature. If people's base values represent the directions in which they would like to move, and the way they would like to be when they have the opportunity, vision is a more concrete, more explicit model of what they are working towards. If values are compass-bearings, vision is a route-map. Just as in any exploration, the route that one takes must be capable of modification in order to cope with the inevitable surprises along the way. Direction must change, goals must be reformulated in the light of experience. Vision directs action and provides criteria by means of which its success can be gauged. Thus when people are attacked for changing their position or not sticking to their guns as they go along, they can quite rightly counter by challenging the presupposition that vision has to be fixed and clear. It is bound to start out hazy, and to be clarified and modified as a result of experience and discussion as it goes along. There is no other way in which it can develop. It is therefore vital that people who are open to change, and who wish to derive ideas for change that are grounded in their own principles and values, should not allow the process to be strangled at birth by either their own or other people's false beliefs.

Idealism is not altruism

This might be the place to note that a concern with vision has nothing to do with being a saint. The assumption that an idealist does, or ought to, act out of pure altruism, is as false as the others. It may be that some idealists are selfless, but it is by no means a necessary requirement. What I am talking about here are the problems faced by teachers who want to operate more on the strength of their own base values, whatever they may be. The goal is not in the first instance to do good but to get more job satisfaction. This discussion is for ordinary human beings who want to feel good in the knowledge that they are doing something they think is worth doing, and doing it tolerably well. Taking cognizance of one's own values is, I am arguing, a better strategy for promoting one's own well-being than trying to pretend they don't exist, and that this applies especially at a time when teachers are feeling pushed around and demoralized. Trying to live by base values as well as face values makes good sense. It is what puts the 'enlightened' into 'enlightened self interest'. What people's base values actually are is not at issue, and anyway it isn't anybody else's business. It so happens that I have not met a teacher yet whose base values are not concerned with the welfare of other people, particularly young people, and with helping them to develop into confident, happy and effective adults. But that is, in the context of the present discussion, incidental. The only base value to which I am confidently appealing here is the commitment that most people have to taking care of themselves and feeling good about themselves, and to working in a healthy and health-promoting environment.

Someone once said: 'There is nothing so practical as a good theory' – though I would add 'provided one wants it to be'. Vision is the source of purposeful action, not an escape from it. Whatever people do, and however they do it, their values are revealed. It therefore behoves them to understand the function of vision rightly, and to attend to the processes of developing the vision they wish to act on, and of clearing away the impediments to such action. But without the first step, that of seeing that, whatever the limitations of the situation, vision can be a practical resource, and need not be depressing or ineffectual, the second two stages cannot get under way. As Ted Wragg reminds us, 'Alvin Toffler pointed out that all education is a vision of the future, and that unless one has such a vision one betrays the nation's youth'.[3]

THE POWER OF REFLECTION

One of the qualities needed for people to be at their most effective in a difficult time is insight: insight into both their base and their face values. The last section argued for the importance of paying attention to base values. Now we need to pursue our enquiry into the effect that face values have in creating a distorted and diminished picture of our capabilities and opportunities. We are back with our old friends the injunctions, whose capacity to undermine energy and integrity we have already exposed. In this section I shall argue further for the power of reflection – this time in bringing these injunctions to light and appraising them. Whilst they remain unconscious we are unwittingly controlled by them, as robots are controlled by their programming. Once these injunctions are unearthed, we are able to choose whether, in this particular situation, we wish to play it safe or to 'go for it'.

It will help to clarify how the face value injunctions operate if we make explicit a distinction between *context* and *content*. Whatever we do or do not do, think or do not think about schools and education, happens within a context of belief. The beliefs we hold about something, whether we are aware of them or not, condition and limit the way we think about it. Surrounding every discussion of how it should be, or what we should do, lies a ring of implicit unspoken assumptions, attitudes or presuppositions that are simply 'taken for granted' or 'obvious'. The context for deliberation and choice (which imply a measure of uncertainty) is a set of beliefs about what is certain. Like the size and shape of the circus ring, this context influences and limits the acts you can put on. Though the size of the ring is a convention, we take it as fixed: *now*, what kind of show can we do?

Beliefs that are part of context derive their power to limit change and prohibit debate from being unrecognized and unexamined. And they are not 'out there' somewhere: they exist only within the minds of people. The first step therefore is to examine one's own beliefs, bring them to light, and acknowledge to oneself those that have been creating self-limiting misapprehensions.

This effect of context on content is not mysterious: it is an everyday phenomenon. It permeates our lives – our thoughts, feelings, perceptions and actions. If the context is 'I like you', then the content of your personal habits and whims is charming: they are lovable. When the context changes to 'I don't like you' these selfsame habits and idiosyncracies become irritating and stupid. Now it seems, all of a sudden, as if the way you butter your toast so carefully and your passion for fresh air are reasons for not liking you. Why did I never notice how 'finicky' you were before? First the context changes, and then the content changes in line with the context. *People perceive, think and act in such a way that the context is reinforced and validated.*

Here is another example (see Figure 3). Look at a: what do you see? Two cubes stacked up. Now look at b: what do you see? Two wedges stacked up. But wait a minute. The bottom 'thing' – whatever it is – is the same in both. That is, the visual information, what you can see of it, is the same. The top block provides

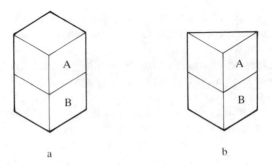

Figure 3

a context within which, without thinking, you perceive the content of the bottom block. Now you think about it, B could be a wedge underneath a cube. But that was not how it first appeared. You are now able to see it differently because you have become aware of the context and its effect. *The first step in the process of changing what people say and do is to become aware of the context: of what they have, usually without knowing it, been taking for granted.* If the circus master wants to change his acts, he may have to make a bigger ring for them.

Context not only influences what people see and say: it determines what they do as well. Travelling on the London underground the other day I watched three boys, aged about nine, eight and six. The two older boys were jumping up and swinging from a handrail attached to the ceiling. The younger boy wanted to do it, but when it came to his turn, he made a pathetic, half-hearted little jump, and smiled rather shamefacedly at the others. The smile said: 'See, I'm only little – I tried – I really did, didn't I? – but I just couldn't do it'. In fact if he'd *really* tried, he could have reached the bar easily, I'm sure. But he believed he couldn't. The context for his trying was 'I can't do it', so he tried in such a way that his belief was confirmed. The boy thought he *was* trying, but from the outside his try looked pretty feeble and phoney. In many spheres of life, grown-up as well as childish, *when efforts to change or improve something consistently fail, that usually means that they are being made in a context of 'it can't be done'.*

When an idea becomes context, when it becomes not part of the debate, but part of the framework within which debate happens and within which solutions are proposed and enacted, then it generates commitment. Ideas and plans are carried through in such a way that they will validate their context. If the context is 'Nothing is going to make any difference' then whatever is done is done in a way that won't make any difference. A child who is trying to learn to read in the context of 'I can't do it' will not learn to read. Teacher and child alike are bashing their heads against a brick wall, and the wall consists of 'I can't do it'. The way this works with children is well documented. A very good example is George Dennison's *The Lives of Children*.[4] Much school learning is ineffective, not because children 'don't want to' or 'aren't trying', but because their efforts are made within a personal context of 'I'm no good at learning'. If it were only those who are openly rebellious who are not learning, schools would be working very much better than they are doing at present.

The basic belief which currently forms the context for school reform in many teachers' minds is 'It can't be done', or 'Not much can be done', or 'Without more money it can't be done', or other variants. After all if it *could* be done, 'they' would have done it already, right? The context 'it can't be done' generates lots of good arguments about *why* it can't be done. The government or big business wouldn't allow it. Bureaucrats and administrators have all the power and they block everything. There's not enough money. Colleagues are too cynical. . . . Even attempts to diagnose the cause of why it can't be done (e.g. not enough money), and to remove the cause ('Fight the cuts'), operate within, and therefore become expressions and fulfilments of the context 'It can't be done'. When what people do occurs in the context of 'It can't be done', 'Why should I succeed where so many others have failed?', 'Circumstances won't allow me to do or say what I want', 'We've just got to make the best of it' etc., then they are only making gestures. A gesture is a solution that is doomed to fail because it lacks commitment. Conversely things that are done in the context of 'I can and will make a difference' are done with commitment, and they carry weight. If it is objectively possible for them to produce the desired result, they will.

Within us, 'It can't be done' is likely to be buttressed by either or both of two personal beliefs 'I can't do anything' and 'I don't know what to do'. Many people, especially teachers, come from a context of 'I know it's a bit of a mess but I don't know how to do anything about it. It's too big a question. And anyway if I did know what to do I wouldn't be able to put it into practice. So it's better not to think about it. I just try to get through till Friday afternoon'. This package is hermetically sealed. It can't be challenged. This is how context works. *If* I can't do anything, it really does make sense not to think about what I might do. And *if* I have no ideas about what to do, no vision, then I can't do anything, can I? The position of 'ignorance' and 'impotence' can be maintained and validated *regardless of the actual opportunities*. And even if I do 'try something out' it will be done half-heartedly, then fail, and I can say 'I told you so'.

WHAT PERSONAL BELIEFS MILITATE AGAINST CHANGE?

It may be useful to summarize here some of the injunctions that block the expression and the development of the personal qualities that teachers need. Everybody will have their own individual set of face values and misapprehensions, so all I can provide here is a general beginners' check-list for people to edit and supplement as they wish. The intention is merely to provide some pointers as to where the internal weeding might profitably begin. The list starts with a reminder of the injunctions we considered earlier in the context of stress.

1. Worthwhile people do not make mistakes. If they do they should pay with shame or embarrassment (i.e. a loss of self-esteem). Public mistakes are especially disastrous.
2. Worthwhile people understand themselves and know what's going on. They pay for ignorance and confusion with a loss of self-esteem.
3. Worthwhile people must live up to their standards and within their self-image. They have no right to upset other people by acting in unexpected ways.
4. Worthwhile people must look cool. They should not show, and preferably not feel, fear or anxiety. Being scared, particularly of other people, is something to be ashamed of.
5. (The clincher): Worthwhile people do not feel guilty or ashamed of themselves!

6. Idealism and enthusiasm are immature. They show that a person is untutored in the 'way of the world' and 'the harsh realities of life'. They are causes for embarrassment.

7. Being disliked, or even criticized, is a disaster, and should be avoided (literally) at all costs.

8. Asking for help is a sign of 'weakness'.

9. People do not have a right to criticize anything unless they have a fully planned and foolproof scheme for doing it better. (You are not allowed to say 'I don't like it' and 'I don't know what to do' together.)

10. Worthwhile people ought to be able to figure out the solutions to problems rapidly and confidently. It is better to invent and defend a position than not to have one.

11. Introspection is dangerous and/or self-indulgent. Worthwhile people are doers, not thinkers or reflecters.

12. Talking in abstract language shows that people are intelligent.

13. Not to be completely integrated and coherent in thought, word and deed is 'hypocritical', and something to be ashamed of.

14. It is better not to think about things that are difficult or upsetting. It is sensible to adopt the 'ostrich position'.

15. It is a disaster if things aren't the way one wants them. One should become obsessional, preoccupied and worry a lot.

16. To accept responsibility is to run the risk of being blamed or of feeling blameworthy (guilty). Assigning blame is an important activity. Because it is painful to blame oneself it is preferable to avoid responsibility or to blame someone else.

17. It is perfectly acceptable to give up on a project or a relationship provided one has 'tried'. One can then escape from the burden of responsibility whilst preserving self-esteem.

18. People's instincts, impulses and feelings are perfectly trustworthy. Not feeling like doing something (even though one may have agreed to do it) is a valid reason for not doing it.

19. If people let us down (whether intentionally or inadvertently) we are entitled to criticize them and are absolved from our responsibilities towards them.

20. Other people, particularly superiors, ought to know what we need and how we are feeling without having to be told. (If

they don't they are imperceptive and insensitive, or deliberately spiteful – and we are entitled to excuse ourselves from
any obligations towards them.)

21.   If someone ask us to do something, we are morally obliged
to do it. If we don't want to, we can either do it, and feel
resentful, or not do it, and feel guilty. So it is better not to
encourage or allow others to ask things of us.

22.   We are entitled to expect our seniors to be concerned about
our well-being and to initiate kindly conversations on the
subject. We are entitled to expect our juniors to be grown-
up enough to look after themselves.

23.   People who disagree with us are less intelligent, less thoughtful and/or less principled than we are. There is always some
flaw in them if they will not behave reasonably and 'see it
my way'.

THE REQUISITE HEAD OF STEAM

Although I have tried to go some way towards explaining about
the influence of unconscious beliefs, merely to have understood
the idea is not going to help. What is needed is a deep perception
into what keeps people's lives static – just like the little boy in
the Tube. Unless we really *see* how context works in our own
lives, we will not be able to shift the context of educational reform.
The same principle applies here as in other areas of reform such
as the attitude towards global problems of hunger and starvation.
For example, Werner Erhard, the founder of an organization
designed to promote a change of heart about hunger, says:

> It is worthless to know that your ground of being contains the belief
> that things are scarce if you know it merely because you have been
> told it or because it makes sense. You need to know it as a result
> of looking inside yourself and actually seeing how the belief in
> scarcity shapes your thoughts and actions. Pierce into your own
> system of beliefs and observe that you do believe in scarcity. While
> confronting this belief, get that it is not true that hunger and star-
> vation persist on this planet because food is scarce.[5]

The premise of this book is that, without such a change of heart
within the teaching force, nothing significant is going to happen
to education, because a teaching force which is dug-in and fed up

has the power to reduce any and every change imposed from without to a mere gesture. Only when large numbers of teachers are in play, participating in the re-creation of education at classroom, staffroom and national levels, will the deep enquiry that is urgently needed achieve lift-off. There is no shortage of ideas about what to do, just as there is no shortage of food in the world. (All the world's hungry could be fed on the grain, fit for human consumption, that is consumed by livestock in the USA each year. Yet 18 children die from starvation and hunger-related causes every minute of every day.) Scarcity is not the problem, either for the persistence of starvation in the world, or for the persistence of educational inertia. In both cases, what is lacking is merely the will of enough people for things to change. To liberate the will it is necessary for individuals to change their stance towards the problem from one of resignation and distancing to one of commitment and participation. This shift of perspective is accomplished by a) doing whatever is necessary to get into good mental shape; b) gaining insight into the previously subconscious conflict between base values and face values, and realizing that the costs of making a blanket commitment to saving face and living a quiet life are, whatever the benefits, too high; and c) developing contact with other people through which one can both derive the essential support that this difficult process requires, and work for change. Personal insight and personal commitment are absolutely necessary: the shift in stance cannot be achieved by exhortation, still less by coercion.

Chapter 6

Changing teaching

What the hell – you might be right; you might be wrong – but don't just avoid.

Katherine Hepburn[1]

The last chapter focused carefully on the frame of mind of individual teachers, and had little to say about the specific kinds of change that teachers might want or need to get involved with, or about the practicalities of dealing with pupils and colleagues. The time has now come to put some practical flesh on the robust skeleton of readiness and positivity that I have been at pains to establish. It is difficult to see, without the use of spies, how legislation can control *how* teachers teach. It can specify up to a point what is to be learnt but not the process by which, nor the atmosphere within which, that learning is to happen. Nor indeed can legislation prevent teachers from attempting to influence policy, both within their own schools and, via associations and pressure groups of various kinds, more broadly. Thus for teachers who wish to experiment with and develop their ways of teaching, to try to persuade colleagues of the value of a different approach, or to have an impact on the general ethos of their school, all is far from lost. Chapters 6 and 7 offer some information and suggestions for teachers who wish to promote change, within their school, in any one of these three areas.

CHANGE IN THE CLASSROOM

For many teachers today there is a real conflict between the way in which the current legislation is pulling them and the direction in which they themselves would like to move in their methods of teaching. There are, of course, many different kinds and levels of change that teachers may wish to undertake, from relatively small-scale changes in classroom organization, lesson-planning or form of assessment, through more comprehensive curriculum develop-ment, to radical changes in teaching style. In some cases these are motivated by the desire to solve particular problems of class control or interest, for example; in others by the wish to raise the overall image of the school in terms of traditional standards of examination achievement or pupil 'behaviour'.

Both of these are perfectly valid reasons for seeking change. But the kind of change that is closer to many teachers' hearts is where even perhaps small modifications to practice, such as those that give students greater responsibility for class management, self-assessment, selection of content, sequence and procedure for study, or move towards more individual, investigative, discussion-based or collaborative forms of work, are a reflection of an under-lying shift in educational values and philosophy, and a reappraisal of both teacher's and student's roles. This shift is commonly seen as moving towards a concern with the testing out and development of students' pre-existing ideas, and with the enhancement of learn-ing ability or autonomy; and away from a preoccupation with teacher control, the acquisition of 'official' knowledge, and exter-nal assessment. In such cases the teacher is beginning to explore an alternative educational *stance* that is as yet not well-formulated (with attendant confusion or uncertainty) and an alternative teach-ing *style* (with attendant anxiety and insecurity). Here the self-chosen, wished-for changes themselves generate exactly the same kinds of demand and pressure that may also be coming from external sources.

Change of this sort, even though it is what the teachers want, is neither easy nor quick, and additional stresses may be created if they suppose otherwise. Personal injunctions which say something like: 'A decent teacher ought to be able to manage change rapidly and effortlessly, and should not experience doubt, indecision and apprehension' are misconceptions that can serve to make the uncertain process of change even more fraught and threatening than it intrinsically is, and thus to undermine further a commit-ment that is, at best, somewhat tenuous. It may well be that, as in the case of stress, a framework for understanding the process of change, and a forum for discussing it within the context of realistic expectations, would be of some help.

This kind of change requires teachers to change at a number of levels. First and foremost, the acid test is their *classroom habits*: planning different lessons, changing the layout of the room perhaps, introducing new activities, trying to respond to pupils' questions and responses in a different way, and so on. Then, somewhat more generally, there will be a shift in the quality of *relationship* with the pupils, which is not just a matter of technique but of the development of a genuine interest in, and respect for, their ideas and interests. Along with this may come a greater trust in the legitimacy and relevance of their needs, feelings and moods.

Underneath this, a concomitant change in teachers' *implicit theories* will be taking place: these constitute the 'underwater' bulk of the iceberg of which teaching style and demeanour are just the tip. Part of the process is to realize (often with a shock) that their previous style has been the outward expression of a mass of inner commitments, beliefs and values. This may be difficult, as it involves calling into question an underlying, unexamined attitude towards one's own practice as being 'natural', 'inevitable', 'obvious' or 'right'. The implicit theories relate to:

- *children* (what they need: what's appropriate for different ages, abilities, backgrounds, ethnic origins and the sexes; the causes of bad behaviour; their ability to handle responsibility; the right attitude to adults);
- *school* (what it is for; where its responsibilities start and finish; the importance of pastoral or 'whole-child' concerns; the relative importance of different subjects and activities; the value and function of school rules; curriculum; assessment);
- *learning* (how people learn; the causes of failure to learn; the role of feelings in learning; why people learn; what kinds of learning difficulties people have; learning to learn);
- *knowledge* (who makes it and 'owns' it; the importance of culture; status of children's own knowledge; how knowledge is evaluated: teachers' role in transmission).

The implicit theories that people hold have a variety of functions. Some of them underline what we say (the opinions we express); some determine how we think, and rationalize our experience; some are the basis of what we do; and some are the sources of how we view and relate to ourselves. Part of the problem with the kind of deep change we are discussing here is that:

a) Do-theories and Self-theories are the most important to modify; but
b) Think-theories and Say-theories are usually more accessible, easier to uncover and articulate; and
c) There is frequently a lack of congruence between the two pairs of theories; what people say they do, or think they are doing, may well not match what they are actually doing, and the same applies to Self; so
d) A change in Say- and Think-theories does not necessarily carry through into Do- and Self-theories.

It is not uncommon for example for people to say they have changed, and even think they have changed, but for that change not to have affected what they do very much at all. Or there is an intermediate form of dissonance where practice has changed somewhat, but in a rather mechanical or rule-bound way that does not actually realize the spirit of the desired change; yet people may think that they have done all that is possible or needed. Student teachers, for example, frequently espouse ideas about teaching – and describe their performance in terms of them – well before they are able to put them into practice fully.

Thus to assist people in uncovering the implicit theories that have been embedded in their previous practice, it is not sufficient to engage in discussion of a merely intellectual kind (for this activates and draws on a form of knowledge that is not the one at stake). Rather they have to be helped to reflect on their own performance, and allow insight into it to emerge, in a more open-minded, experimental way; and the context in which this occurs must be one where people are helped to tolerate the uncomfortable dissonance which such self-observation may create, between the reality and the private rhetoric of their classroom presence. It may be the unwillingness, or even the inability, to acknowledge the details and implications of what one is actually doing that prevents people from realizing the desirability and possibility of change in the first place. Honest self-appraisal is one of the prerequisites for self-motivated change.

In fact, 'reflection' is a good example of the point I have just been making. It is currently a very fashionable notion – largely as a result of the influential writings of Donald Schon.[2] But its incorporation into educational rhetoric has not yet been matched by a real increase in the abilities to be self-aware and constructively self-critical.

WHAT STAGES DOES CHANGE INVOLVE?

It will be impossible to specify any precise set and sequence of changes that teachers go through in the course of reorienting and reintegrating their educational stance and practices. That said, a sequence such as the following does seem to be quite common, and to represent teachers' experience:

Stage	*Feeling*
Entrenchment	Uninterested, dismissive
Opposition	Argumentative, irritated, resistant
Possibility	Doubtful, sceptical, private wondering
Dabbling	Uncommitted, interested, 'give it a go'
Agreement	Acceptant, 'like the idea'
Commitment	Enthusiastic, hopeful, talkative
Clarification	Puzzling, 'what does it really mean/involve?'
Introspection	Self-questioning, self-doubt, 'what have I been doing?'
Planning	Innovative, 'what can I try out?'
Experimentation	Nervous, feeling 'odd', excited
Reaction	Surprised, disappointed
Deflation	Disheartened, second thoughts, 'stuff it!'
Projection	Angry, blaming, betrayed, misled
Reappraisal	Objective, 'sense of proportion', 'not so simple, but . . .'
Recuperation	Recharged, encouraged, 'feeling better'
Reaffirmation	Persistent, more realistic, more solid commitment
Extension	Inconsistent, fragmented, double standards

Evangelism	Preaching, over-enthusiastic, bumptious
Limitation	Judicious, perceiving limits of new approach
Consolidation	Confident, integrated, 'I've really got it'
Permeation	'I'm different': flexible, creative

We could illuminate these stages a little with a 'case study', say of a female history teacher, eight years into her career, on top of the job, traditional style, coasting along nicely, looking for promotion. One or two colleagues come back from a course very excited about a new teaching approach but she doesn't pay much attention – 'it's nothing to do with me' (*entrenchment*). But they keep on about it and start discussing in her presence the beneficial effects on the pupils. She finds their enthusiasm rather naive and irritating, and begins to get drawn into arguments (*opposition*). Privately, while still affecting hostility, she starts to wonder if there might be something in it; glimmers of self-doubt about the real value/success of her own method appear; she veers between being dismissive and, despite herself, increasingly interested (*possibility*). Next she (perhaps privately) decides to try something out ('give it a go') but without any sense of commitment: just sticking a toe in the water. If her lukewarm attempt fails (i.e. does not bring instant benefits) she may retreat into 'I thought so . . . stupid idea . . . never work with my kids' and revert to a (reinforced) entrenchment (*dabbling*). If she passes dabbling, the next stage may be open assent to 'the idea' but perhaps some reservations still about its practicability and whether she has the time to take it on board seriously (*agreement*). Then she takes the plunge and decides to 'go for it', a decision that liberates enthusiasm and energy (though not without some private misgivings) (*commitment*). With commitment come the next three phases. She works away at what the whole idea is really about – thinking, discussing with like minds, reading perhaps (*clarification*). She begins (with some discomfort) to reflect on her previous teaching style, becomes aware of the limitations and attitudes it embodied, and re-evaluates her 'educational philosophy'. Periods of strong condemnation of the 'old way', of herself for having followed it, and of other teachers for not having seen the light, may recur (*introspection*). There is a search for ideas and advice about how to be different, with a feeling of exploration and innovation (*planning*).

Then comes the plunge (*experimentation*) where she dares to try different activities and approaches in the classroom and struggles to behave/react in ways consistent with the new approach, but which are constantly subverted by old habits. She feels excited, apprehensive and 'a bit odd', not yet feeling that the new role is 'really me'. Some things will go well; others may have unwanted outcomes – most significantly the loss of classroom control – that confirm her worst fears, or consequences that are unexpected and therefore unplanned for. She feels surprised, disappointed or shocked (*reaction*). After the initial optimism, she feels disheartened and demoralized. She has second thoughts and wants to pack it in. 'If I'd known what was going to happen I'd never have started' (*deflation*). She may feel angry with people 'whose stupid idea it was', and believe that she was misled or duped (*projection*). Drop-out is a real possibility at this stage, but if she weathers the rough passage she may get her sense of proportion back and see her experience from a more objective (and less black-and-white) point of view. She can distinguish between disaster and 'setback', which, during deflation and projection, she couldn't (*reappraisal*). Her spirits rise again (*recuperation*) and her commitment re-emerges in a more solid, realistic form. She now knows what she's in for – 'it isn't going to be easy' – but is ready to go ahead (*reaffirmation*).

She may for a while cycle through all the previous stages back to clarification, but with a general feeling of making progress and 'getting the hang of it'. She has the confidence to extend the fresh approach to new topics, classes and situations, but may, at the same time, be uncomfortably aware of the breadth of the repercussions of what she has taken on, and of how 'local' her own grasp of it still is. She notices inconsistencies in her approach from class to class, or even between different aspects of her conduct with one class. For example, she may be teaching in the new way, but suddenly realize she is still giving the kinds of 'tests', or making written comments on homework, that come from her old style. She feels 'patchy' and her struggle now is to follow through the implications and applications of the new way wherever they lead (*extension*).

Somewhere along the line she may fall into the trap of *evangelism*, where she sees the new method as the only way forward and adopts the role of preacher in the staffroom. She is blind to the limitations of the approach and to other people's right to think differently. She becomes boring, predictable and self-righteous, and does more to turn people off the approach than to invite their interest. Having avoided or passed through this stage, she begins to be more level-headed and to see limits to the approach without feeling that this undermines her commitment to it. It may well not be right for all educational purposes or all ages or types of student (*limitation*). Gradually she comes to feel 'all of a piece' again, and confident in her ability to put her new philosophy into practice (*consolidation*). Finally the spirit of the approach pervades her whole life as a teacher. She can rely on herself to act and talk in ways that are congruent with what she thinks and believes. She need not rely on methods or prescriptions, but she naturally and flexibly finds ways of putting the ideas into practice whenever she thinks they are appropriate (*permeation*).

Whether this sequence matches the experience of all teachers going through any kind of change in their teaching style is less important than the assumption on which it rests: that change is a process which takes time, is unpredictable, involves misgivings and setbacks, and requires patience and perseverance to see it through. To the extent that teachers underestimate or ignore these characteristics of change, they are setting themselves up to become disheartened, and to drop out when things turn out to be tougher or slower than they expected.

MISGIVINGS

This brisk outline skates over a process that may take years to complete – if indeed it can ever be said to be finished. To illustrate its complexity let us concentrate on just one component, albeit a recurrent one, and explore further the vital role of reflection.

Suppose that a teacher has reduced her stress to the point where she can begin to think about initiating some self-chosen change in her own way of teaching (some or all of her classes) and/or in the policy, organization or ethos of the school. She has some idea about what is desirable, the direction in which she wants to move, and she also sees, however, slight, some chink or window of possibility. She is approaching the change with some energy and enthusiasm, feeling keen and committed. Is it all going to be plain sailing from then on? Far from it. There will almost certainly be plenty of misgivings and difficulties along the way. It is unlikely that she will set out without some apprehension, and equally unlikely that all her tacit expectations about what the process is going to be like will be met.

People generally suffer some self-doubt concerning their ability and their right to be different. Their train of thought, somewhat compressed, may run like this: 'Isn't it arrogant to presume to know better than the textbook or the received wisdom? Who am I to say what's wrong and what's right? Surely things can't be as much in need of change as I feel them to be? If they were, wouldn't other people be showing their dissatisfaction and frustration too? I must be hypercritical: we can't we wasting pupils' time as much as I sometimes think – "they" would never have let it get to that state. And what right do I have to experiment with the education of my pupils? These aren't chemicals we are talking about: they are real people. I think I know what's for the best – but do I really? What if it turns out to be a complete fiasco? I could actually damage people's education with my fancy ideas. Even if I am on the right track, what gives me reason to believe that one person can really make any difference? Everyone else is going to be teaching them in the same old way, so what hope is there for little me to have any impact? Anyway, I don't really see myself as a pioneer: like it or lump it I don't think I've got it in me. I'm just not the kind of person who sticks their neck out like that. Talking of which, what happens if I lose control and the head walks in? It'll be all round the staffroom that I've lost my touch and that I'm trying out some hare-brained scheme with the third years. And it certainly won't do my chances of becoming head of department when Sheila retires next year any good.'

Taken together, and taken at face value, the links in such a chain of thought may seem to provide a strong case against bothering. Looked at more closely, however, the case is less strong. Teachers' concern about their perception of the present situation, and what would constitute an improvement, is fair enough (though, as we have seen, the reason why other people aren't speaking out may have nothing to do with their lack of private dissatisfactions and everything to do with the stance th͟ adopted to cope with their own stress). It is inevitable that u͟ changes people are contemplating will have unpredictable effects. But this argues not for inactivity but for implementing the changes with care, patience and a lot of attention to how they are working. It also argues for the need to talk to others about what you are doing, to check out your plans and perceptions, to get advice, and to receive support and reassurance.

The worry about using the pupils as guinea-pigs is exaggerated. They are just as likely to be damaged if you ignore your doubts about the conventional way of teaching a subject as they are by any small experiment you might devise. It is likely that they will have a better educational experience with someone who is teaching with thoughtfulness and gusto regardless (up to a point) of what exactly the method is. And besides, the fear about the damage you might do is contradicted by the doubts about whether 'little me' will be able to make any difference at all.

We have met misgivings about what colleagues or superiors might say before. If people are generally more concerned about face values than base values it is unlikely that they will be contemplating any changes that might make them conspicuous in the first place. Yet nearly everyone will have some such apprehensions which will be more or less well-founded. The key perhaps, as Jill Jones comments in Chapter 2, lies in the teachers' own security: security provided by their status, by knowing that their generally favourable reputation could withstand one or two knocks, by feeling confident enough to be able to explain what they are up to, if needs be, without getting embarrassed or defensive, and by knowing that, if the class does get a bit out of hand, they will be able to revert to the old way without having done any lasting damage. The importance of this underlying self-confidence, which enables people to be innovative, or to speak out despite their misgivings, reminds us that we should not expect too much from people new to teaching or to a particular school, who have not yet found their feet. Nor should we forget that many of the risks they fear, both social and practical, are entirely justified. What teachers are embarking on when they change is a delicate juggling act in which they are trying to keep all the existing balls in the air whilst adding a new one. Their fraught goal is to introduce a bit more 'base' to what they do without sacrificing too much 'face'.

The misgiving that we have not so far commented upon is the one that concerns self-image: 'I'm not the kind of person who . . .', 'It wouldn't be me to . . .'. Here are echoes of the injunctions that we spoke of in Chapter 3 concerning the needs to be *consistent* and *coherent*. Part of the uncertainty that is produced by change is that, in order to do something different, people have to run the risk of being, or becoming, different. Just as the unprecedented situation they are creating may be disconcerting or threatening for pupils and colleagues, so it is for the changers themselves. As events take their course, they may find themselves reacting in ways that feel out of character, or behaving in ways that may feel artificial or even phoney. A person's own responses form part of the experiment, and new ways of operating and relating may have to be forged which lie outside the bounds of the comfortable and familiar self-image. Thus a transient period of feeling a bit strange, or of finding oneself behaving inconsistently, as one moves backwards and forwards between 'normal' and 'experimental' settings, may be another hazard to be dealt with. This in its turn can produce further uncertainty in dealing with other people. The relative predictability of everyday encounters can be disrupted if, even in small ways, one is not one's normal self. Others may be startled by the change, and resistant to it, if one suddenly becomes more forthright or more friendly, or moves from an 'expert' to a 'chairing' mode of operating in the classroom. Again, these reactions are real, and teachers who want to change their *modus operandi* should expect such repercussions and be prepared to ride them out. The strength of people's initial reaction to a proposed change may reflect in large measure their disquiet about the general instability you are producing in their worlds, and may say little or nothing about the longer-term feasibility or desirability of the particular change in question.

Whether the fact that people find themselves behaving or thinking in new ways becomes a real problem depends not on the initial feeling of strangeness but on whether they are able to expand the boundaries of their self-image to include this unfamiliar persona. Like a new set of teeth, there may be some discomfort to start with but which soon settles down. But it is also possible that the 'act' never comes to feel like 'me', and it continues to grate, in which case it is likely to cause an overall increase in stress. There are many teachers, concerned not with change but with basic survival, who are unable to feel comfortable with the *only* way they have found to be an effective teacher, and for them, as we saw in some of the quotations in Chapter 2, the only solution may be to leave teaching.

SPREADING THE WORD

The second kind of change that teachers can work for is the spread of a teaching approach that they believe in. In secondary schools this will mostly involve trying to 'sell' the approach to colleagues within the same subject department. Let me start by recalling some particularly apt lessons that we learned in early chapters, lessons that apply to anyone – colleague, adviser, inspector, educationalist, bureaucrat – who is trying to get other people to change their ways. First I think we should now assume that the only kind of change worth promoting is self-chosen change, where teachers have somehow got over the barrier between 'I should change', or 'I've got to change', and 'I want to change'. It seems to me that the evidence is abundantly clear that imposing change on teachers, however well-intentioned and well-formulated the change might be, is doomed to failure. Particularly in a climate where teachers feel pressure from many different directions, any prescription for change will feel not like a 'solution' but as another burdensome part of their problem – unless they have been given the time, opportunity and support to make the change their own. And as we saw in the last chapter, any change enacted in this state of mind will be begrudging or even subverted, so that its failure is guaranteed – and it can then be rejected with a sigh of relief. Many curriculum innovations, in science, maths, humanities and elsewhere, have foundered for this reason. It is not that they were not good ideas. It is not even that teachers (on the whole) did not like or agree with them. It is because the complexity, emotional demands and support required to 'take them on board' and 'see them through' have been consistently and greviously underestimated. Any programme of innovation or 'in-service education' that does not recognize and respond to the personal realities and difficulties of change condemns itself, I would argue, to be an expensive flop.

The crucial sticking points to be overcome, therefore, are the transition from resistance to commitment, and the likelihood of drop-out following dabbling or disappointment. The following guidelines for change-agents may help to ease the transition into, and to maintain, commitment amongst their colleagues. Do not, under any circumstances, do anything to make colleagues feel that they are bad, inadequate or old-fashioned for doing things the way they are currently doing them; for not wanting to change; or for feeling misgivings, or even for giving up, once they have started. Do not lecture them or proselytize: nothing turns people off faster. Do not affect an air, however subtle, of self-satisfaction or superiority. Do not allow your department to become polarized into an in-group of enlightened, courageous, forward-thinking, right-minded teachers, and an out-group of the others. You will buy your cosiness and support at the cost of increased isolation and resentment from those you are seeking to influence. The whole message of this book is that change will occur, and can only occur with conviction, from a position of strength, when teachers themselves feel ready, willing and able to change. People are much more likely to move when they feel themselves to be moving on to greater competence than when they are being bullied or embarrassed out of apparent incompetence. As a change-agent the most effective thing you can do is to create a climate within which people can feel able to think about what they are doing for themselves, without feeling that they are bad or being attacked.

One of the ways to do this is by showing a genuine interest in and respect for what your colleagues are doing. Unless you are absolutely certain that they are made of wood, it is likely that, whatever stance they are adopting to deal with the pressures, they are trying to do a good job, just as you are. The interest you show must be genuine or they will become suspicious of you. If it is authentic it is likely to have several effects. First, your 'target' feels flattered that what they think should matter to you. Second, they feel powerful: you have put yourself in a position in which you may have something to learn from them. Third, you have at least initiated a more productive kind of conversation than the usual mixture of panic and gossip. And fourth, it becomes increasingly difficult for colleagues who you are treating in this way not to express an interest in *your* ideas and approaches. When they do so, it is a mistake to pounce. Maintain a soft-sell approach:

play hard to get, so that you have to be persuaded (but not *too* hard, or they will give up) to talk about what you are doing. Make it sound a little mysterious, as if you are somewhat baffled by the success you seem to be having.

The next step, according to my informants, is crucial. It is to get your colleagues to actually *see* you teaching in your new style. You might casually suggest that, if they are interested, they might like to sit in on one of your lessons – you would appreciate their reactions and comments on the approach. Again this puts *them* in the position of power, rather than you, and increases the likelihood that they will accept. The alternative strategy is to offer to take one of their classes for a lesson or two. You might say that you want to 'try it out' on a different group, to see if it works, and again you would be grateful for their perceptions. This has the added advantage for your colleague of giving them a lesson or two they don't have to prepare. And it has the added advantage for you that, if things go well, they have seen it work with *their* class, and they are not then able to say: 'Ah yes, it's easy enough with 3X, but it would never work with my 3Y'. Whichever way you do it, actually seeing a new approach working in practice is a much more powerful stimulus to change than any amount of encouragement or rhetoric.

All the way along it is important to let people feel that they can retreat if they want to. You are leading them into the unknown, and it is helpful to remember how you would feel if you were gingerly exploring a dark passage and a door banged shut behind you: immediately all your energy goes into retreat rather than exploration, avoidance rather than approach.

When you do feel you can talk to people about your new approach, it is more helpful for them if you talk about your *experience* with it, rather than simply to describe the fruits. Especially share with them your own misgivings and set-backs, so that they have an accurate picture of what is involved, and also, without making a big song-and-dance about it, they can see, through your example, the way in which your commitment has paid off. Let them know what you will probably genuinely feel: that it wasn't easy, but it was worth it.

This kind of approach is particularly important if you are in a position of power with respect to the teachers you are trying to influence – as head of department, adviser, INSET co-ordinator or whatever. If you set up meetings which they have to attend, present them as opportunities for *you* to learn from *them* about current practice and their perceptions of it. If the change you want to promote is to stand any chance of gaining their whole-hearted support, it is bound to fit in with their own dissatisfactions, and you can then present it, tentatively, as an answer to a question that they have raised, and not as your own pet rabbit pulled out of a hat. Research by Jan Harding on teachers' reaction to proposed curriculum development projects showed that a positive response depended on the project being seen as a *feasible* and *relevant* answer to a felt *dissatisfaction*.[3]

The final point that is influential in persuading teachers to take change on board was also reflected in this research: teachers have to feel that the *resources* they are going to need will be available. These comprise resources of material, resources of time, resources of support and resources of advice and information. It is taking the providers of in-service training a long time to wake up to the fact that the short course consisting of a pep talk and a demonstration and time-for-a-few-questions is a hopelessly inadequate preparation for change. For the schoolteacher trying to promote change amongst colleagues, the provision of time and money may be beyond their control. But they do need to be prepared to offer as much support, and as little advice, as they may be asked for.

Chapter 7

A change of climate: a climate of change

> Somewhere there is the exception that may become the norm, the dream that may become reality, the radical that may become established. We may not be able to predict which innovation will blossom, but at any time it is possible to look back twenty years and identify major changes that have taken place in and around the schools. *These changes are not dependent on shifting a massive, central educational bureaucracy* . . . (They) have spread from the margin, from teachers free to experiment and often jealous of their right to do so. Somewhere there will be an experiment that may be picked up and swept into popularity. (*Emphasis added*)
>
> Marten Shipman[1]

What I wish to focus on more closely in this chapter is the way in which an individual teacher can promote a general climate of greater openness to change amongst the staff. Often, teachers will be working for change in an ethos that does not support them in their intention. Part of their job must therefore involve working to create a more supportive atmosphere for themselves – and for anyone else who wishes to participate more fully in debate. Many of the points that I shall make will also apply to other campaigns, both those for different kinds of atmosphere shift, and those for the promotion of particular policies on matters of organization and curriculum. Whether your concern is to put stress on the agenda, or to promote community studies, or language across the curriculum, à la Bullock and now Kingman, you will need to be astute about your methods.

First, let us review what teachers may be up against – what characterizes, say, a stressed institution. What kinds of corporate, as well as individual, attitudes may change-agents encounter? The first move is to know the opposition. Then we can look at what people can do to try to turn things round.

131

THE STRESSED INSTITUTION

The stressed institution is characterized by a breakdown of community and an increase of *disunity*. The staff begins to break up into factions whose identity relies on espousing a simplistic point of view and/or a disparagement of other subgroups. The structure and functioning of the staffroom begins to resemble old rubber: lumpy, crumbly, hard and non-resilient (in contrast to the 'healthy institution' which, like a new sheet of rubber, is all-of-a-piece, and capable of sustaining and integrating conflicting forces without cracking up). Some of these cliques, or some individuals, begin to adopt a stance of *non-participation*. From their position of resignation and/or paranoia it makes sense to opt out of involvement in the formal decision-making processes of the school, and to sit silently in staff-meetings looking ironic or bored, whispering audibly to each other, or passing notes and chuckling like pupils at the back of a class. Having opted out, such groups then feel able to *disown decisions* and, in the privacy of their own interactions, to ignore or subvert them, to make gestures that deliberately fail to fulfil the intention of the decision, or even to express directly to pupils their opposition and disaffection. Like cancer cells in a body, such teachers are 'in' the school but not 'of' it.

In place of public participation, teachers in a stressed school become more involved in what Stephen Ball has called 'micropolitics'.[2] Though they may have resigned from direct promotion of their own interests and causes, they may continue their campaigns indirectly through the informal media of humour, rumour and gossip. Opposition is no longer confronted at the level of issues, but now becomes a matter of *personalities*. Reputations are established or undermined by the stories that are told about people: they are turned into caricatures, so that they are seen as being merely figures of fun, crawlers, bolshy lefties, time-servers, or whatever. Denigration, slander and ridicule are used as a form of moral arbitration and of social control by competing groups and individuals. The rumour-monger is further able to reduce uncertainties and solve apparent mysteries by providing reasons, causes, motivations and explanations to fill the gaps. The respect that is accorded to what people say in meetings is filtered through these informal reputations, and is enhanced or (more usually) reduced accordingly. 'Well she would say that, wouldn't she?' becomes a powerful enough reason for ignoring what it was she actually said. But while colleagues are discussed endlessly in corners of the staffroom there is a professional closing of ranks which prevents the public acknowledgement of individual responsibility, let alone culpability. Up to a point we might say that the private language of a stressed school is lay psychology, whilst its public language is lay sociology.

The tendency to personalize extends to the way that decisions are made about pupils, too. Instant diagnoses for low achievement or 'bad behaviour' are offered in terms of the most superficial *psychologizing*. Causes are confidently attributed to personal character or family background, and are rarely sought publicly in the school organization or in the relationship with individual teachers.

Decision and policy-making processes themselves come to be 'aversive' rather than 'attractive'. The processes are stimulated by the attempt to manage crises, solve particular problems or diminish dissatisfactions. Changes are suggested that are 'away from' rather than 'towards'. No collective vision exists to inform these discussions, so that the organization of the school develops in a piecemeal fashion, constantly being patched up or modified in a variety of ways which do not cohere, and do not amount to development in a consistent direction. The decisions that are taken (in so far as democratic decision-making remains a reality in the school) are therefore determined by a combination of the most urgent problems and the most forceful personalities. Indeed, it is not only that vision is lost: there may even be a collective belief that the display of personal values in meetings, whether ethical, ideological or political, is unseemly and inappropriate. Everyone must *appear* to be pragmatic and disinterested. When values surface it is as if one were improperly dressed: speaking from the heart, rather than from pseudo-rationality and phoney objectivity, may be seen by some as a source of acute embarrassment. No explicit corporate vision can be developed because individual vision is off the formal agenda, whilst in private, face values come to dominate and overwhelm base values.

It is interesting to look at today's schools in the light of a now classic study of stressed institutions by Isobel Menzies from the Tavistock Institute in 1970. Her report, entitled *The Functioning of Social Systems as a Defence against Anxiety*,[3] focused on the way in which the organization of nursing, and particularly nurse training, could be seen as having developed to cope with the considerable anxieties that nurses experience. She found that the coping strategies that had become institutionalized were those of denial and projection, rather than of acknowledgement and mastery. The *sources* of anxiety were similar to many experienced by teachers: uncertainty, apparent lack of control over some aspects of life coupled with a heavy sense of responsibility and personal judgement, frequent proximity to distress, sudden changes of setting and emotional climate, coping with relatives and dealing with personal desires, including sexual ones.

She summarizes her conclusions thus:

> The characteristic feature of the social defence system . . . is its orientation to helping the individual avoid the experience of anxiety, guilt, doubt and uncertainty. As far as possible this is done by eliminating situations, events, tasks, activities and relationships that cause anxiety. . . . The intense anxiety evoked by the nursing task has precipitated . . . individual regression to primitive types of defence (i.e. avoidance and denial). These have been projected and given objective existence in the social structure and culture of the nursing service, with the result that anxiety is to some extent contained, but that true mastery of anxiety by deep working-through and modification is seriously inhibited.[4]

In the late 1980s one could safely substitute 'teaching' for 'nursing' without falsifying these conclusions.

Amongst the strategies she discovered were several that are common in schools, some which we have met before and some new ones. In some ways, the relationship of the providers (nurses, teachers) to the receivers (patients, pupils) was *depersonalized*. For example, although providers talk about the receivers a lot, they do so in ways that focus only on receivers, and ignore or deny differences in the way the providers *feel* about them. Nurses are not supposed to *like* patients differently, to become attached to them or to want more for one than another, so to admit these natural human feelings is to be somehow unprofessional. Likewise, teachers' feelings about pupils (with the exception, interestingly, of negative ones such as frustration or irritation) are submerged beneath a professional ideal of fairness and impartiality. Furthermore the attitude of both groups of providers focuses almost exclusively on giving, and allows little public acknowledgement of the extent to which the providers are also receiving from their patients and pupils. Providers are expected to have an air of detachment from the receivers: their 'professional distance' stops them from getting 'over-involved'. They are not expected to mind too much when pupils move on or patients get better. In ward and staffroom many kinds of emotion – particularly the 'soft' and positive ones – are suppressed. Teachers and nurses are perpetual liars about their own feelings, and it is only with some anxiety that they occasionally 'dare' to express how they really feel.

Relationships between seniors and juniors were characterized more by reprimand than by support. Yet Menzies found that the authoritarian attitude of senior staff masked not an insensitivity to the stresses and anxieties of the juniors, but *a lack of personal confidence* to deal directly and effectively with the feelings of which they were distressingly aware. This guilt formed one aspect of the particular stresses experienced by the senior staff. Another was created by the tendency of insecure juniors to *delegate upwards*: to avoid the pressures of responsibility by affecting to be less competent or less autonomous than they were. This tactical underachievement forced senior staff to take on fairly routine tasks in addition to their own appropriate duties. Interestingly they were often only too willing to do this – perhaps because 'having to take on' these routine tasks allowed them to shelve some of their own more difficult responsibilities; and they therefore colluded with the juniors in 'not being able to trust' the competence of subordinates. In general, although the providers often felt that their professional lives were over-organized and full of routine tasks which they had to do, responsibility, when it came to the crunch, was frequently obscured, so that individuals could not be singled out for 'blame'.

The common myth that 'nurses (like teachers) are born not made' was seen to serve the function of allowing seniors, particularly those with a responsibility for training, to deny the possibility – and therefore the need – to help juniors deal with their complex and difficult feelings. Emotional resilience was seen as something that people just had (or did not have), and about which little could be done.

Lastly, and perhaps most importantly of all for our present discussion, Menzies noted a pervasive *resistance to change* which was born both of anxieties about change itself (the increase of confusion and insecurity) and of fear about feelings which routine served to contain, and which therefore threatened to be released by change. She suggested that:

> Resistance to social change can be better understood if it is seen as the resistance of groups of people unconsciously clinging to existing institutions because change threatens existing social defences against deep and intense anxieties. . . . The service tries to avoid change whenever possible, almost, one might say, at all cost, and tends to cling to the familiar even when the familiar has obviously ceased to be appropriate or relevant.[5]

The mood in stressed staffrooms is often explicitly anti-change, as we have seen already. The air is one of entrenchment and resistance – not principled but reflex. When issues of change become unavoidable, proposals tend to be greeted with *cynicism*. Cynicism masquerades as maturity: it sees itself as opting into realism, not as opting out of commitment. Cynics are very willing to offer criticism, and they may even play a useful role in probing the coherence of the enthusiasts' bright ideas. But their intention, and effect, is frequently not to contribute to the development of policy, but to prevent it. They do not wish to be personally involved with experimentation, preferring to espouse a world-weary certainty, and to snipe at the players from the safety of the sidelines. Thus other people's attempts to promote change are denigrated and any show of enthusiasm is treated with contempt. When an individual proposes a new issue or a review of current practice they may be attacked for unnecessarily rocking the boat and their attempts to change resisted because they create additional demands and unpredictability in casual encounters or in meetings.

Enthusiasm is threatening to the cynics' position because it implies that the cynical stance is not the only possible one. This threat becomes all the greater the more the enthusiasm is seen to be getting results: its success gives the lie to the cynics' belief that enthusiasm is necessarily naive and out of touch with reality. People who are prepared to experiment in the face of uncertainty are distrusted. If their experiments succeed, people will be resentful because they are implicitly reminded of their lack of courage and the low standards for which they have settled. If the experiments fail, the cynics adopt a smug 'told you so' attitude that expresses their own relief, or the more cunning ones may seize the opportunity to convince you of the hopelessness of the situation whilst appearing to commiserate. However it is possible for the cynics defence to become more vicious and more personal, depending on how rattled they are getting. They will point out that any success is only due to the perpetrator's position as the headteacher's 'blue-eyed boy' (or girl), or to their blatant sucking-up, obsessive ambition etc.

As the climate deteriorates so *hostility* becomes more indiscriminate: relationships are sacrificed over minor differences of opinion or even misunderstandings that are never cleared up. Each individual's list of others with whom they do not communicate lengthens. If you have time they can reel off to you a long list of grievances about people who let them down, went behind their backs, abused their goodwill or ripped them off. One's own or other people's predicaments are analysed and explained with unwarranted but hotly-defended confidence. 'Let me tell you what's wrong with this place . . .', people are only too willing to begin, especially when they can buttonhole a newcomer who has not heard the story before and is more likely to believe it. Questions always have a quick answer: 'It's obvious' or 'That will never work'. An air of unarticulated collusion may arise, in which the collective reflex of the staff is to reassure each other, or outsiders, that 'things aren't too bad really', and in which the gap between public face and private thoughts becomes wider. In a different school, or a different corner of the staffroom, the conventional view might be the converse: that 'this school is the pits' and that the time for constructive attempts to improve it is long past.

Thus the defensive institutional ethos not only fails to address the inevitable anxieties that the providers feel; it also creates additional stresses, in just the way that the strategies which individuals use to cope with stress may serve inadvertently to increase rather than decrease their overall stress level (see Chapter 3). Delegation upwards increases the workload of senior staff. The plethora of petty rules creates additional anxiety when people feel they are inhibited from expressing a natural caring attitude or from using their own common sense. Decreased individual responsibility leads to a lessening of personal satisfaction. The authoritarian style squeezes out the expressions of appreciation which people at all levels of the hierarchy are hungry for. The implicit requirement to subscribe to the institution's forms of defence jars with individual ways of coping, and may lead to further outer or inner conflicts. These institutional pressures mean that it is often the most mature, thoughtful and independent providers who leave the profession, which ensures that outmoded orthodoxies remain unchallenged. Helpful change is successfully avoided, so that existing pressures are not lessened, nor is satisfaction increased. And finally, the quality of the service naturally suffers. It is well documented in the medical profession that the recovery rate of patients is related to the morale of the nursing staff. And although there is no comparable objective measure of success in education (exam-passing being, for most people, too narrow an index of teachers' performance), it is plausible to suppose that the same principle applies.

SUPPORT: THE ESSENTIAL BACK-UP

What, then, can individuals do to turn such a situation round? They need to ensure that they are, personally, in good shape. When they get stressed or disheartened, as they will, they need to be able to put down the burden of 'change' and do what they need to to get back into good shape. They need to be patient and judicious. They need to be prepared for the fact that, whatever they do, some people won't like it, and open to the possibility that unexpected allies and sources of support will appear.

They also need to organize support, either within the school or elsewhere, which will provide a continuing source of validation for their commitment to their base values, and of encouragement and remoralization when they feel like giving up. (Tony Jacklin, the golfer, was asked years ago in a newspaper interview what the key to his success was. He said it was the persistent refusal to give in to the frequent urge to say 'Sod it!'.) It seems to be the experience of teachers who have persevered with the intention to change that the most helpful thing to do is to attempt to set up conditions, particularly social conditions, that strengthen or encourage the expression of their 'positive' qualities whilst simultaneously minimizing the power of the 'negative' ones. Thus setting up support is the means, as well as one of the aims, of the person who wishes to stay open and enthusiastic in a difficult time. It is something to be argued for at an official level, and also the means by which one retains one's commitment to the argument.

What exactly do I mean by 'support'? I mean a forum within which the following characteristics are present:

- the intention to change is reinforced by being accepted as rational and desirable;
- there is a general (though not necessarily detailed) consensus about the direction of change;
- there is a general understanding of the practical difficulties that is based on experience;
- people are sympathetic to the misgivings that inevitably arise, and encourage each other through them;
- experiences of varying degrees of success, and their associated feelings, can be shared without judgement;
- participants can share ideas about what might work and strategies for dealing with institutional opposition;
- discussion of educational values and ideals is taken seriously;
- people are not criticized for being confused or half-baked in their ideas;
- it is accepted that people undergoing change will feel uncertain about their identities, and are vulnerable in a variety of ways;
- there is a general understanding of the process of change; of the setbacks that may arise; of the feelings that change arouses; and of the role that one's personal belief system can play in blocking learning;
- the promotion of insight into one's implicit theories is fostered, and disentangled from self-criticism.

It is important, for reasons already discussed, that this forum:

- avoids lapsing into merely intellectual debate: any arguments which are implicitly concerned with promoting agreement, and with 'right and wrong ideas';
- avoids becoming an exclusive club that promotes a 'We're Right, They're Wrong' feeling within an institution.

When this forum consists of a group of teachers, rather than just one other person, my experience leads me to suggest the following additional ground rules for the creation of such a support group:

- it should meet regularly, preferably not less than once a month;
- its meetings should last for between two and three hours;
- each meeting should be conducted informally, but should have a *Chairperson* who reminds the group of the ground rules and of any explicit agenda, who stops discussions 'wandering off' and who keeps time;
- people who miss a meeting should be contacted soon by someone who was there to find out if they are all right, tell them what happened and give them details of future meetings;
- one person should agree to be the *Custodian* of the group's aims and intentions. It is their job to see that what the group wanted to happen, and agreed would happen, does happen *even (or rather especially) when members' enthusiasm or commitment wavers*. (This person has a long-term responsibility. The Chairperson can change from meeting to meeting);
- at least to start with, numbers should not be greater than about 16;
- the group should agree on the confidentiality of meetings;
- the success of the group may be jeopardized if it contains too many people, especially of unequal status, from the same institution. The requisite feeling of safety is harder to create, and matters of school detail and gossip, 'personality issues' and so on may begin to intrude.

Groups which are run on these lines are often called *Peer Support Groups*. An ongoing structure such as this provides continuing support and fulfils the important condition that the people who are undergoing change (the 'insiders') feel they are managing and monitoring the change themselves. If they feel that the change is being directed or taken over by 'outsiders', and that they are being pushed or controlled by people who do not respect their wishes, intentions and difficulties, then commitment is likely to be undermined. Such support is necessary on every level of the educational tree in order to clarify values and priorities, relieve feelings and share ideas. Because the nature of the demands are different at different levels, a range of provision is required. Support of this sort is no less important for headteachers, advisers and school inspectors than it is for junior members of a school's staff.

THE CRAFT OF PERSUASION

The first things which teachers must do to create a climate of involvement and energy, therefore, all are concerned with achieving and maintaining the right frame of mind to do so. They may be 'background' but they are vital, both to the success of the venture and to the preservation of teachers' own mental health. One might argue that the natural expression of this frame of mind is courage, commitment and ingenuity – or, less formally, being ready, willing and able to act on one's base values. The tips that follow are merely suggestions which may be overridden or superseded by a teacher's own sense of what it is desirable and feasible to attempt. In addition to the ones I shall list here, many of the points to do with colleagues changing their practice and which we have already considered, also apply to the promotion of particular policy changes amongst the staff at large: getting people to articulate a dissatisfaction or a need to which your proposal provides a plausible answer; offering it in a tentative manner that does not make people feel steamrollered into it; but taking repeated opportunities to indicate or demonstrate how relevant your solution might be.

1. Try to get stress as an issue on to the formal agenda of the school. This is an attempt to open up institutional discussion of the demands that people are experiencing, the extent of the pressure and overload that result, and the ways in which the situation might be improved. Sooner or later some such move is inevitable, whether the particular issue is stress, as in our example, or anything else. Support and energy are necessary but not sufficient for change to carry through into policy. Unless issues are addressed and acted on formally, as a result of discussions and decisions arrived at in staff meetings, good intentions can continually be frustrated.

   What should one be lobbying for, exactly? For the staff as a whole to take the issue seriously. Some presentation to colleagues of ways of thinking about stress – such as those contained in Chapters 3 and 4 of this book – which make it more understandable as a phenomenon, and less a matter of personal shame, might be useful in this context. A Baker day on the subject, led by a trainer from outside, might also be a start – but it will be no more than that. It would be ludicrous to suppose that you have ever 'done' stress; some ongoing provision is vital if a genuine shift in attitude is to take place. And this provision needs to be not only supportive but also organizational. Efforts need to be made to identify sources of stress in the school such as lack of clarity about roles and responsibilities, or particular tensions between departments, and to tackle these directly and explicitly.

2. When the time is right, be open about your own stress and fallibility. It may be interesting to know, and useful to quote, research which shows that 'better' teachers – as rated by a combination of pupils, parents, colleagues and headteachers – report a *higher* level of stress than do others.[6] This, at first surprising, finding is interpreted as showing that the 'better' teachers have the professional confidence to admit openly to the stress they experience. They are more able, because of their stable self-esteem, to tolerate being thought of as weak by others. Conversely the less secure teachers are, the less willing they are to risk that judgement. Being honest about your anxiety or confusion creates the opportunity for others to begin to own up – but caution is required, because it also opens you up to attack.

3. When the time is right, initiate conversations, either with groups or individuals, about their feelings on education – as it is and as they would like it to be. And listen.

4. When the time is right, express your feelings and thoughts, even if they are going to sound waffly or romantic. But do it as 'This is what I think/feel' not as 'This is what you ought to be thinking/feeling'. Practice the art of not getting defensive when people start sneering or taking the mickey. One ploy for dealing with the cynics' counter-attacks is to agree with everything they say, but without getting upset about it. If you can do this it will be they, not you, whose blood pressure goes up.

5. Resolve to start noticing and appreciating what others do, even if it is only small things. Do this especially with the people who won't expect it, and with people senior to you in the hierarchy. There is no need to be enormously effusive: if

anything be the reverse. You must be genuine. There are two rewards for doing this. The best is when this habit becomes contagious and starts to spread. The consolation prize is to disconcert some of the cynics, who will be desperate to know what you are up to.

6.   When it seems appropriate, ask for other people's advice or support in some way which is not going to burden them unduly. This has the dual effect of (a) modelling for them someone who can ask for help without feeling ashamed, and (b) giving them the chance to feel flattered that you should respect them and value their opinion. This is very effective when directed down the hierarchy, with seniors seeking the help of juniors.

7.   When you have time, break out of your normal pattern of socializing. Chat with people you don't know so well. You may sometimes be rebuffed, but probably far less often than you fear. Students and other visitors to staffrooms often view them as massively indifferent and lonely places, and a little spontaneous friendliness can transform their feeling completely. But do not make a rule for yourself that you have to do this, or it will become another burden.

8.   When you have the energy (perhaps in situations where you might seem to have an excuse, like on a school outing, in the pub, or at a party), see if you can repair relationships that have gone sour with people whom you respect, or whose friendship you used to value. Your expression of wanting to have a better relationship is what counts: it is both the trigger and the risk. Where you go from there depends. You might get the brush-off, in which case at least you've tried. You might agree amicably to 'let bygones be bygones'. Or you might risk opening up the original issue to explore it and perhaps resolve it at a deeper level.

9.   Become interested in the process of meetings and committees, in order to become more skilful at promoting your point of view through the formal decision-making channels of the school. Observe who gets their way and how they do it: who to oppose, when to defer, how to frame issues, when to be

cool and when to get heated, who to lobby and who to try to isolate, when to compromise and when to keep quiet.

10. Become interested in the self-interest of others, especially those whose support you want, and present your issue in such a way that it feeds into those self-interests. Like yourself, people will become interested in change not because they are being harangued about what's wrong with them, nor out of appeals to their better nature, but because they can see something in it for themselves. John Holt wrote, in the first edition of the magazine *Growing Without Schooling* which he produced during the last years of his life:

> In areas they feel are important, people don't change their ideas, much less their lives, because someone comes along with a bunch of arguments to show that they are mistaken, or even wicked, to think or do as they do . . . most of the time, as a way of making real and deep changes in society, this kind of shouting and arguing seem to me a waste of time.

It was, fittingly, in Holt's home town of Boston that I first met the American concept of the Car-pool Lane – an idea which seems to embody very nicely the principle of promoting change 'for the better' by capitalizing on self-interest. On the freeways into Boston there is one lane that a driver can only use, during the rush-hour period, if the car contains at least three people. They can therefore cut their journey time considerably by setting up for themselves car-sharing schemes with their neighbours and colleagues: that is the incentive. But the *effect* is to reduce fuel consumption, pollution and traffic congestion. Another example, from education this time, was the production in London a few years ago of a package of materials for school pupils on equal opportunities. What distinguished this from other such schemes was that it was called, not 'Give Girls a Chance' or some such, but 'What's in it for Boys?'.[7]

11. Target particularly senior members of staff who you think are likely to be sympathetic. Especially if you yourself are relatively junior, powerful allies are invaluable, both because they have the opportunity to influence the other powerful people in the school, and because they may be more difficult to undermine by micropolitics than you are.

12. It may be possible to use the mechanisms of micropolitics to your own advantage. You might, for example, be able to put the cynics on the defensive by making *them* into the figures of fun, to be labelled, nicknamed ('Ah! Here come the Wet Blankets') and caricatured. Their negative attitude can be commented on openly and neutralized by being treated lightly. It is even possible to use the formal machinery of the staff meeting to combat their dispiriting effects. The way students are treated in the staffroom, and the negative socialization they are being subjected to, for instance, can properly be turned into the focus of an institutional discussion. By using these means, the influence of powerful mood-setters in the informal arena of the staffroom can be diminished.

13. A related point to work at is the extent to which micropolitics are allowed to influence the official decision-making process. The Maori people of New Zealand have an excellent principle to guide their important discussions: if it's not said in the meeting, it doesn't count. No amount of lobbying or shady dealing *outside* will influence a decision unless the arguments are put openly *inside*.

14. In addition, as the campaign progresses, it may be possible to slowly shift the ground rules of the debate, so that discussion moves from a consideration of the proposal in principle to an exploration of the ways in which it could be implemented in practice. This amounts to a reversal of the process of 'insight', where presuppositions that once formed part of the *context* of a habit or a pattern of thought are unearthed and turned into matters of *content*, and capable of being challenged. In this reverse process, you change the tone of the discussion from 'whether' to 'how', by talking in a way which assumes agreement in principle. Over a period of time, if you are successful, the mood will shift so that people begin increasingly to take your approach – or something like it – as the natural or obvious way of looking at the issue.

15. A worthwhile long-term (and it is long-term) project is to work on getting better at dealing with conflict. Many people are depowered by their own feelings of anxiety and inad-

equacy about confrontation – although teachers in the course of their jobs get as much practice at coping skilfully with opposition as anyone. It is useful to make small experiments in being assertive (or even to take a course of assertiveness training), and to use the support group to work through the results.

16.   Although I have been advocating, by and large, a softly-softly attitude to change-promotion, there is also a place for being awkward. But it should usually not be the first strategy, because it causes antagonism which hardens opposition; and it should be well thought out. It is no use being awkward if the people you want to change can avoid or neutralize your awkwardness, or if they have the power to be even more awkward back to you. You need to find a place – maybe only a small place – where you can effectively create a big nuisance, and from which you cannot be dislodged, so that giving you what you want becomes an attractive option. A caricature of the suffragette story would say that their eventual success was due in large measure to their tactic of digging up golf greens, and leaving large messages cut into the turf saying 'No Votes, No Golf'. Women were given the vote because important men got fed up with having their playtime disrupted.

17.   Educate the headteacher.

WHAT HEADS CAN DO

Many readers may have been thinking: all very well, but nothing can really be done about the ethos of a school without the consent and support of the headteacher. If the head is dictatorial and traditional, all our attempts to change will be doomed to failure. This is largely true: headteachers in the British systems hold a great deal of power to decide on 'what goes' in their schools, and in some ways the Education Reform Act seems to increase that power still further. Depending on how they use that power, and particularly the extent to which they devolve it, an individual teacher's elbow-room – their scope for innovation in their teaching, and their ability to contribute meaningfully to debate – may be large or small. If your headteacher is an authoritarian recluse who doesn't remember your name, if you have no idea what the 'philosophy' of the school is, and if staff meetings are a travesty of democracy, it may be that the only thing left for you to change is your job.

Many heads, however, are more open than their staff give them credit for, and than they sometimes appear. In approaching headteachers, it is useful therefore to understand something of their special predicament. Pressures conspire to make heads appear more certain than they actually feel. They may be trying to live up to the impossible standard of having all the answers all of the time. They may feel that a head has no right to be confused or conflicted. And there may well be some teachers who agree: who *need* the head to be omniscient and omnipotent as part of their own self-protective game plan. There are some teachers who are preoccupied with their own teaching, and for whom discussions of policy are far too abstract. They just want to be left alone to get on with what they construe as the job, and policy is an irrelevance provided it does not interfere with what they do in the classroom. And there are others who much prefer to let the head make all the decisions – and who then complain about the awful decisions on which they were never consulted. A headteacher who wishes to promote a climate of greater debate and greater participation may well experience fierce resistance to attempts at power-sharing from these two groups, which may – provided they are not too big or too influential a lobby in the staffroom – have to be by-passed.

I attended a meeting about five years ago at which there was a headteacher from a large comprehensive school in south London. She was young, tall and boldly but elegantly dressed, with the kind of classy, assured manner that gets served first in busy restaurants. After about half an hour of people talking about their current experience of education she made her first contribution. 'I frequently find myself sitting in staff meetings', she said, 'and I listen to five people express five incompatible views on an issue. . . . and I find myself agreeing with all of them.' She paused, and then said, with feeling, 'I don't know what to do. I often just don't know what to do. And I'm paid to know. So what am I supposed to do?'. If this paragon of self-confidence has such private doubts I cannot believe she is alone.

If the first thing to remember about heads is that they are probably experiencing as much doubt and uncertainty as their teachers, the second is that they are just as subject to stress, if not more so, and have just as much right to be. It is therefore quite possible that their reluctance to enter the staffroom, their aloofness and their dictatorial pronouncements pinned to the staff noticeboard are just as much a reflection of their anxiety as are your critical projections and attachment to your own special seat. For many, the frost that descended during The Action, and which damaged trust and goodwill between them and their staffs severely, has not yet completely thawed. On top of this there are the demands of being the person with whom the buck stops, of being the court of appeal for teachers, pupils and parents. There are the demands of making difficult allocations of scarce resources – which *somebody* is bound to oppose. There are the demands to be soft and caring when they are looking 'inwards' at their own staff while simultaneously being tough and warlike as they protect their school, as best they can, from the cuts, criticisms and impositions issuing from the LEA or the Governors' meetings. Heads these days can feel that every time they turn round, the goal-posts have been moved again. Headteachers frequently say how lonely and beleaguered they feel; and if teachers are tempted to reply 'that's what they are paid for', or 'they *chose* to be in that position' they should remember that the same unfeeling ripostes could be made to their own complaints. And even though the head is inevitably in a position of authority, it makes no better sense for teachers to withdraw their goodwill than it would for the heart to decide to starve the brain of oxygen.

But by the same token, if headteachers want the support and participation of their staff, it behoves them to listen to what their teachers have to say, to create opportunities for their voices to be heard, and to meet them on a human as well as on a managerial plain. I once told a group of teachers that I was shortly going to have the opportunity to talk to a group of headteachers, and I asked them if they had any messages that I could transmit which they might have difficulty expressing so clearly within the confines of their own schools. They gave me several pieces of constructive advice about how heads could improve their relationships with their staff.

This is what they wanted me to pass on:

1. First and foremost, be a human being. If you can acknowledge some of your mistakes or uncertainties, we will feel
   that we have permission to be a little bit fallible too. And
   when that happens you may be surprised at how much energy
   and ingenuity is forthcoming.

2. So you don't need to pretend that you have all the answers.
   You only make things worse, because we can see, when you
   bluster and fudge the issues.

3. Particularly, please don't cloak a decision you have already
   made under the guise of discussion. We don't expect to be
   consulted about everything – far from it – but when you do
   ask our views we will not give them if we think you are just
   going through the motions. We can tell when you are doing
   it, and our trust in you, and our willingness to participate
   next time, are damaged as a result.

4. Likewise we don't expect a free rein in what we do: it is
   your school and you are answerable for what goes on in it.
   But when you do give us responsibility, make sure it's real.
   If you don't trust us with a duty, don't give it to us. It is
   threatening and invalidating to feel you are being checked
   up on all the time. How would you like it if the Chief
   Inspector kept making surprise visits to your office to look
   over your shoulder?

5. But when you have good grounds for thinking that something
   isn't right, tell us. We may not like it, but we would rather
   know. We won't be straight with you if you aren't straight
   with us.

6. Conversely, let us know when you like what we've done.

7. We suspect that part of your humanness is that you would
   like the odd bit of recognition or the occasional compliment
   too. Can you let us do it, or do you have to be strong and
   silent?

8. Get to know us. Don't only make contact with us when
   we've done something wrong, or by sending messages down
   the hierarchy. Don't hide in your office all the time. It is
   hard to trust yourself to a stranger, when you don't even
   know if he has any children, or what kind of music she likes.

9. We may not choose to come and weep on your shoulder, and would resent it if we were forced to. But it would be nice to know that you were genuinely available if we wanted to, and that we could talk, even up to a point 'off the record', without feeling that our careers might be jeopardized if we said the wrong thing.

10. Keep some direct contact with the pupils. If you are out of touch with classroom life, and talk only in educational rhetoric, we will know, and we will feel that you are out of touch with us, with our daily experience.

Teachers who wish to create a climate which supports their own desires to improve education could consider ways in which these, or other, equally direct messages, might be communicated to their headteacher. But it is important that it is done in such a way that the head may feel able to consider them coolly. If there is an underlying message of 'You've got to change' or 'You're not doing a good enough job' they will react defensively and stop listening – just as you would. There is a well-known brand of pop psychology called 'transactional analysis' which claims that when we are dealing with other people we can be in one of three states, called Parent, Adult and Child.[8] It is very easy for people whose work roles have a superordinate–subordinate relationship to fall into a Parent–Child kind of interaction, especially if either or both are not on good form. Messages such as the above can be positive, but only if the 'sender' does everything she can to ensure that both she and the 'receiver' are in the Adult mode at the time; otherwise somebody is going to end up feeling scolded. For this reason the strategy of photocopying the previous list and sending it anonymously to your head is quite likely to misfire. It would be better to engineer a situation in which you can deliver your message directly – but that of course runs the risk, if you are spotted walking out of school with the head on a Friday evening, of being branded a creep by the more negative of your colleagues the following Monday morning.

The conditions implicit in these messages are only a start. For the teacher who wishes to push harder, or for the head who is more ready, there are structural and policy alterations that can be made. This chapter concludes with a few further suggestions.[9]

1. Move from a hierarchical form of management to a more participative democracy. Question the technological and managerial approach to change, much vaunted at the moment, which attempts to preplan the whole exercise. (Define objectives → Plan learning experiences → Select learning content → Assess learning outcomes → Evaluate programme.) By ignoring the inevitability of surprise, and the importance of both teachers' and pupils' attitudes and values, the technological approach renders itself both neat and ineffective. The rise and fall of Lawrence Stenhouse's famous Humanities Curriculum Project demonstrates the fate of a good idea that was imposed on teachers, subverted and quietly dropped. A considerable amount of time and money went into the project, and 4000 packs were sold to schools. Because little money was spent on working with the teachers who were expected to use them, it is doubtful whether a single one of those packs is still in use today.

2. There must be open forums for debate about change, and time for people to chew proposals over, get used to them, assimilate them and if necessary modify them.

3. Agendas for formal meetings should be fixed democratically, not autocratically. Staff should feel that they are able to place their concerns and ideas before colleagues in a formal way.

4. Heads might devolve agenda-setting to a small sub-committee which contains junior as well as senior teachers. They might propose to this committee two items for the agenda: an open discussion on stress, and an 'open door' item in which individuals or groups of staff can have, say, 10 minutes of every alternate meeting to present any topic they like. Plans for innovation in their own teaching or department would be made especially welcome.

5. Each year, one or two working parties, comprising staff from different departments and of different seniority, should examine a major issue of school policy. These parties should give progress reports to the staff meeting as they go along, take account of comments made, and present a final report with clear recommendations. Headteachers should of course make a significant input to these working parties, but should not

pre-empt their outcomes, nor attempt to nobble them. Topics for consideration could include: the school's 'vision' (though this might appear too abstract for teachers conditioned to be very pragmatic, at least at first); the use and organization of space; the structure of the timetable; the organization and grouping of pupils; tutoring and special needs provision; record-keeping and assessment.

6. One special working party might focus on the management and decision-making structure of the school. This might report on such questions as the following: At each level in the hierarchy what work is delegated and how is it delegated? Do people typically delegate chores and retain power? To what extent (for example) is financial responsibility delegated? How is work divided and co-ordinated? Are work-loads compared or equated, and if so, how? What counts as 'work' in this process, and what does not? Are 'integrated' courses really integrated, or just a collection of fragments? Do the rules and procedures of the school help people to do what needs to be done, or frustrate them? What different kinds of meetings are there? How are they organized? What power do they have? Who decides who chairs them?

7. One outcome of this might be to clarify the distinction between the 'management team's' status as Legislature and Executive: the Legislature decides on what policy shall be, and the Executive sees that agreed policy is carried out. In the technological/hierarchical model, heads and their senior staff have combined both functions. In the organic/participative model, they retain the (by no means unpowerful) function of the Executive while broadening the constituency of the Legislature, to include, on some if not all issues, the staff as a whole. It is the head's right to decide which issues to retain legislative control over, and which to open up to general debate. The success of this democratization depends crucially not on how much responsibility is devolved, but on the genuineness of the offers that are made to the staff.

8. Time for regular reflective meetings must be made *during normal working hours*. In addition a two-day 'retreat' away from the school should be organized for the whole staff once

a year, with overnight stay strongly recommended, the agenda for the retreat being set by the staff as a whole (following time for debate about it at earlier staff meetings). The amount of work done, and goodwill generated, by such retreats can be phenomenal.

Crafty change-agents need to be pursuing their campaigns, whatever they are, on three levels. They need to keep on good form. They need to keep working on the ethos and power-structure of the school, so that its mood and procedures come into line with the values that underlie their campaign. And they need to be promoting their particular issues. The third component is obvious, but campaigns often fail from lack of attention to the first two. It is for this reason that the present chapter has focused on them. But we cannot put off any longer a discussion of the particular dissatisfactions that teachers are experiencing, and the emerging directions for change which underlie many of the innovations that are currently interesting (rather than depressing) the educational world.

Chapter 8

The articulate critic

Education, n. That which discloses to the wise and disguises from the foolish their lack of understanding.
Learning, n. The kind of ignorance distinguishing the studious.
Ambrose Bierce[1]

The bulk of this book, the first part, has focused on the process of change. The major emphasis has been, quite rightly I think, on the personal side of teaching: what it is like being a teacher, and what teachers can do to assume such power as may be available and congenial to them. So let us assume that the car is out of the garage, ticking over nicely, with a full tank of petrol and brakes that are not going to stick. All that is lacking now is a destination and a map. If teachers in large numbers felt able to bend the system in which they work to their own will, how would they bend it?

As I have said before, the changes that any individuals – teachers or otherwise – would like to see are expressions of their own values and beliefs, and as such, the clarification of the direction for change is their personal business. Vision is developed out of dissatisfaction with current practice, which stimulates (in a healthy climate) *reflection* on improvements that are expressions of, and latent within, a personal philosophy; and *communication*, which serves to test out and clarify ideas in the light of other people's reactions and alternatives. In these last two chapters, I shall summarize what some of the prevalent dissatisfactions are and attempt to sketch out the direction for the development of education in which they seem to point. In coming to focus at last on what some people, especially those in the business, see as being in need of change, my intention is not to launch yet another attack on hard-pressed teachers, but to articulate what it is that many of them are feeling in their bones.

154

There will be few surprises: most of the worries I shall mention will be familiar. And the analysis will not be based on the latest research or theories in psychology and sociology. We do not need more sophistication. Most people are well aware of the basic ways in which education is falling short. You do not sit down and ponder the law of gravity as the truck rolls towards the pram. So the main purpose of this brief review is to remind you, the reader, of your own critique. Which of these concerns do you share? Which do you discount or dispute? And what have I left out which is important to you? What things worry you, at the heart of education, which may not have been touched by GCSE, PSHE, TVEI, CPVE, the subject curriculum reviews, work experience and records of achievement? When we have achieved some sort of a critical picture, we can go on, in Chapter 9, to explore a non-technical framework which pulls these disparate concerns together into a unified critique, and offers a practical sketch of the way forward.

WHAT'S WRONG WITH SCHOOL?

Question: what have the following worthies got in common? Four professors, six headteachers, senior representatives of the Catholic, Anglican, Methodist and Jewish religions, a past president of the British Association for the Advancement of Science, the directors of the Commonwealth Institute, the National Children's Bureau and the University of London Institute of Education, the chairmen of Cadbury Schweppes and EMI, Peter Maxwell Davies, Jonathan Miller and a former Tory Minister of Education? Answer: they were all signatories to a full-page feature in *The Times Educational Supplement* of 30 January 1981, headed *Manifesto for Change*, which spelt out 12 criticisms of secondary schools that needed urgent attention. The article began

> We, the undersigned, believe that the vigorous transformation of secondary education is of immediate and profound importance for the future of young people and our society.

> In spite of much dedicated work in schools, the educational habits of the past cannot meet the demands of the future – for competence in life and work, for flexibility in the face of change, for developing

the inner resources needed to make constructive use of increased
free time.

We further believe that the depression within the secondary system,
the motivation problem which plagues many schools, the anti-social
attitudes found among some young people, and a great deal of under-
functioning in industry and commerce, are consequences of a hiatus
between the traditional secondary system, and what we need as the
outcomes of secondary education.

The necessary changes affect 12 areas of schooling in particular. We
urge that not only individual schools, their parents and governors,
but whole LEAs should, as a matter of immediate importance,
embark upon programmes of discussion and change, to bring the
secondary system up to date as quickly as possible.

Let me paraphrase their criticisms. Fundamentally they believe
that it is in such areas as practical ability and the ability to get on
with others, and such necessary attributes for a full and effective
life as 'judgement, responsibility and reliability' that secondary
education, seen as a whole, is falling short of what young people
and the nation need. They argue that the traditional curriculum
of isolated subjects develops specialisms at too early an age, and
is inadequate for the modern world. 'Today we need to educate
minds that are . . . practised in finding and using information in
the solution of real problems.' The ability to adapt to the constantly changing situation, they say, 'calls for openness of mind,
flexibility and imagination far beyond what was necessary when
the traditional style of secondary education was first laid down.
All too often today, curiosity is dulled rather than sharpened by
schooling. The curriculm has to be confidence-building and not,
as is often the case at present, confidence-breaking'.

So they see the job of the secondary school as being not to
concentrate on narrow, specialist study, but rather to provide a
broad, integrated education which can serve as a good grounding
for *any* specialism at the tertiary stage or in later life. Subjects
should be broadened into experiences which draw out, within the
same context, intellectual capacity, feeling, aesthetic appreciation,
practical application and social responsibility. And they believe
that it is for lack of such enrichment and life-relatedness that
students often condemn what they have to learn as 'irrelevant'.
'The isolated specialist, teaching in the isolated classroom, in the

isolated school, cannot provide the right educational environment for young people growing up in an interrelated world.'

In fact many of the skills necessary for effective living – being able to get along with others and be sensitive to their needs and rights, making choices, facility in oral as well as written communication, self-discipline and so on – cannot be effectively *taught* at all. They have to grow from the 'encounters of purposeful community life'. Most important, the traditional curriculum too much neglects the development of moral insight and values. The manifesto argues that the time is past when young people would accept authoritarian edicts on trust as the basis for their lives. Instead we have to offer them real experiences that will help them to frame viable philosophies of life for themselves. Yet many schools today are too rushed, too stressed, too impersonal and too exclusively dedicated to examination goals to provide this essential diet of meaningful, collaborative work.

The exam system comes in for particularly harsh words. They say that this system,

> upon which young people's personal status in society depends, is becoming increasingly inappropriate. It distorts the curriculum, excludes vital elements in education, generates a damaging sense of failure among a large section of the student population and positively rejects – at great risk to society – some 10 to 20 per cent of the 'least able'. It also trains young people in intense academic competitiveness at a time when cooperative skills are everywhere in demand. . . . We cannot build a responsible, self-confident and productive community on the basis of an examination system which labels hosts of young people as inferior human beings.

As if that weren't enough the Royal Society of Arts has been promoting, since 1980, its own campaign, called *Education for Capability*, signalled each year by a large newspaper advertisement, and signed by dignitaries from industry (Sirs Campbell Adamson, Terence Beckett, Michael Edwardes, Monty Finniston and Ian MacGregor), the arts (Lindsay Anderson, Sirs Richard Attenborough and Peter Hall) politics (Lord Eccles and Neil Kinnock) and the media (Jeremy Isaacs and Donald Trelford), numbering over 200 in all. They state that:

> Young people in secondary and higher education . . . acquire knowledge of particular subjects, but are not equipped to use knowledge in ways that are relevant to the world outside the education system. . . . A well-balanced education must include the exercise of

creative skills, the competence to undertake and complete tasks and the ability to cope with everyday life; and also doing all these things in cooperation with others.

It might be possible to write off these complaints as the querulous musings of old fogies, though they come from all quarters of society and from all colours along the political spectrum. Or as out-of-date, having been answered by the current changes to the curriculum and to forms of assessment. Do we not now have a system which is more vocationally orientated, and a higher pass rate in GCSE? Is there not more scope for choice and for collaboration in project work? It is true that things have changed over the last eight years – but nothing like enough. Young people know as well as employers that the important thing about failure is that it is *relative*. It doesn't matter a bit whether you call it F for Fail or for not as good as A to E: the 'low achievers' probably understand the game better even than their more successful peers. The sense of having been required to compete and do badly in a race they were never cut out for remains. The fact is that the comments in these public statements continue to mirror quite accurately the private misgivings of many of those within the secondary system itself. Many teachers, for example, sympathize with the pupils' frequent experience of mystification and confusion. Jill Jones in her interview with me said:

> I think I don't do a bad job and most teachers don't do a bad job really, and that most kids come out sort of all right: but there's an awful lot of them that don't, and that's where we fail. Like for instance when you know you're teaching them something that's totally meaningless to them you think to yourself they're going from lesson to lesson learning all these meaningless things and they come out at the end with a Grade E GCSE and they've forgotten everything and you think: What's the point?

Ken Young, a headteacher from Tower Hamlets in London, was quoted in *The Times Educational Supplement* (11 October 1985) as saying of his pupils:

> They come into school with lively enquiring minds, but they don't leave with them. . . . God created the universe: he separated light from darkness and land from water. Then he stopped. He didn't say a word about history and geography or maths and physics. . . . He knew when he'd done a good job . . . subjects can't be didactically decreed; they grow up from the ground, like children, not from universities and the DES.

When you look at it, the whole organization of secondary schools seems antiquated and odd – certainly not designed for the kind of committed and communal investigation of real problems that *The Manifesto for Change* was calling for. Despite the recent changes to content and assessment, you still find, with few exceptions, that the standard format is a division of a large number of 11 to 18 year-olds into lumps of about 20 to 30 each. Schools are built as a collection of boxes to accommodate such lumps, and such lumps only, except perhaps for a hall which will take the whole lot. Everyone in each lump is about the same age, which minimizes the opportunity for each pupil to learn from another or to instruct another. The lumps are shifted at fixed intervals, usually each hour, from box to box, in each of which they are confronted by an adult who spends all of his or her working week in these boxes. During each block of time, the adult presents knowledge and experiences of various sorts to the children. If they do not catch the knowledge, or extract the desired meaning from the experience, it is gone. The syllabus comes past but once. In the course of a week each lump meets between five and ten of these ephemeral adults, and each adult between five and ten lumps, amounting maybe to about 250 children. What one adult says to a lump usually remains unknown to the other adults. At the beginning of each year the lumps re-form, and it is a matter of chance whether a child meets any of the previous year's adults again.[2]

It appears that the standard timetable is based on some rather dubious assumptions, which some schools, to their credit, are struggling to break away from. Yet it remains true, in the vast majority of cases, that pupils are treated as relatively passive, in need of constant supervision, and unable to select and organize learning experiences for themselves. The welcome element of choice in GCSE projects, for example, boils down in practice to a menu of options from which the *teacher* can select, and within which individual pupils may sometimes be allowed to opt for one project from a choice of two or three. Freedom of this kind is a token, not a reality.

Then again, despite the attempts here and there to produce integrated and cross-curricular courses, the national curriculum reinforces the belief that knowledge is like a patchwork quilt which has to be doled out a piece at a time by an expert in each colour, and which can be cobbled together in the learner's mind by some unspecified processes which 'bright' pupils are better at than the 'less able'; and that it is possible for teachers and learners to generate a sense of partnership and continuity as the kaleidoscope of knowledge constantly shifts. At its worst, as one teacher put it to me, you feel as if you are practising taxidermy on living things – removing their natural organs and replacing them with dead stuffing which bears no functional relationship at all to the needs of the individual or its species. No wonder, he said, that many of them still end up immobilized and glassy-eyed – despite project work and TVEI.

Even when the pupils can make sense of what is going on there is no denying that many find much of school boring. Patrick Eavis, a headteacher from Newcastle-upon-Tyne, commenting on an HMI report in *The Times Educational Supplement*, said:

> The truth is that most kids are bored out of their minds with this stuff. It's OK for those who know they only have to put up with it for a few years to get a nice job like mine, but what are the other 80 per cent here for? Nothing in this report is going to cause a revolution in terms of motivation; getting kids interested in what they are doing and actually wanting to do it. What I am concerned about is just what sort of science we should do and how we can make it relevant to the twentieth century, let alone the twenty-first.[3]

A report published in *The Daily Telegraph* (typical of dozens) on 25 August 1986 agrees, and immediately goes on to demonstrate just the sort of defensive reaction that is so common.

> *'Switched off' pupils condemned as unhelpful* – Headteachers have condemned as 'unhelpful' a claim by Mr Baker, Education Secretary, that too many fourteen and fifteen year old pupils are bored and 'switched off' in school. Mr David Hart, general secretary of the National Association of Head Teachers, said yesterday, 'The reason so many are bored is because the curriculum provided for non-academic children is wrong and needs to be radically changed. The implication of Mr Baker's comment is that boredom is the result of inadequate teachers. That is categorically wrong. Until we feed children a much more relevant curriculum we shall never get over the problem . . .'.

Many teachers (and observers) attribute this lack of interest and meaning to a narrowness of the curriculum in two senses: a disconnection with pupils' real likes, real needs, real interests and real desires for competence; and an over-concentration on intellectual performance to the detriment of other areas of human development. At a down-to-earth level, Jill Jones echoes the concerns of the two choruses with which this chapter opened. I asked her: what is it that some pupils are not getting that you think they should get as they grow up? She replied:

> Something that's relevant to them. Something they can feel, not that they've learnt *about*, but they've learnt the way to go about things so they can tackle things better in their everyday lives with a bit more gusto, if you like, rather than just thinking 'Oh, I don't know about that'. I'd like them to get more *confidence*. I talk to loads of kids who have left school and they still feel that they know very little – that they haven't got anywhere. And I've spoken to kids who have gone on to Colleges of Higher Education as well as those who have gone into jobs, and for *them* school's not relevant. There are very few people who I've spoken to who actually say 'School was a good thing for me' – except perhaps for those who go on to university or poly. School works for the 'brightest' and for the rest . . . not really.

Of all the forms of knowledge, skill or human quality that could be focused on by school, the intellectual remains pre-eminent. Some other forms are present in school, but by their weight on the timetable and the form of assessment, they are very clearly signalled as second-class. Certain types of physical skill, for example, are acknowledged, though even here there is a pecking order, with football or netball better than surfing or dancing, and playing the piano better than the drums. Art and music are second-division activities, though you can upgrade them to GCSE or A-level subjects at the cost of allowing them to be infected with the virus of intellectualism, and turned into something you can mug up and write essays about. Two recent letters in *The Times*, one from John Bratby, RA, and the other signed by a dozen professors of art and principals of art schools and colleges, bemoaned this stultifying influence of knowledge-based exams on the selection of young applicants for art school.

There is evidence that the domination of intellectual and verbal modes of operation damages not only aesthetic and artistic ability, but creativity in general. Allowing for the fact that we have not really the faintest idea what creativity tests (or intelligence tests, come to that) actually measure, 'creative' pupils are generally less academically successful, and less well-liked by teachers, than 'intelligent' pupils.[4] Research has revealed some of the factors that appear to inhibit creativity:[5]

pressure to conform
authoritarian personality
ridicule and sarcasm
over-emphasis on evaluation
excessive quests for certainty
hostility towards divergent personalities
over-emphasis on success
intolerance of play attitudes

It is not surprising that creativity does not flourish in school, where teachers are either required to operate under at least some of these conditions, or they feel that, for their own sanity, they have no choice but to do so.

Emotional and social development loom larger in the rhetoric of many schools than they do in the day-to-day reality. The dominant ethos in many schools for the pupils (as also for the staff) is one not only of conformity but of toughness. For both boys and girls the most acceptable social style is a macho one in which brashness, snappy come-backs and public self-confidence are at a premium, while tenderness, fearfulness, insecurity, sadness and dependency are feelings to be expressed in corners or hidden in shame. Even in the welcome spread of Personal and Social Education, feelings are treated as things to be thought about and discussed, rather than as rich, inextricable threads of life to be accepted and learnt from in school as much as elsewhere. Whether a genuinely more mature and convivial attitude to life is actually developed by artificially stimulated discussion is highly questionable.

One particular concern is the way in which, when children transfer from primary to secondary schools, they are implicitly expected to leave the faculty of visual imagination behind them, as if it were now developmentally passé, to be superseded by the more adult medium of symbolic reasoning. Where fantasy and symbolic play were everyday sources of fun and resources for learning, they now dwindle to an element of 'creative writing' or drama, and after the age of 14 may peter out altogether. Yet imagination and intuition remain invaluable tools for learning, and could be developed still further if they were encouraged and exercised. In some areas of growth, like the acquisition of virtuosity in sport or music for example, visualization is much more suited to 'mental practice' than is conscious thought. The obsession of school with the latter (even in the realms of art and literature) handicaps young people in two ways: by allowing a valuable resource to atrophy through neglect; and by conveying the implicit message that analysis and deliberation are the best ways to tackle any problem. The waiting-rooms of counsellors are full of people who are in despair because the tools of analytic reason, which are the only ones they know – short of physical or emotional duress – are quite unable to fix their relationships.

People are also concerned that schools do not do enough to make young people critical consumers of information and ideas. True, they may well do a project in English on 'advertising', but the healthy scepticism that may be raised is not fostered in other activities and does not seem to carry through into everyday life. It is not surprising that school fails in this regard, for young people have little opportunity or encouragement to be critical consumers of their own education. Teachers on the whole do not wish to be repeatedly reminded of their own doubts by the pupils. It seems needlessly depressing to be repeatedly forced to consider questions of relevance or meaning that you already know you have no good answers to. Most pupils quickly learn that the best policy is to keep quiet and get on with what they have been told to do, moment by moment, regardless of its apparently fragmented or meaningless nature. And because they have no overall sense of where they are going, and why, it is quite understandable that they will adopt a docile and dependent attitude towards their studies – or an angry and resentful one.

At its worst, perhaps not as rare as we would like to think, pupils' experience of school may become profoundly perplexing and invalidating. As John Holt, at his most chilling, says:

> the limits we put in many schools on freedom of speech, movement, and even facial expression are far more stringent than anything we would find even in a maximum security prison. . . . This would be a very effective punishment if it were meant as such. But the child is forbidden to think of it as punishment, or to ask why he should submit to this inhuman treatment. He is forbidden to think that these people who are doing these things to him are in any way his enemies or that they dislike or fear him. He is told to believe that they care about him, that what they do, they do for his sake, for his good. He is made to feel that if he resists these orders not to speak or move, or even to change the expression on his face, or turn his head away

from the teacher for even a few seconds, that if he even resents or questions these things, he is somehow bad, wicked and really deserves harsher punishment.[6]

Not only are people worried that school is failing to develop many valuable competencies and qualities in young people – social, emotional, mental, practical and physical; there is also concern about its degree of success within its own pinched terms. This is what the 'levering up of standards' is all about. Statistics about the extent of adult illiteracy, for example, are hotly disputed, but many people, employers and others, are clearly concerned. *The Daily Telegraph* (perhaps not surprisingly) is full of stories of alarm. In the months of January and February 1987, for example, it carried the following stories:

'. . . Average competence at sixteen is represented by a miserable CSE grade four, and at any one time 100,000 native English speaking British adults, most of whom have been through eleven years of compulsory schooling and still can't read, are taking basic literacy and numeracy courses.' (14 January)

'Colleges generally find that one in five first year undergraduates require some form of remedial English.' (2 February)

'An outline of the principles for awarding marks, produced by the Associated Examining Board, says that in answering questions pupils do not have to use correct English spelling, or even write in sentences.' (9 February)

'As many as seven million Britons may be unable to read and write . . . 26% of children are "not HOPELESSLY illiterate, perhaps, but so abysmally poor at reading and writing after 11 years of compulsory schooling that I do not think they can function in our society".' (9 February)

'Errors of grammar by averagely able, older teenagers studied in an education project were so serious that almost a third of what they wrote was rated "unsatisfactory" said a report yesterday.' (21 February)[7]

The Independent's figures are lower, but not dramatically so.

'Of more than 6 million adults in the UK with severe difficulty in reading, writing and doing simple maths, 40% received no special help from their schools.' (3 June 1987)

Whatever the statistical truth, I know of no teacher or commentator who thinks that school, even within its own narrow terms, is doing a good enough job; nor anyone, other than politicians and union officials, who does not understand that part of the problem is precisely the narrowness of the terms. School operates under a rubric which seems automatically to exclude most things that teenagers need and want to know. Even real issues of current concern are squeezed out by 'the syllabus', and by many teachers' feeling that somehow they ought not to become controversial. Science teachers may allow themselves to be sidetracked in to a discussion of last night's programme on the dumping of nuclear waste, acid rain, or the production of man-made deserts by multi-national greed, and then, for lack of time and encouragement, it's back to the Universal Indicator, hydrogen's 'squeaky pop' and the habits of the woodlouse.

For many people, as we have seen, the 16-plus exams are the villain of the piece. They lock teachers into a way of teaching at least from age fourteen upwards, which emphasizes retention of knowledge and the acquisition of specified skills. They inhibit the following of interests and questions that naturally arise – and GCSE represents a tiny shuffle in the right direction, when what is urgently needed is a giant stride. They label and grade pupils in a pernicious and often irrevocable fashion. They act as quite inadequate predictors both of young people's real-world competence and qualities and (even more unforgivably) of future academic success. And they generate for many pupils, regardless of their likelihood of winning or losing in the paper-chase, an incredible burden of stress and anxiety, one which the coursework assessment of GCSE now smears across two years but does not remove. Many pupils would clearly like to go back to the bad old days when you got it all over with at once, and you didn't have the constant black cloud of evaluation hanging over you. Now you have the worst of both worlds, with this nagging anxiety building up to a terminal exam that still counts for most of the marks. The first year of GCSE showed many pupils responding to the shift to coursework by overworking, sometimes quite dramatically. And while the rhetoric promised the assessment of a greater variety of skills – projects, creative writing, library research and so on – so that the less able would have more ways in which to show their capabilities, by the same token they now have more ways in which to be, and feel, inadequate. This is quite apart from the concern that these other skills will give the pupils from 'middle-class' backgrounds an even greater head start than they enjoy already.

Everyone in the business is painfully aware of the way in which both the future and self-esteem of the 'failures' is blighted. We shall return to that in a moment. But the 'successes' too are likely to achieve their status at some cost if they become convinced of their own superiority, and take their examination passes as an index of their personal worth. They may become addicted to a cut-throat and conservative way of operating which can reveal itself in many ways, from ruthlessness in business dealings, through insensitivity to those less privileged, down to an unwillingness to share thoughts or resources with each other. As James Hemming put it: 'however much (the school) may talk of *esprit de corps* on the playing field, or in out-of-school activities, the principle for the classroom is *esprit de moi*'.[8] And they are at risk of becoming 'success-junkies' in which the only way to insulate themselves against unthinkable failure is to stick slavishly to a narrow and unadventurous lifestyle, the only arena within which the necessary diet of achievement can be guaranteed.

The short-term emotional toll that exams take on the potential winners is at least as severe as it is for the resigned losers, who may well have already developed alternative ways of defending or defining themselves that will take the sting out of the anticipated failure. If your identity revolves around your relationships and you are looking forward to leaving school and getting a job in a shop, GCSE becomes a drag rather than an assault. But if you have been labelled as 'bright' and you want to be a doctor, then you have further to fall. An article in *The Independent* of 9 July 1987 documented several deaths of 16- and 18-year-old students from anxiety attacks brought on by exams. Suicide amongst the under-25s has risen by 24 per cent in the last decade, and is 50 per cent higher for Oxbridge students (who have the farthest to fall of all) than for other young people of the same age. In 1986 the Samaritans dealt with 20,000 calls from people under 16, most of which were to do, at least in part, with exam pressures.

It is not only exams which frequently make schools scary places for young people to be. A survey of school truants in South Wales found that the reasons why youngsters decide to bunk off predominantly reflect the unbearable anxiety of being in school.[9] Bullying, intimidation (by pupils and teachers) and the stress of an enormous depersonalized environment were commonly mentioned. On an average day nearly 10 per cent of the total school population is absent from school, either truanting or 'school-phobic': afraid to go.

For many pupils, even the relatively successful, the day-to-day reality is the recurrent experience or threat of failure. Like the bathers in *Jaws*, it is not long before that familiar theme music of apprehension starts up, and everybody (apart from the 'hard-nuts') races for the firm, dry land of a Right Answer or a Good Try. Some are good enough swimmers to make it most of the time. Some keep getting caught. Some have been bitten so often that they have learnt to blend into the beach, or to stay very close to the 'sure', captive within their own cramped paddling-pool of pre-existing confidence.

Contrary to some simple-minded opinion, it is not failure *per se* that lastingly undermines people's courage, curiosity, creativity and self-confidence. It may be an unfortunate, but not a crippling, fact of life that in order to learn you've got to make mistakes, and that everybody can't be as good as everybody else at every-thing they attempt. Sometimes you get it wrong, and sometimes you are way down the class. To be able to learn you have got to be able to handle these things when they happen. So to pretend that everyone can be successful – for example, by grading exams A to G with no 'fail', or to give each school-leaver an individual 'profile of achievement' as some counties already do – is a trans-parent lie through which pupils, parents and employers will see without any trouble. The fashion for profiles or records or certifi-cates of educational achievement, as well as creating new ways for young people to become a formal failure, is also based on the false assumption that their manner or accomplishment in school bears a predictive relationship to their attitude or potential else-where. However disguised the language, this trend simply extends the school's pernicious habit of labelling and grading ever more deeply into pupils' private lives.

In the normal course of events you can choose to persist in what you are not very good at if you want to get better; or to give it up if you either don't need it or don't like it. This may be a difficult decision but it is not a threat to identity. It is only under special conditions, like those of a school, that failure becomes a personal assault; when academic success is confused with personal worth; when everyone is busy telling you that 'your future hangs on it'; when the atmosphere is individualized, competitive and comparative; when failure may be persistent and inescapable; and when the things you aren't good at are 'the only games in town'. To the extent that these conditions do not obtain, failure is at worst frustrating and at best challenging and informative. Let me illustrate with a story that David Hargreaves tells in *The Challenge to the Comprehensive School*.

> I was not successful, during my schooldays, at woodwork. Slowly I grew to dislike and then to hate the subject at which I was failing. . . . Naturally I gave up woodwork at the earliest opportunity and forgot about it. But . . . I had been able to consign my experiences in woodwork to distant corners of my subconscious only because in most of my other school subjects I had been relatively successful. My conspicuous failure had been drowned in a sea of moderate success.

But he goes on to muse about how different things might have been if the experience of failure had been more pervasive and inescapable.

> The nearest I can come is to imagine a school in which the aspects in which I was least successful (the physical–manual) replace those aspects in which I was most successful (the cognitive–intellectual). In this nightmare my secondary school's timetable is dominated by periods of compulsory woodwork and metalwork, gymnastics, football and cricket, drawing and painting, technical drawing, swimming and cross-country running. Sandwiched between these lessons, but only in thin slices, appear welcome lessons in arithmetic and English, in French and history. Some of these, however, cease to be available to me after the third year: they clash with the more important subjects of technical drawing and gymnastics which I need for higher education and a good job. I enjoy most lessons very little; I am bored and make little effort in areas where I seem destined to fail. The temptation to 'muck about' in lessons, and even to truant, is almost irresistible. My friends soon matter to me much more than anything else in school and our greatest pleasure is in trying to subvert and mock the institution which we are forced to attend for five long years. I don't think my teachers, who seem so strong and so clever with their hands and feet, really understand me at all. Quite often they are kind, but I know they look down on me and think it's all rather hopeless in my case. I'll be glad to leave school.
> Is this too fanciful? Or do we all have within us the making of our own nightmare through which we might catch a glimpse of how easily, had the education system been built on alternative narrow premises, we might be such very different people?[10]

Though it is 40 years since Hargreaves was a schoolboy, the

changes over the last three, 10, or 20 years have done little to alter the experience.

The majority of young people who find school boring, confusing, depressing and invalidating come from poor or working-class or 'ethnic minority' families. For some white middle-class boys school is like this, but for girls, to some extent, and for poor and black youngsters certainly, the chances are much higher. How could it be otherwise? Anyone whose home culture has not prepared them for, or is at odds with, the intellectual culture of school is going to have a harder time of it. Some pupils and their families try to adjust, to become more aligned with the aims and activities of the school – though it may be too hard or too late – while many others either cannot or will not do so. You do not have to be too cynical an observer of education, and of the politicians' attitude to it (irrespective sadly of which party), to suspect that its prime function may be not as a training for life, but as an obstacle course whose hurdles are specifically designed to be familiar and congenial to the children of powerful parents, and alien or distasteful to the rest. According to one's politics, one will find this situation either inevitable or intolerable. Whichever, the double tragedy is that many of the losers are not only socially disadvantaged but psychologically damaged by the process. The false premise of comprehensive education – that everyone has a fair chance, and that if they are 'bright' enough and work hard enough they can win – almost guarantees that the losers not only lose, but they feel personally responsible for their failure. To quote Hargreaves again:

> My argument is that our present secondary-school system, largely through the hidden curriculum, exerts on many pupils, particularly but by no means exclusively from the working-class, a destruction of their dignity which is so massive and pervasive that few subsequently recover from it. To have dignity means to have a sense of being worthy, or possessing creative, inventive and critical capacities, of having the power to achieve personal and social change. When dignity is damaged, one's deepest experience is of being inferior, unable, and powerless. My argument is that our secondary schools inflict such damage, in varying degrees, on many of their pupils. It is not intended by the teachers, the vast majority of whom seek and strive hard to give their pupils dignity as I have defined it.[11]

It is hard to see how anybody's morality could condone an education system in which social injury is compounded by personal insult in this way – anybody, that is, who is neither the most cynical of beneficiaries nor the most despairing of fatalists. Nor is it even practical. Teachers lose, because their job is soured by having to try to control the increasingly desperate attempts of some young people to salvage a few shreds of self-respect by active or passive opposition to the teachers' efforts to teach. Even the winners lose, as 'their' culture is forced to devote time and money to dealing with the fall-out from disaffection. There is much more that can be, and has been, said about what is wrong with school. But I wanted to stay fairly close to what many teachers are themselves thinking and feeling, whether out loud or in private. To complement this, I wish now to take a quick look at things from the pupils' side.

THE PUPILS'-EYE VIEW

Instead of spending their time in school learning skills and qualities that are of use in the world outside, many pupils are unwittingly forced to devote most of their energies to devising ways of coping with school itself. The emotional pressures conspire with the dearth of opportunities for real choice and relevant learning to create a complex, multi-dimensional *problem* for pupils, in which the content of the lesson they happen to be in plays only one part. Pupils develop their own stance, or repertoire of stances, toward school which represents their best solution to this problem, and which is influenced by a host of considerations. Do I like the teacher? Is the subject intrinsically interesting to me? Is it too cold or too hot in here? What opportunities for mischief are there? What do I want to be when I grow up? Does school have anything to do with what I want to be? Do I need to do well in this subject to get a qualification? What do my parents want for me, and how much do I care? How much do I want to be popular with the other kids? How miserable do I get if I feel lonely? What else am I good at? Am I 'bright'? Am I 'thick'?

Who in the class am I scared of? What do you get laughed at for around here? Am I good-looking? What else is on my mind? How good am I at learning stuff for exams? How much support/ peace and quiet do I get if I want to study at home? What does this teacher put up with? If I'm cheeky do I get treated by the class like a hero or a jerk? Do I understand what the teacher is on about? Do I think I *could* understand if I made the effort? How easy is it to be invisible in this class? Who am I sitting with? What do we have in common? Do I want them to be my friends? Does the teacher help when you don't understand, or do you get sneered at? What reputation do I have? How do people expect me to behave? What kind of exams are there going to be? What kind of learning do you need to do to pass? Will I get bullied if I look like a swot? Can I find a way of studying and trying whilst *not* losing social brownie points?

What fun-things might I have to sacrifice if I decide to 'go for it'? How do I want to be like/not like my brothers and sisters? Do I hate feeling confused? Am I tough enough to be a 'rough kid'? What makes me anxious? What are my friends good at? What jobs have I not done yet? What have we got next lesson? Where is Barbara today? And so on and so on. Out of this pile of considerations – long-term and short-term; weighty and trivial; intellectual, emotional, vocational, practical and social – a personal style must be constructed that fulfils as many needs and wishes, and avoids as many threats, as possible. And how, and how much, pupils actually learn, how obliging they are, how resourceful they seem, and how chatty or cheeky they are, all emerge as facets of this tacit but sophisticated decision-making process. Thus it is not surprising that demeanour and performance in school bear so little relationship to a young person's character and capabilities outside: nor that what *is* learnt in school so often fails to transfer to out-of-school contexts. Even if it were useful – which most of it is not – it was not learnt for its use, but as part of a package of measures to cope with the peculiar demands of school.

For many pupils in school, the combination of social stresses and intellectual fog leads them, rationally but tragically, towards a stance that requires them to *sacrifice* learning opportunities, and to destroy or stunt the natural learning abilities they arrived with. Most secondary school teachers I know are deeply saddened by the self-destructive transformation that happens to so many youngsters between the ages of 11 and 14. Some become controlled, earnest and dependent swots, maybe paying for their open commitment to the curriculum with a loss of social standing in the class. (It is striking, in workshops for teacher-trainees, how many of them regularly confess to having been lonely adolescents.) Some flounder in a game but ineffectual way. Some seem to switch off their gumption at the start of every lesson. (Teachers frequently find themselves in a desperate, incredulous and self-defeating battle to switch them on, not realizing that for kids to *take part* and *try*, to mobilize the intelligence which the teachers quite rightly know they have, would be to jeopardize the game plan.) Some become invisible, some become babyish and some become truculent. Some become depressed. Some start truanting. If you have a good memory, bright friends, supportive parents, and teachers who explain things clearly and listen to your questions carefully, it is more likely that your game plan will coincide with the school's. Otherwise school is about something quite different. And, from the pupils' point of view, necessarily and sensibly so. If they cannot make much sense of the lessons, and feel pessimistic about their chances of doing so, then the options that are left are to focus on what is left – the people, and one's relationships with them – or to adopt a stance of self-protection, either through hiding or through active opposition.

Thus the pupils' predicament, though different in content, comes to resemble that of teachers in form. Instead of being interested in expansion, both young and old are propelled by the social forces in a direction that they do not like: towards the saving of face and the containment of feeling. Like their teachers, adolescents may find themselves becoming dull and harsh, bemused and depressed, cynical and unadventurous. Feeling impotent, the seemingly insuperable mountains of learning and change are ignored, and replaced instead with the blow-up molehills of gossip and small damage-limitation exercises. Many teachers and pupils find themselves huddled at opposite ends of the same boat: a boat that lacks a rudder, and which is holed below the water-line. They cannot steer, and must keep baling to prevent their self-esteem from becoming swamped. Small wonder that in such a situation they fall to bickering. The young feel they have precious little control, and the teachers feel either powerless or scared to give them any more (lest they become 'unmanageable'). Thus trapped pupil starts behaving badly to pupil, teacher to teacher, and both groups to each other. In the storm of stress, the whole idea of education – the empowerment of the young –

gets watered down or washed away. For some teachers their work continues to deliver satisfaction. For some pupils their studies and their socializing are pleasant and successful. But for teachers and pupils as a whole, the balance sheet of education is in debit.

IN A NUTSHELL

Despite recent and projected changes, deep and all-too-familiar concerns remain about the job that schools are doing. The social context of the late twentieth century is crucially different from that within which our schools were conceived. The job that schools need to be doing to equip young people – not just some, but all of them – for successful adulthood is likewise different. Traditional stabilities based on agreed values, on clearly defined social classes, on the need for labourers, clerks and managers, on bodies of knowledge that it was good to know – all have crumbled, leaving young people with vastly increased senses of opportunity, responsibility and insecurity. Time was when to fail at school meant you would find it very difficult to move into a different lifestyle, or to do a different kind of job, from the one your parents had. Now those traditional cultures and industries are going or gone, and there is nothing clear-cut for the 'failures' and their mates to fall back on. The world is individualistic, opportunistic, entrepreneurial – yet the necessary skills for crafting a life of one's own are not taught or developed. J. Krishnamurti summed it up while talking one day to the young people at the school he founded at Brockwood Park in Hampshire.

> If you are not being educated to live, then education has no meaning. You may learn to be very tidy, have good manners, and you may pass all your examinations; but to give primary importance to these superficial things when the whole structure of society is crumbling, is like cleaning and polishing your fingernails while the house is burning down. . . . As you spend day after day studying certain subjects – mathematics, history, geography – so also you should spend a great deal of time talking about these deeper matters.[12]

Schools are being primped with social skills and the new vocationalism, but the mood in the classrooms, behind the desks, has not improved nearly as much as was hoped. The problems run deeper than curriculum: peace education and anti-sexism and open-ended project work and negotiated assessment and multi-faith approaches to RE and . . . and . . . and . . . all seem to suffer the fate of new wine poured into unrinsed bottles. What is needed is an education that equips young people to deal with precisely the kind of situation that is now facing their teachers. So perhaps we can learn, from reflecting on the pickle that teachers find themselves in, what such a process of empowerment would look like.

Chapter 9

Good learning

> It is the thesis of this book that change – constant, accelerating, ubiquitous – is the most striking characteristic of the world we live in and that our educational system has not yet recognized this fact. We maintain, further, that the abilities and attitudes required to deal adequately with change are those of the highest priority and that it is not beyond our ingenuity to design school environments which can help young people to master concepts necessary to survival in a rapidly changing world.
>
> N. Postman and C. Weingartner[1]

Not only must schools change; they must become *about* change. Before young people are equipped with skill and knowledge from the exercise of which they can derive satisfaction and employment, they must be given the equipment with which to equip themselves. They have to have the tools to learn. In a world of changing circumstances, values and demands, they need not just spanners and screwdrivers but lathes and milling-machines with which they can fashion their own tools. Young people need to be helped to become good learners. Once that indestructible foundation has been laid, then teachers may assist them in acquiring particular areas of expertise, whether it be writing poetry, doing clean experiments or fixing cars. But if the laying of this foundation is being ignored by schools these days, they are criminally negligent. And if what they are doing instead actually undermines such bases as young people already have, they are guilty of criminal damage.

In some jobs, it is true, the ideal employee is docile and biddable. Cynics argue that schools are in fact doing a good job of training people for a working life of quiet (or noisy) boredom. But the public complaint of employers, signatories to the *Manifesto for Change* and others, is the reverse: that school-leavers behave irresponsibly and unintelligently. Too many seem unable to ask sensible questions, take sensible initiatives, and to lack the confidence that breeds the satisfaction and pride in a job well done. School-leavers themselves are dismissive of a system that offers, as the alternative to continuing academic failure, training in stacking shelves and advice about applying for jobs. The hole in the heart of their school experience has not been filled, for these young people, by the appearance of TVEI and other ostensibly more 'relevant' courses. Studies of TVEI have shown that it has failed to improve both pupils' motivation and their exam results.[2] These are attempts to build a superstructure on a base that has been ground down, over the previous years, from rock to sand. And teachers themselves, as we have seen, know deep down that what they are constrained to do is, for many young people, at best a modicum and at worst an insult. They know that it is not right that the effect of school, whatever its intention, is to stupefy a lot of young people, including the so-called bright ones. University teachers complain as much as employers about the decline in cultural awareness and general nous over the last twenty years, and they in their turn have been trapped more and more into the factory-farming approach to education.

All in all I assert that the core of the widespread disaffection with schools is that they are not helping pupils to become good learners. They are bored, not so much because they are not learning anything, but because their *powers* of learning are not being stretched. They are lazy and irresponsible because, after a while, they become ashamed of their own ineptness in the face of problems and uncertainties, and seek to avoid being exposed. That is why they mumble, giggle, mess about and switch off. And when people react defensively to their own incompetence, incompetent is what they remain. Hiding and blustering are useful for saving face in the short-term. But the more these ploys are used, the more they *have* to be used, because they prevent the development of the mastery that could make them redundant.

If we go *right* back to basics, we find that it is in everyone's interests for young people to become good learners, and for education to hold that as its primary goal. Teachers will have more fun, employers will get recruits who are quicker on the uptake, and young people will be better able to amuse themselves. ('Amuse', I read in one dictionary, derives from the Old French for 'to hold one's muzzle in the air' – which I take to mean to be curious, sniffing the breeze, looking for and open to learning opportunities.) The protection and fostering of learning ability is the bottom line of education, prior even to reading, writing and arithmetic. The earnest and well-intentioned attempt to train people in the 3Rs when they are not ready, willing or able to learn them can easily destroy those people's confidence on their ability to learn. Distaste and distress increase and transform what was originally the parents' or the teachers' impatience into a *real* learning difficulty. It is not that one should not teach the 3Rs, nor that one should not try to encourage people who are having difficulty. The point is that if teachers are insensitive to the learners' signals of resistance and anxiety, and plough on regardless, they are doing more harm than good. When children are in 'mastery-mode' they love being challenged and stretched. When they are in 'survival-mode' your challenge becomes a threat; your 'stretch' becomes an indictment. The 'back to basics' call does not go far enough back if it allows its obsession with 'standards' and uniformity to create this debilitating insensitivity.

GOOD AND BAD LEARNING

Pupils adopt a wide range of modes to cope with the perceived demands of school. Each mode gives rise to an attitude towards classroom 'work', and a style and level of performance, which may mirror quite accurately, or not at all, the way a person might tackle a similar task, and with what success, in a different context.[3] Of all these modes, I wish to contrast here just two which obviously represent the ends of a fairly complex continuum: the ones I called just now 'mastery-mode' and 'survival-mode'. These have been researched extensively by Carol Dweck of the University of Illinois and her team, who have developed some compelling ideas about their origins and effects. She summarizes them thus. (She refers to them as 'mastery-oriented' and 'helpless' patterns.)

> The adaptive ('mastery-oriented') pattern is characterised by challenge-seeking and high, effective persistence in the face of obstacles. Children displaying this pattern appear to enjoy exerting effort in the pursuit of task mastery. In contrast the maladaptive ('helpless') pattern is characterised by challenge avoidance and low persistence in the face of difficulty. Children displaying this pattern tend to evidence negative affect (such as anxiety) and negative self-cognitions when they confront obstacles. . . . *Children displaying the different patterns do not differ in intellectual ability.*[4] (*Emphasis added*)

This finding is at first sight surprising – though teachers find it less so than others. 'Bright' children are as likely to become upset, give up, have tantrums and feel badly in the face of difficulties as 'less able' children. So if it is not lack of ability that throws children into survival-mode, what is it? Dweck suggests one answer; I shall suggest another, complementary, one. Both of them have to do with our old friends, people's *implicit theories* and *injunctions*. Dweck says:

> Basically, children's theories of intelligence appear to orient them toward different goals. Children who believe intelligence is a fixed trait tend to orient towards gaining favorable judgements of that trait (performance goals), whereas children who believe intelligence is a malleable quality tend to orient toward developing that quality (learning goals) . . . with performance goals the entire task choice and pursuit process is built around children's concerns about their ability level. . . . That is, if the goal is to obtain a favorable judgment of ability, then children need to be certain their ability is high before displaying it for judgment. Otherwise they will choose tasks that conceal their ability or protect it from negative evaluation – personally easy tasks on which success is ensured or excessively difficult ones on which failure does not signify low ability. . . . They attribute errors or failures to a lack of ability . . . and view them as predictive of continued failure. . . . (They) are significantly more likely than children with learning goals to view effort per se as indicative of low ability. . . . Worry about goal attainment may well overwhelm any intrinsic interest the task may hold for the child. . . .
>
> In contrast, with learning goals the choice and pursuit processes involve a focus on progress and mastery through effort. . . . Children with learning goals chose challenging tasks regardless of whether they believed themselves to have high or low ability . . . they are willing to risk displays of ignorance in order to acquire skills and knowledge. Instead of calculating their exact ability level and how it will be judged, they can think more about the value of the skill to be developed or their interest in the task to be undertaken. . . . They tend to use obstacles as a cue to increase their effort or to analyse and vary their strategies . . . which often results in *improved* performance in the face of obstacles.[5]

(It is worth noting that although she uses the word 'children' throughout, the pattern is being clearly replicated with college students.)

What Dweck does not focus on explicitly, but which must be present, is the *injunction*, which we met in Chapter 3, which links success, or 'being bright' to personal worth. Even if people saw ability as being fixed rather than malleable, there would be no reason to get upset unless 'high ability' had been accepted as an index to being a better person than 'low ability'. For example 'height' is fixed rather than malleable, but most people do not get defensive about being short (though interestingly even here some people suffer from an injunction about what is a 'good height' to be, for a man or a woman).

The two beliefs, I suspect, lock together in an interesting way. If you believe that 'ability' means 'worth' (and therefore that 'lack of ability' threatens shame or rejection from others) *and* that ability is fixed, then you are likely to find yourself in survival-mode when you meet or anticipate obstacles and problems. But if you *either* don't buy the idea that you've got to be smart all the time to be lovable, *or* you think that it is possible to get smarter if you try, then there is less to be afraid of, and more to be gained, from grappling with tough tasks than from avoiding them. The trap closes if we add in the rest of the injunctions. If people are going to wrestle with challenges, and to bootstrap their own learning-power by doing so, they have to be prepared to tolerate, not just the possibility of failure, but of feeling confused, unconfi-dent, uncomfortable, and perhaps not-quite-themselves as well. These are the occupational hazards of someone in mastery-mode.

Now remember that injunctions and implicit beliefs derive their force from having been picked up unwittingly. People rarely say 'Ability is a fixed trait, you know', or 'You're a bad person if you feel confused'. Instead we learn them from the *way* people speak, and from the way they react to us when we get tongue-tied, behave unexpectedly, or say 'I don't know'. I do not have any evidence, except the grim nodding of hundreds of teachers when I have suggested it, but I am convinced that many pupils' experi-ence in school is absolutely saturated with the beliefs that it is not just more pleasant but *better* to be competent, clear, confident, comfortable, in control, consistent and coherent (the same beliefs, you remember, that were implicated, in Chapter 3, in the pro-duction of stress), than the converse; and that ability is a fixed personal trait, like having red hair or hazel eyes.

What Dweck calls the 'entity theory' of ability is actually com-pounded of three sub-beliefs. The first, which is the one she has focused on, is the idea that ability is *immutable*: if you are bright you will stay bright; if you are dim you will stay dim. The second says that ability is *pervasive*: if you are bright in one subject you will, all things being equal, be bright (or at least 'capable of being bright') in other subjects; and your 'ability level' in school reflects your 'ability level' outside. The third says that ability is *monolithic*: that it is an integral, unitary quality and not compounded of a variety of constituents, each of which might become available in different circumstances, and be capable of being exercised and developed separately, or in sub-groups. These beliefs are demonstrably false, and now widely known to be so by many teachers and educationalists. Yet they remain embedded in the way people still suppose that so-called 'diagnostic tests' can be used as dipsticks with which to gauge pupils' future attainment, or to predict their performance in quite different settings. The major tragedy of the 7, 11 and 14 tests will be if they enshrine these mistaken assumptions even more firmly in educational mythology and practice. And just as dangerously, they remain dissolved in the way teachers inadvertently talk to pupils, to each other, and write reports. If teachers were not unconsciously wedded to these assumptions they would not be as frequently disconcerted as they are by their pupils' variability. 'Can we really be talking about the same Dianne?' they say, or, after a field trip perhaps, 'You know Jason must really have some brains somewhere: he amazed me by . . .'.

The first and greatest condition for someone – teacher or pupil – to be a good learner is therefore *emotional resilience* in the face of uncertainty. To the extent that this has been eroded by injunctions and other false beliefs, people are going to switch from mastery-mode to survival-mode whenever the going gets tough. Commitment to the base values of learning, growth and mastery, which are only achievable through persistence, effort, ingenuity and inquisitiveness when confronted with a challenge, is weakened by the socialized commitment to looking good and appearing bright. John Holt again says:

> The person who is not afraid of the world wants understanding, competence, mastery. He wants to make his mental model better, both more complete, in the sense of having more in it, and more accurate, in being more like the world out there, a better guide to what is happening and may happen. He wants to know the score. . . . And so he is willing, and eager, to expose himself to the reality of things as they are. . . .

The fearful person, on the other hand, does not care whether his model is accurate. What he wants is to feel safe. He wants a model that is reassuring, simple, unchanging. . . . The trouble with such models is that they don't do what a good model should do – tell us what to expect. The people who live in a dream world are always being rudely awakened. They cannot see life's surprises as sources of useful information. They must see them as attacks. . . . such people fall back in many ways on the protective strategy of deliberate failure. How can failure be protective? On the principle that you can't fall out of bed if you're sleeping on the floor, you can't lose any money if you don't place any bets.[6]

When young people are not afraid of uncertainty, they will naturally develop the emotional and personal qualities which are the basic prerequisites for good learning: judicious curiosity; an increasingly accurate sense of what is valuable and what is too dangerous to explore; patience and persistence, coupled with the ability to give up or change tack without guilt; open-mindedness and perceptiveness about what they see; a healthy scepticism about what they are told; a perfect willingness to ask questions, seek help and admit confusion; and the ability to see and explore other points of view without losing a hold on their own.

Let me spell this out a little more clearly. There is a good deal of educational rhetoric about helping young people to be good learners, but until we move beyond the rhetoric to a more precise specification of what this means, we will not be in a position to know how to achieve it. First, as we have just seen, young people need an accurate intuitive sense of what ability means. Second, they need an attitude of tolerance towards their own frailty – their mistakes, anxiety, confusion and uncertainty. If you cannot allow yourself to dive into the cloudy waters of learning, you will not learn. Third, learners need an attitude of openness towards themselves – they need to have a flexible and provisional self-image. If you have made up your mind about who you are, then certain limitations and prejudices become enshrined within that self-definition and therefore serve as blocks to future development in those areas. 'I'm hopeless at drawing', 'I hate maths', 'I've got terrible co-ordination' and such-like are conditioned beliefs that have blocked off for many people potential areas of growth, competence and fun.

Fourth, young people must develop an 'internal locus of control' (in the jargon of the trade): a realistic sense of their responsibility for their own lives and learning. If they grow up believing that it is mostly fate, or other powerful people, who control what they can do or become, then their initiative and energy are crippled. Their stance tends to become passive and fatalistic. And fifth, learners need an attitude towards knowledge that is a blend of respect and scepticism. They need to be willing to study what other people have discovered or thought without swallowing it hook, line and sinker. Any school system that does not preserve and enhance these learning-positive attitudes will be sowing whatever it teaches into mental soil from which the nutrients have been leached.

The second compartment of the good learners' tool-kit contains their *strategies* for learning. Tools, in the literal sense, are amplifiers of people's natural abilities. Saws and scissors amplify our natural ability to tear. Pliers and hammers amplify our abilities to grasp and push. Microscopes and telescopes amplify our natural ability to see. And the repertoire of learning strategies that we acquire from infancy onward amplifies our natural ability to respond with the right mixture of circumspection, curiosity and intelligence to strangeness. Again, recent thinking in psychology has helped us to identify these strategies, and the conditions under which they develop best, more closely. Most basic perhaps are the strategies for inspection, for gathering information. Science teachers sometimes claim that one of the main purposes of their lessons is to 'teach children the skills of observation' – apparently unaware that children have become virtuoso observers before they ever set foot inside a school.

Good learners have learnt the value of scrutinizing and watching, waiting for a strange event to repeat itself, or a new object to perform. They have developed some skill in concentration, which is the ability to sustain observation despite frustration or confusion. They are expert at exploring: the art of discovering new things to study. They become skilled at making predictions – using what they already know in order to guide a selective search for data which will corroborate a tentative hypothesis. They acquire a useful repertoire of simple ways to 'prod' things so that they reveal themselves. Young children, like scientists, quickly develop a set of initial tests to be applied to a strange thing, which will give them information to work on. Chemists pass it through a flame or bubble it through lime water. Young children smile at it, poke it, chew it, throw it and ignore it. Most valuable is the developing ability to observe other people and to mimic what they do – a skill which begins in the first year, and will eventually be of great help to the candidate teacher, or windsurfer, or politician. Imitating provides a ready-made (though by no means foolproof) source of ideas based on how other people do it. Children learn a vast amount from watching each other as well as adults.

We develop methods for experimenting with our own reactions, so that we can come up with good guesses about what might work in each new situation we meet (i.e. *every* situation). A good guess gives us a working hypothesis about how to get along with something – new teacher, unfamiliar dog, first cigarette – that generates hunches about how to behave while simultaneously minimizing the risk of getting shouted at, bitten, run over or sick. Young people develop strategies for refining their theories and actions. They practise until an effect can be produced with reliability, and then they play at altering the situation in small ways to increase the scope and the elegance of their responses. They also begin to be able to use metaphor: the process of searching their existing store of knowledge for ideas that may be useful, even though they may not look too similar to the present problem on the surface.

In the next sub-compartment we find the very useful learning tools of intuition and imagination. There are times when the best way to proceed with a problem is to stop being busy, both mentally and physically, and turn the whole thing over to the subconscious, allowing things to simmer away on the fringes of awareness. Knowing when and how to intersperse your 'wise activity' with what Aldous Huxley called 'wise passiveness' is essential for any kind of creativity. Whilst with the ability to *visualize* comes another powerful learning amplifier, one that enables you to run things through in your mind first, so that the risks of getting laughed at or fouling up are reduced. As we have seen, this compartment of the learners' tool-kit tends to get ignored once they have moved up to secondary school.

Learning may sometimes proceed as a solitary activity, but there are many times when it must be, and is more effective when it is, social. The use of language is vital in both individual and social contexts, but the kind of language, and the particular sort of facility that is needed, is rather different. Covert language, or thinking, provides a vicarious test-bed for ideas, in one corner of which stands the powerful tool called 'logic' which enables the last drops of potentially useful information to be wrung out of whatever one has gathered. In collaborative learning on the other hand, people need, in addition to thinking, to have a certain level of verbal confidence and oral fluency – but they may not need to be able to write elegant or logical prose. School pupils, for example, are very busy practising the important skill of advancing tentative opinions into a discussion to test their popularity, in such a way that they can be quickly withdrawn and dropped, if they are not liked, without much face being lost. In fact the majority of playground chat involves such games of reversible chess, in which pawns of opinion are cautiously advanced, and hastily withdrawn if friends think it's 'stupid'. There is evidence too that small group discussions in science lessons are controlled more by these social processes than by the objective, rational search for truth.[7]

Only when these groups of learning strategies are well established, *and are still being practised and developed*, do the intellectual capabilities that so dominate the school curriculum begin to take a hold. The increasingly disembedded skills of logical thought and logical expression that are required in all subjects, and their basis in the 3Rs, are important general purpose tools, but their development must be seen within the context of the broader portfolio of the six 'Is' – the skills of Inspection, Ingenuity, Intuition, Imagination, Interaction and Intellect. If vital experience of the situations in which the other learning strategies are appropriate is squeezed out by too much concentration on Literacy and Numeracy, and worse, if people's emotional resilience for learning is damaged by demoralizing and mishandled experiences with books or sums, then the preoccupation with the 3Rs needs to be reassessed.

The general sub-groups of these strategies begin to be developed more or less in the order in which I described them, but each continues to be useful and exploitable through life, and certainly throughout school. Once the emotional climate for learning has been established, it is the school's primary responsibility to help each pupil to develop his or her repertoire of learning strategies as fully as possible. These include the 3Rs as strategies of central but not overriding importance. They also include the skills of listening, studying, discussing, fossicking, organizing, explaining and figuring out. These skills have to be explored, tested out and integrated within each individual's 'mental model', to use Holt's phrase (one now used extensively by 'cognitive scientists'), and they cannot therefore be neatly transmitted in a well-articulated, pre-processed package. But neither need they be ignored in the vain hope that somehow they will automatically develop in the course of normal school work. Clearly, for many pupils they do not. The effective middle way is deliberately to create environments within which pupils are stimulated to exercise their learning strategies to the limit, to go beyond them, and to shape their discoveries through practice, informal conversation and peer instruction. The teachers' powerful role is to contrive suitable situations and to offer subtle nudges and suggestions.

The development of learning strategies in a special, 'off-the-job' environment like school runs into an enormous problem: that of transfer or, more usually, the lack of it. As John Nisbet and Janet Shucksmith have recently pointed out:

> Strategies like these are sometimes taught in school, but children usually do not learn to apply the strategies beyond specific applications in narrowly defined tasks. Effective learning demands more than this: skills and strategies have to be learnt in such a way that they can be 'transferred' to fit new problems or situations not previously encountered. Being able to select the appropriate strategy, and to adapt it where necessary, is an important part of this definition of good learning.[8]

If school is to become a powerful preparation for life, it must, as almost everyone is saying these days, become more permeable to life. If pupils only develop learning strategies with respect to problems that have no real-life counterpart, then they will not be accessed in real life, even in situations where they might be potentially applicable. It is like building an aeroplane in a workshop and then not being able to get it out of the door: it is of no use, and you cannot even tell whether it will fly. The hangar doors between school and life have got to be wide open, so that what is developed in the workshop of school can be taken out and tested; and what is intriguing or problematic in the everyday world can be wheeled into school for a period of more intense tinkering and exploration than is possible in a shed or on the street. The frustration that both teachers and pupils feel with schoolwork that is boring or irrelevant is thus symptomatic of time being wasted on two levels. Not only are the pupils not learning what they need or want to know, but they are also failing to develop a portable set of strategies for finding things out. And as Dweck's work so strongly suggests, it is only through the personal engagement which interest or need generates that people's learning powers are truly and transferably enhanced.

The third major compartment of the good learners' tool-kit is labelled *monitoring*. It is on this that Nisbet and Shucksmith's work has focused. As they point out:

> Learning to manage the process of learning involves *being aware of what one is doing*, or being able to bring one's mental processes under conscious scrutiny and thus more effectively under control. . . . Though learning is largely intuitive, the learner should be able to move from the intuitive to the deliberate when some difficulty intervenes, stopping to consider the source of the difficulty and to select a strategy to deal with it.[9]

It is the ability to be reflective about one's own learning that comes to the aid of someone in mastery-mode, and is so conspicuously unavailable in survival-mode. In the former, people, when they encounter difficulties, become conscious and progressive. In the latter, when the same difficulties become what Robert Pirsig in *Zen and the Art of Motorcycle Maintenance*[10] calls 'gumption traps', they become self-conscious and regressive. To use Pirsig's example, what happens when you are trying to take a motorbike engine to bits and you burr the head of a screw? In mastery-mode you sit down quietly with a cup of tea and chew over the alternatives (use a drill, ring someone up, take it to a garage, cut a new slot . . .). In survival-mode you look around guiltily to see if anyone saw you, feel upset and angry, kick the stupid bike, knocking it over, breaking an indicator and stubbing your toe into the bargain, and become sulky and withdrawn for the rest of the day. A teacher's job in school is to avoid creating the conditions in which survival takes precedence over mastery and to try to ensure that learners, when they do hit a gumption trap, do as little damage as possible, behave in not too ridiculous a fashion, and snap back into mastery as quickly as they can. Usually the most effective ploy is not to make a big emotional deal out of it but to have a break and rehabilitate the dented self-respect by talking about or doing something different, or simply by leaving the sufferer alone for a while, so that they can drift back from being worried about people to being interested in the problem.

Various authors, including Nisbet and Shucksmith, have tried to analyse what the important elements of this monitoring or self-awareness (as distinct from self-consciousness) might be. They include initial *planning* in which the problem, if a tricky one, is mulled over and one tries to look at it from all sides. Then there is *checking*, which means staying alert, as you work on the problem, to how things are going, rather than mindlessly ploughing on with the selected strategy to the bitter end. As a result of this might come *reviewing*, when you take stock and decide that it might be better to try a different tack (in which case you may revert to planning and reassessing the options, like the motorcycle fixer). Finally comes *evaluating*, when you look critically at the answer to see whether it makes sense, or whether it actually does what you want it to. *Estimating* is a useful skill here, which involves doing a rough check of the problem to see if the answer you have come up with is 'the right kind of thing' or 'about the right size'. John Holt's classic *How Children Fail* provides many detailed examples of schoolchildren who lack, in the classroom, the 'ability' (remember the reason for the quotes here) to carry out even the most rudimentary of commonsense monitoring processes.[11] These are the ones, in maths and science especially, who will look you in the eye and say it takes 19.43 men to dig the hole, that the apples cost £49.7 each, or that the melting point of wax is 2.3×10^4 degrees centigrade.

Self-awareness (not losing one's presence of mind in the face of obstacles or set-backs), like the other two aspects of good learning, cannot be taught directly. It is an intuitive faculty that grows out of the experience of spotting one's own errors, figuring out alternative approaches, and uncovering mistaken assumptions – and doing so with some success. My use of the image of a tool-kit is unfortunate if it leads to the assumption – which is a fashionable one – that the next thing to do, having identified some skills, is to put them in order and try to train them one by one. This is wrong-headed and ineffective, for the simple reason that the human being is organism, not mechanism, and its learning cannot be assembled piece by piece, just as flowers are not best produced by a succession of grafts. But again this does not reduce the teacher's role to zero. It redefines it but does not deny it.

BEING A MENTOR

We should now try to summarize what the implications of the last two chapters are for teachers who are interested in helping young people become good learners. I should warn you that some of these implications are practicable within existing situations, and indeed reflect established methods of working for some teachers, or projected changes that are definitely espoused. I hope that the discussion here might help teachers who are in these positions by clarifying, amplifying or making more coherent the rationale for their preferences. Other implications, however, point quite clearly towards the need for a different kind of educational structure from the one that currently predominates. These are therefore more in the nature of pipedreams. My belief, in line with the spirit of the book, is that this does not make them worthless. Such ideas may add to the current debate from which the education of the future will arise.

Everything we know about human beings – especially, but not exclusively young ones – suggests that we are built to learn. We do not have to be coerced, encouraged, or trained. Put us in a new situation and we will set about learning. *What* we learn depends on the resources we bring, the needs we have, and on our perception of how safe and/or interesting the situation is. We can learn to avoid it, neutralize it, control it, play with it or exploit it. And as we learn, so inevitably we are learning *how* to learn. This process cannot be created or transmitted: it can only happen, and must happen, as we go about dealing with the endless succession of questions that daily life fires at us.

But this is not to say that the growth of learning cannot be influenced. Adults can affect it dramatically through the environments they (wittingly or unwittingly) create; the models of a learner (courageous or timid; open- or closed-minded) they present; and the way they interact with the young person's own learning efforts. If the environment is chaotic, the model a bigot and the interactions moody or repressive, then the natural search for expertise is choked off, and the thrill of exploration replaced by the fear of exposure. The teachers' – or as I shall call them, the mentors' – job is to orchestrate the world, model attitudes and interact with the learners in such a way that the latter's skill in learning, and enthusiasm for it, becomes a flood, not a trickle.

The word 'mentor' has become over-used recently, perhaps because there are so few alternative words for teacher. My *Concise Oxford Dictionary* defines mentor as 'an experienced and trusted adviser' and says it comes from the Greek root 'to think'. That captures some of what I want, so I shall use mentor as my word for someone who helps another to become a better learner. What does it take to be a mentor?

Emotional resilience

Above everything else comes the need to consolidate in pupils (for want of a better one I will keep this word) a sense of confidence and interest in learning. This means distinguishing clearly between success and worth so that nothing the mentor does puts pupils off learning. It does not mean always praising: far from it, because praise trains learners to need someone else's validation and feedback. It creates an emotional and intellectual dependency. There is evidence that if pupils are rewarded, with praise or materially, for doing what they would naturally have chosen to do, when the reward is withdrawn they stop doing what they had previously enjoyed.[12] For a mentor, neither success nor failure is *personal*. Instead both are interesting, and failure is often a lot more interesting than success. Confusion is something to tolerate and trust. Learning to inspect and describe one's own mental fog is a valuable activity, whether by doodling on bits of paper, keeping a scrapbook of weird or useless thoughts, or by half-baked conversations. Being stuck is, for the mentor, a state to be cherished and shared.

De-stressing

Learning is a taxing, and sometimes inevitably stressful activity, and mentors may well make available to their pupils some of the stress management techniques – such as those we reviewed in Chapter 4 – that they know of. They might use 'alarm calls' – and suggest to pupils to use them on each other – to help pupils spot when they are getting frustrated and tense with their learning, and to take some remedial action *before* they have got to the stage of being angry or upset. They might use some 'affirmations', preferably getting the pupils to generate their own, to combat the tendency of the lurking injunctions to promote face values at the expense of base values. They might use, as a matter of routine, exercises for relaxation.

Effort

In case the above presents too romantic a sketch, we must remember that, even without being worried about the reviews, learning is an uncertain and risky business, and people have a right to become apprehensive and fed up. A good mentor must stay in touch with the fine line between excitement and anxiety, challenge and threat. If pupils come to feel in any way that it is not acceptable to give up, they will come to select only those tasks they already think they can complete. If you are allowed to drop something for a while, there is a good chance that you might pick it up again. (Most creative adults, I suspect, have projects of this sort that they have 'on the back burner' and come back to from time to time.) And even if the problem is not solved, the mentor is not bothered, because while success feels good and keeps you going, it is the travelling rather than the arriving that is the real point. However, provided this freedom to give up is clearly given, a mentor can encourage persistence and effort. Appreciation of trying is certainly more helpful than applause for succeeding – and the injunction which such applause tends to smuggle into learners' minds. One of Carol Dweck's conclusions from her research is that 'a focus on ability judgments can result in a tendency to avoid and withdraw from challenge, whereas a focus on progress through effort creates a tendency to seek and be energized by challenge'.[13]

Empathy

Mentors need to be sensitive to both emotional and intellectual aspects of pupils' worlds. In particular, they need to learn the signals that pupils use to mark a shift from mastery-mode to survival-mode. Young people show discomfort and boredom in different ways, and they need to know that their mentor (a trusted adviser, remember) is not going to push them too hard at the wrong times. The mentor has, in getting to know his or her pupils, to recognize that the time to ease off is when Michelle goes quiet, Polly gets fidgety, Courtney wants to go to the toilet and Gordon gets angry. (The importance of this emotional trust, based on knowledge, between mentor and pupil is one of the main reasons why it is so frustrating to want to act as a mentor in a secondary school. The structure seems almost designed to prevent teachers from getting to know any more than a handful of pupils – usually their own tutor group – well enough. Their time is spread so thinly that the requisite trust simply cannot develop.)

Interest

Mentors have to know something about the interests and concerns of the pupils they are working with in order to be able to introduce them to topics or questions that they might find captivating. But even more important than being able to second-guess the pupils' interests is a disposition to listen: to find out what puzzles the pupils and to capitalize on these clues in an impromptu fashion. In the present system there are of course enormous limitations of time and resource on what can be followed up. But a climate in which pupils feel at least some sense of ownership and authorship about what is going on is likely to breed a higher level of participation in the classroom, just as it does in the staffroom. As Nisbet and Shucksmith claim:

> the most effective teachers . . . engage in continual prompts to get children to plan and monitor their own activities, but with the intention not of retaining total control for themselves but of passing it over to the children as they become ready and able to take responsibility.[14]

Self-examination

Just as they are interested in pupils' implicit theories about the world, and in helping them to inspect and improve them, so mentors need to be aware of their own. In particular they need to be constantly monitoring their own language, and non-verbal responses to pupils, for the presence of embedded beliefs about ability and worth. Conscious intentions often run ahead of unconscious habits and, as with any form of prejudice, its traces are likely to remain in spur-of-the-moment comments, reactions or jokes long after a contrary viewpoint has been deliberately, even wholeheartedly, espoused. This is true for men and women who believe in the importance of non-sexism, or blacks and whites who have repudiated their own racism, and it is equally so for people who wish to create, through their presence, a safe climate for learning to learn. In particular they must learn to be very careful in their use of words like 'ability', 'less able', 'intelligence', 'lazy', 'motivated', 'bright', or any other description that attributes a personal characteristic to a pupil, and/or that threatens a judgement of 'better' or 'worse' in terms of personal worth, on the basis of differences in performance or attitude.

Example

Central to the mentors' role is their being ready, willing and able to exemplify for their pupils the attributes of a good learner. They themselves need to be genuinely resilient in the face of obstacles or uncertainty. They must not be defensive about their own errors and ignorance, and be willing to engage openly in floundering and fossicking. They must, up to a point, actually enjoy being in the dark, so that, like young children playing a party game, the pupils dare to creep about in their own darkness, knowing that a self-confident adult is nearby. Mentors must also possess a good range of learning strategies, so that pupils can watch them being modelled, and get a feel for the kinds of problems that each is good for. It is very useful if mentors develop the habit of thinking out loud as they decide how to organize the classroom, or to set about investigating a particular problem. They need to develop an unusually high degree of awareness of their own learning processes, so that they can articulate more clearly what in an 'ordinary' learner need only be intuitive. In doing this they are not *teaching* pupils how to solve problems, but *demonstrating* the entire process, both intellectual and emotional, of learning.

It would even be a good idea, if mentors have the time, to bring their own projects which they are working on into the classroom. Pupils who are taking a break from their own enquiries can hang about and watch a real adult really learning – something they may not see too often, and almost certainly never on television – and they may even be able to reverse the roles by offering advice or support to the mentor, an experience of power that pupils usually enjoy enormously and rarely get.

Mentors do not need to be perfect, only human. With the best will in the world they will have off-days, get cross and lapse into survival-mode, just as the pupils will. Their responsibility then is to keep on being open about their own process, and perhaps with some measure of ironic detachment from their own grumpiness or vulnerability. 'I'm in a bad mood, today, SO WATCH OUT', they might say, half-joking but half-serious. Or 'Is anyone else feeling as fed up as I am?' A mentor must retain the awareness that feelings are not an occasional nuisance in the context of learning, but its life-blood. And they must apply to the pupils the same rule that they themselves operate by. To be in mastery-mode you have to be on reasonably good form: adventurousness is born of self-confidence and self-respect. So when you are not on good form the most helpful thing you can do to get back to learning is to take care of whatever is undermining or upsetting you. (Paradoxically, but by no means necessarily, the thing that 'takes you out of yourself' may be a different learning experience. But the golden rule for mentors helping pupils to recuperate from an upset or a setback is to do what works, not what they think ought to work.)

Questions and alternatives

Mentors are extremely miserly with information and answers. If pupils are used to more conventional teachers they will find a mentor very frustrating and evasive. They will have met teachers before who refuse to tell them what the answer is – but they will have learnt that the teacher *knows* the answer, and that if they wait long enough they will be told. But mentors will usually have set things up so they don't know the answer, if only because such situations are more interesting to *them*. (The opportunities for such a commitment to process at the expense of content are of course more limited when the teacher or the syllabus has predetermined the course of study.) If a pupil asks directly how to spell a word or where to find something, there is no sense in being needlessly obstructive. The mentor's more typical reaction, though, will be in terms of questions and alternatives. 'That's a good thought . . . where does that take us?' 'How could we find out?' 'Are there any other problems you've solved that remind you of this one? . . . How did you tackle that one?' 'I haven't a clue. Let's ask Azra and Trish.' If a pupil has got a solution one way, the mentor might ask them to see how many different ways they could do it – 'for fun'. They might invite pupils to gain greater control over their learning strategies by deliberately creating 'wrong' answers – and challenging their friends to figure out what the mistake is and how they made it. (The behaviourists' fear that wrong answers are habit-forming is only justified when learners aren't *thinking*.) Often the mentor will encourage conferences amongst the learners themselves to test out and explain their own ideas and to chew over each other's.

Work patterns

Mentors will allow pupils time to loaf about; they know that learning is seasonal, and that there is a time to lie fallow. And they also know that there is a fluid balance between being a star in your own learning production, and being a spear-carrier in someone else's. The current emphasis on objective and comparative assessment puts all pupils in the role of prima donna all the time. And indeed the whole individualistic ethos seems to teach young people that there is something intrinsically better about being a leader than a follower. They also serve, who only stand and hold the spanner; but more importantly at school, they also learn. They learn the satisfaction of joint achievement, and they also learn that 'star' and 'supporter' can be *roles* that may be freely chosen, and happily played. They do not have to be rejected on the basis of crude slogans about 'elitism' and 'inequality of power'. You can learn as much, and with as much pride, by printing the programmes, as you can by rehearsing your lines – perhaps more.

It would be an oversimplification, though one containing a large amount of truth, to say that what I am suggesting is that secondary school teachers should operate more like primary school teachers, and that secondary schools, in their organization and ethos, should be more like primary schools. Which brings us back to how schools are organized.

SCHOOLS FOR LEARNING

Commitment to good learning inexorably pushes us beyond what is currently possible into the realm of what is conceivable: the organization and structure, especially of secondary schools, is not suited to the whole-hearted promotion of good learning. The whole apparatus of fixed groups, fixed timetables and fixed subjects points the wrong way, so it is only possible to be an intermittent and restricted mentor in schools as they are. I wish to close, therefore, with some brief comments about how schools might change. The main purpose of these remarks is not so much to promote my particular vision – though of course that is part of it – but to offer you something to react to, in the pursuit of your own vision. As I have been trying to argue, the exercise of thinking up alternative ways of doing school need not be depressing. On the contrary it can help teachers to clarify their own values, indicate possible first steps, and gives them something to talk about with each other. Here, for example, is a simple picture which would be much more conducive to learning-to-learn than the one we predominantly have at the moment.

I put forward, as a sample only, one possible reorganization. There may be better solutions. The one criticism of this sketch that I will not accept is that it is not practical: the present system is not practical, but continues to operate.

In this scenario for secondary education, there would again be lumps of some 20 to 30 children, only this time they would be of as diverse an age range as possible, 11 to 17. Associated with each lump would be three adults, each of whom is allowed to work as a teacher only half-time. The other half can be devoted to running a family, working in a shop, farming, contemplative thought, fishing, anything except teaching. That prohibition on full-time teaching is intended to keep the school in touch with the larger society. The three adults will overlap through the week, having at least one day when all are present. They will work with only one group of children, except where their group combines with others. They will be with that group as long as they are in the school, which should be years. The groups will never die: as some students leave, others will join, and as one teacher goes another will come while the other two will be there to provide continuity. There will be no sharp transitions, no annual spill of positions, no yearly stop-start.

What must the students learn? First and foremost, to become independent learners. For compulsory content, my choice would be basic numeracy (not a feature of the present system); reading, in the widest possible sense of the term; writing; speaking; public affairs; and the natural universe. To these I would add whatever else suits the interests of the teachers and the students: cooking, crafts, accountancy, languages, Roman coins, Chinese history, anything. Though not compulsory, these chosen fields of interest must be seen as important, not to be squeezed out by the basics that all must acquire. A lot of time will be spent outside the school, observing and doing, in order to keep the school learning in touch with the larger world. That will be easier to arrange than it is now, where a lot of the difficulty in getting away from the school lies in arranging times with other teachers. Under this arrangement there are no other teachers, no bells, no periods to work in.

New methods will become feasible, indeed, necessary, as the teachers will rarely want to talk to the whole group at once. They will spend a lot of their time talking with, not to, students, explaining information which the students have acquired from books and other resources such as computers and finding out far more than they can do now about their students' understanding. The teachers will have to watch over each student's progress, but they will have time to do this and will find it easy as they come to know their students very well. One thing they will not have to worry about is control. Discipline is largely a problem created by uniform age blocks and traffic management associated with the period system, and would not be an issue in this arrangement.

That is the merest sketch of one scenario. I believe it would produce greater learning, less waste, happier schools, and a better society. Others are possible, though one that does not fit the lessons from recent research is the present form of organization of schools.[15]

In such a setting it would be much more possible to be a mentor. But its achievement as a mainstream model is a long way off. A few brave schools and authorities – such as Stantonbury in Milton Keynes, or Sheffield LEA, for example – have moved significantly in this direction. Sheffield has planned to abolish the traditional subject boundaries entirely, replacing them with much larger blocks of time devoted to 'creative and recreational studies' or 'social and community studies',[16] though how these plans weather the Education Reform Act remains to be seen. In fact it is interesting to notice that educational provision which is not so far away from this model does exist – but on the margins of the school system, in special units, support centres, off-site units and so on. Education of this kind is provided, as a last resort, for pupils who cannot or will not tolerate the normal diet, but in order to get it they have to pay the price of being labelled deviant or inadequate in some way. It is my experience that such units are frequently staffed by teachers who have been unable to find a way, or a place, to be mentors in the mainstream system, and who have marginalized themselves in the interests of their own integrity and mental health. Their commitment is not so much to the value of such provision for the young people who end up there, as to a personal model of teaching that they were unable to realize in ordinary secondary schools.

I would like to suggest one modification that makes the idea of mentorly schools significantly more practical (even given testing at 11 and 14). That is to reduce the scope of this kind of education to the 10 or 11 to 14-year-old age range. This seems to be the part of our education system that we have got most badly and most consistently wrong. It is the period when many young people's confidence as learners is undermined, whilst also being the golden opportunity for the expansion of their learning powers. People of this age are becoming ready and eager to take on responsibility in varying degrees, and are on the way to being able to co-operate with each other in undertaking sustained practical and intellectual challenges.

The majority of 11-year-olds, when they enter a comprehensive, are bright-eyed and bushy-tailed, easy to enthuse and open about their thoughts and interests. After three years of anonymity and confusion, having a conversation with many of them is like pulling teeth. Whereas if their enthusiasm and energy were harnessed, if they were allowed to make real choices and take on some real responsibility, if school and community interpenetrated like a coast of fjords, if they were allowed gradually to explore further *for themselves* the difficulties and benefits of being sociable, then an inviolable rig of competence, confidence, curiosity and conviviality would be established, capable then of being floated into any area of subsequent learning and delivering the goods. In this

Intermediate Education the protection and structure of primary school would be slowly peeled back, but without being immediately replaced with the tight prescriptions of secondary school. It would be a time of finding their own feet and learning to run as learners, no matter if only round in circles for a while.

Such schools would cater for roughly the same age group as the 'middle schools', but they would not be the same. Middle schools have failed to prosper because they lack a rigorous philosophy which distinguishes them from both primary and secondary schools. Their introduction was prompted as much by the need to cope with some of the logistical problems posed by the implementation of comprehensives in some areas as it was by a coherent educational rationale. They failed to carry through from primary schools the continuing close relationship between a teacher and a group of pupils. And they failed to give pupils any real choice and real responsibility for their learning – which are at the heart of my proposal. Such power must be handed back to learners, by someone who knows them, at a rate they can handle. It is through learning to exercise that power to choose that the power to learn is developed. Learning cannot be made more interesting by being made more 'relevant' – which is what many current reforms assume. Relevance is not a property of material. You cannot design a 'relevant' curriculum. Relevance arises when a person with a desire meets an apparent opportunity to fulfil it. Because desires are individual and ephemeral, the learner *must* be allowed some freedom to decide what to pick up and when to put it down. The existence of developmental trends means we can predict in general what young people of different ages will find interesting. And luckily we can rely up to a point on their being open to persuasion. But engagement cannot be engineered and without it, whatever we do, and as teachers see every day, learning will only proceed in a superficial fashion.

At 14, something more like the present system could be introduced in which teachers who wished to, and were equipped to, would coach expertise and impart specialized knowledge to groups of young people who had opted, from a wide range of choices, to follow a particular course of study. From age 14 to 16, school would still be compulsory, but discipline problems would now be rare. Pupils would (a) learn faster, and be more absorbed and less intimidated, because they were better learners; (b) be willing to put up with some hard, even boring, study because they had been genuinely responsible for choosing it; and (c), if they get fed up, they could – in my system – freely opt out and go and read and chat for a while. There would be no reason and no opportunity to get back at the teachers by refusing to learn.

At this 14 to 16 stage some sort of small core plus a large array of intellectual, practical and aesthetic options should be available. If this requires a big school, so be it. Provided they can keep just a few good friends with them, 14-year-olds are much more able to cope with a shifting and anonymous world than are 11-year-olds. I would also strongly suggest that secondary schools carry through the principle, firmly started in intermediate, of young people taking an increasingly substantial role in the running and maintenance of the school. They should prepare communal lunches, clean up, garden, decorate and run real small businesses of which the school would take two-thirds of the profit and the pupils the rest. This of course is completely pie-in-the-sky: the unions would never allow it, and too many people have come to believe that because children often *act* irresponsibly when they are *treated* as irresponsible, they are therefore incapable of *being* responsible. *The Independent* of 23 September 1988, for example, reports on a scheme in Droitwich High School where sixth-form *volunteers* are being paid *on the normal wage scale* to clean the school – because the school is unable to get adult cleaning staff. 'The action has been condemned by a union leader as child labour . . . Jerry Bartlett, an area officer for the public employees' union NUPE, said . . . "I'm extremely concerned at the precedent for increasing unemployment by substituting child labour in adult employees' jobs." ' Apparently we still live in an age where 16 to 18-year-olds are thought of as children, and in which they should not be given opportunities to take on adult responsibilities and rights – to work and be paid for it – for fear of pushing up the unemployment figures.

The big advantage of this idea of intermediate schools is that it allows (though it also forces) *teachers* to choose which kind of teacher they want to be. Some will want to be experts, and to go into the 14 to 16 secondary schools. One would like to think that they would experience more often than at present the delight of teaching what they know and love to groups of people who want to learn. But many teachers I know would even more strongly love to be mentors, and to work in the intermediate schools, learning alongside the youngsters with the excitement of unpredictability and the warmth of greater personal contact. There would need to be substantial in-service and initial training, partly on the job, partly reflective, for people who wanted to be mentors, to show them how to talk *with*, rather than *to*, young people, to tell them something of the early adolescents' world, to give them a hamper of ideas to put on display, and to explore ways of containing and managing such a lively and incandescent situation without inadvertently resorting to the traditional fire-blankets of 'All right, if you can't be quiet we'll have to do some copying' or 'If you can't make up your minds I'll have to *tell* you what to do'. A large number of the teachers and ex-teachers who have found themselves unable to operate with any integrity in secondary schools, and who have been forced out into the margins of special units, youth work, EFL, and even into other careers, would jump at the chance to work in my intermediate schools.

THE BEGINNING

Secondary schools as we now know them are not good places for young people to learn how to learn. They are characterized by stress, conservatism and disaffection, conditions which for both teachers and pupils are the very antitheses of learning. Many teachers and pupils dare not be enthusiastic for fear of being called names; they dare not be adventurous for fear of making a mess of it; they dare not hope because they see no possibility.

Where then are we to begin? What happens when the irresistible need for an education that empowers and enables, meets the immovable objections to change? I can see no other thing to do than to dwell in, and dwell on, the predicament. Perhaps such resignation is premature, born of a collective unwillingness to be seen to be at a loss. Out of our own reluctance to be learners we have allowed secondary education to be turned into a rigmarole and have, in doing so, set the next generation an example of adults who are too proud to say 'We don't know', and who tout instead a glossy menu knowing full well that there are only tins in the kitchen. Albert Einstein said once that the only rational method of educating was to be an example. And he added: 'If one can't help it, be a warning example'.[17] It would be sad to think that that was the best we could do.

Teachers need to learn to be good learners for three compelling reasons. The first is for their own sanity. The strain of trying to do an incredibly demanding job without really believing that what they are doing is worthwhile is literally killing some teachers and depressing and agitating thousands more. The situation will continue to degenerate unless those thousands start standing up and saying: 'It isn't nearly good enough. Something substantial urgently needs doing. And we don't know what to do, or how to do it'. This *is* the stance of a learner. 'I want to do something: and I don't know how to do it' is the only starting point for setting up your own business, entering a new relationship, fighting stupid policy, writing a book. Difficult though it may be, teachers, for their own good, need to come clean.

The second reason is to save education. It doesn't look as if anybody else is going to do it. Politicians and pundits are mostly an irrelevance. Standards are not the point. Teachers' pay is not really the point. Doing something that you believe in your heart is worthwhile, doing it well, and being respected for it – that is the point. The only people who know what is going on in schools are teachers and pupils. Nobody takes 'the kids' too seriously: if they complain it is due to the 'decline of deference' (as the sociologists say) or the fact that they aren't brought up to respect their elders and do what they're told any more (as a lot of the parents say). So if the teachers do not start the enquiry, nobody will. The vague suggestions I have made in the last two chapters are not the answer. We do not yet have an answer. And it is only by patiently but vociferously inhabiting and exploring the question that answers, or at least directions, will begin to emerge which will be as unexpected as they are worthy of consideration.

The third reason is for the pupils' sake. For my own belief is that education must help people to become good learners or it is a travesty. Before the 3Rs come the 4Cs: *Curiosity* (interest and pleasure in meeting challenges); *Confidence* (the courage to go into uncertainty and confusion); *Competence* (a repertoire of learning strategies); and *Conviviality* (the willingness to join with others sociably and non-defensively in learning). These qualities are eroded by the presence of powerful others who do not possess them. And conversely they are strengthened and consolidated by the example of people who are themselves good learners. In helping young people to adopt a learning stance to life, the teachers' first job is to adopt it themselves.

To want young people to be good learners is not a political position: it is not designed to help one person learn to be stronger, richer, more self-aware, more powerful than, or at the expense of, another. In a time of uncertainty you need to be a good learner to clarify your own values, to make friends, to retrain for a new job, to make difficult family decisions, to bring up children, to know why you distrust so many of those faces on TV. Everybody needs a comprehensive Learners' Starter Pack from school, not a learnectomy, if they are even to belong anywhere these days, let alone achieve.

Appendix

Making a Relaxation Tape

Here is a script which you can use to make your own relaxation tape. It is adapted from a version of this widely used type of exercise given by Jack Dunham in his book *Stress in Teaching* (Croom Helm, 1984). I suggest you read through the script to see whether it sounds right to you, and change any parts that you want to. Then just record it on to a cassette in a calm voice, leaving pauses at the points where there are strings of dots.

'Sit comfortably, in a relaxed position, and let your mind follow these instructions . . . take a deep breath, and as you let it out, allow your eyes to fall shut . . . let your body begin to relax and unwind . . . take another deep breath, and as you breathe out, let it carry all the cares and tensions out of your body . . . allow a feeling of peacefulness to come over you . . . a pleasant, enjoyable sensation of feeling comfortable and at ease . . . now turn your attention to your body, and begin to pay close attention to the sensations and signals you can detect . . . find the place or the muscle that feels most tense and gently allow it, if you can, to let go of its hold . . . do not force anything . . . just see if you can allow some of the tension to melt away . . . begin to let all your muscles, all over your body, give up their hold and go limp. . . .

Now direct your attention to the top of your head and allow a feeling of relaxation to begin there . . . allow it to spread downwards through your body . . . let the small muscles of your scalp relax . . . let the muscles of your forehead relax . . . devote special attention to your forehead and feel the muscles there softening and relaxing . . . feel your eyebrows sagging and your eyelids getting very heavy . . . let all the muscles around the back and sides of your head relax completely . . . now let your jaw muscles relax and allow your jaw to drop a little . . . don't deliberately open or close your mouth, just allow your jaw to float freely . . . allow the muscles of your cheeks and lips to go slack . . . now all the muscles of your face and head are giving up their hold and are getting very relaxed . . . now let the muscles of your neck relax, especially the ones running up into the back of your head . . . feel as if your head is gently floating on your neck . . . let your shoulders become heavy and sag downwards . . . notice any spots of pain or tension and just let your attention soften those spots . . . let the feeling of relaxation continue down your back to the base of your spine . . . let your awareness dwell on any aches you find and see if you can allow them to melt away. . . .

Tell the muscles of your chest and back that they do not need to be tensed up . . . they can relax safely . . . let your shoulder muscles go completely limp, and let your arms go heavy and hang loosely in their sockets . . . relax all the muscles of your forearms . . . hands . . . fingers . . . now let the feeling of relaxation spread down into the muscles of your stomach . . . let your stomach go . . . let it soften up so that you can breathe more deeply . . . now be aware of your breathing for a few moments . . . do not try to make it different . . . just notice the rise and fall of your chest and stomach as you breathe in and out . . . see if your breathing becomes a little slower and deeper just naturally, without any effort on your part . . .

Now feel the sensation of pressure in your buttocks, and the feel of your hands lying on your thighs or in your lap . . . allow any tension inside your stomach to unwind . . . now relax the large muscles of your thighs . . . let them go completely limp . . . feel all your muscles so relaxed they begin to feel like jelly . . . let the muscles of your calves relax . . . just soften all the muscles in your lower legs . . . let your ankles feel free and loose . . . now wiggle your toes very very gently, and let the muscles of your feet give up their stiffness . . . the feet are very important . . . allow any tension there to ease away. . . .

Now your whole body is really relaxed we are going to concentrate on certain areas to see if the relaxation will go even deeper still . . . pay close attention to the sensations in your arms . . . first the right . . . and then the left . . . be aware of the feelings of warmth and see if you can quite naturally let that warm feeling increase and spread . . . feel the warmth spreading into your fingers, melting away the last shreds of tension . . . let your arms feel very heavy . . . just watch the sensations of warmth and heaviness and very gently encourage them . . . now let those same feelings of warmth and heaviness spread through your legs . . . concentrate closely on the sensations in your legs, and let them become very, very heavy . . . very warm . . . arms and legs becoming so heavy and so warm . . . your entire body is profoundly relaxed, and you feel just a pleasant overall feeling of heaviness, warmth and peacefulness. . . .

Now turn your attention back to your breathing for a moment . . . without interfering in any way, simply observe the rise and fall . . . watch the slow rise and fall of your stomach as the air flows in and out, without any effort at all . . . don't try to hurry it up or slow it down . . . just observing with curiosity and respect . . . wait patiently for each breath to arrive . . . and watch its passing, like waves on the beach . . . notice any brief periods of quiet between the outbreath and the inbreath . . . now continue to observe this natural process of breathing, and begin to count the breaths as they occur . . . as the first one comes in, just watch it closely and hear yourself say in your mind 'One' . . . wait patiently for the next one, and as it arises say 'Two' . . . continue until you have counted to 'fifteen', trying quietly to keep your attention on the feeling of the breath, and not to let other thoughts distract you . . . if thoughts arise and carry you away, don't worry . . . just gently come back to the awareness of breathing when you realize you've drifted off. . . .

Now be aware of the peaceful feeling that permeates your body and mind . . . pay attention to it as if you were trying to remember it carefully . . . store the entire feeling of your whole body in your memory, so that later you can call it up and fall into the relaxed state quickly and easily . . . let your mind drift wherever it wants for a few moments . . . now you are thinking about coming back

to the world of activity . . . before you do, take some time to
wake up your body and bring it back to its normal state . . .
wiggle your fingers and toes . . . shrug your shoulders . . . move
your arms and legs a little bit . . . keep your eyes closed for just
a few moments longer as you do this . . . move your head around
a little bit, and make some faces so you can wake up the muscles
of your face . . . now take a nice deep breath and feel your body
fully alive and flowing with clear energy . . . in your own time,
slowly open your eyes, slowly stand up, and have a big stretch.'

Notes

CHAPTER 1

(1) Edmund Burke, quoted by Oxfam in their publicity.
(2) S. Milgram, *Obedience to Authority* (Harper & Row, New York, 1974)
(3) D. Woodhouse, E. Hall and A. Wooster, 'Taking control of stress in teaching.' *British Journal of Educational Psychology*, 1985, 55, pp. 119–123.
(4) Machiavelli, *The Prince* (Dent, London, 1958, pp. 30–31)
(5) D. Lessing, *The Sentimental Agents of the Volyen Empire* (Cape, London, 1983, p. 138)

CHAPTER 2

(1) D. Hargreaves, 'The occupational culture of teachers.' In P. Woods (Ed.); *Teacher Strategies* (Croom Helm, Beckenham, 1980, p. 126)
(2) D. Hargreaves, *The Challenge for the Comprehensive School* (Routledge & Kegan Paul, London, 1982, p. 198). Hereafter 'CCS'.
(3) J. Holt, *Instead of Education* (Penguin, Harmondsworth, 1977, p. 177)
(4) K. Armstrong, *The Guardian*, 17 November 1984.
(5) *Time Out*, 5 November 1986.
(6) D. Hargreaves, CCS, p. 193.
(7) E. Wragg, *The Sunday Times*, 20 October 1985.
(8) C. Lacey, *The Socialization of Teachers* (Methuen, London, 1977, pp. 139–142)

(9)   J. Ryder and L. Campbell, *Balancing Acts* (Routledge, London, 1988)

CHAPTER 3

(1)   J. Watts, 'The changing role of the classroom teacher.' In C. Harber, R. Meighan and B. Roberts (Eds), *Alternative Educational Futures* (Holt Education, London, 1984, p. 54). Hereafter 'AEF'.
(2)   For example, H. Selye, *Stress without Distress* (Hodder & Stoughton, London, 1975); F. Capra, *The Turning Point* (Wildwood House, London, 1982)
(3)   E. Berne, *Games People Play* (Penguin, Harmondsworth, 1968)

CHAPTER 4

(1)   Quoted in S. Hayward (Ed.), *Begin It Now* (In-Tune Books, Crows Nest, New South Wales, Australia, 1987)
(2)   J. Dunham, *Stress in Teaching* (Croom Helm, Beckenham, 1984)

CHAPTER 5

(1)   From the song 'How?' on the album *Imagine*. Lyrics published by Northern Songs, 1968.
(2)   T. McIntyre, 'The relationship between locus of control and teacher burnout.' *British Journal of Educational Psychology*, 1984, 54, pp. 235–238.
(3)   E. Wragg, 'Education for the 21st century.' (AEF, p. 11.)
(4)   G. Dennison, *The Lives of Children* (Penguin, Harmondsworth, 1972)
(5)   W. Erhard, *An Idea Whose Time Has Come* (The Hunger Project, San Francisco, 1981)

CHAPTER 6

(1)   Quoted in S. Hayward, *op. cit.*
(2)   D. Schon, *The Reflective Practitioner* (Basic Books, New York, 1983) and *Educating the Reflective Practitioner* (Jossey Bass, San Francisco, 1987)
(3)   J. Harding, *Communication and Support for Change in School Science Education* (PhD thesis, Chelsea College London, 1975)

CHAPTER 7

(1) M. Shipman, 'The political context of educational alternatives.' (AEF, p. 166.)
(2) S. Ball, *The Micropolitics of the School: Towards a Theory of School Organization* (Methuen, London, 1987)
(3) I. Menzies, *The Functioning of Social Systems as a Defence against Anxiety* (Tavistock Publications, London, 1970); reprinted in I. Menzies Lyth, *Containing Anxiety in Institutions* (Free Association Books, London, 1988)
(4) *Ibid.*, pp. 24–25.
(5) *Ibid.*, pp. 21–22.
(6) J. Smilansky, 'External and internal correlates of teachers' satisfaction and willingness to report stress.' *British Journal of Educational Psychology*, 1984, 54, pp. 84–92.
(7) 'Equal Opportunities: What's in it for Boys?' A conference report and resource pack published by ILEA/Schools Council, 1984. Discussed in C. Watkins, 'What can the pastoral curriculum do?' In C. McLaughlin, C. Lodge and C. Watkins (Eds), *Gender and Pastoral Care* (Blackwell, Oxford, 1989)
(8) See E. Berne, *op. cit.*
(9) The majority of the points here are derived from ideas presented in talks in 1986 by Peter Mitchell, formerly head of a London comprehensive and director of initial teacher training at the London Institute of Education; and by Patrick Bailey of the University of Leicester.

CHAPTER 8

(1) A. Bierce, *The Devil's Dictionary* (Dover, Toronto, 1958)
(2) This characterization is based on R. White, 'The end of schools as we know them,' *SET: Research Information for Teachers*, 1984, 1, pp. 6–11.
(3) Quoted in CCS, p. 50.
(4) D. Mackinnon, 'The nature and nurture of creative talent.' *American Psychologist*, 1962, 17, pp. 484–495.
(5) R. Hallman, 'Techniques of creative teaching.' *Journal of Creative Behavior*, 1967, 1, pp. 325–330.
(6) J. Holt, *What Do I Do Monday?* (Pitman, London, 1971, p. 55)
(7) These quotations appeared in the journal *Education Otherwise*, vols 53 (June, 1987) and 54 (August, 1987).
(8) J. Hemming, *The Betrayal of Youth: Why Secondary Schools Must Change* (Marion Boyars, London, 1981, p. 90)
(9) K. Reid, *Truancy and School Absenteeism* (Hodder & Stoughton, London, 1985)

(10)   CCS, pp. 63–64.
(11)   *Ibid.*, p. 17.
(12)   J. Krishnamurti, *Think on These Things* (Harper & Row: New York, 1964, p. 41)

CHAPTER 9

(1)   N. Postman and C. Weingartner, *Teaching as a Subversive Activity* (Penguin, Harmondsworth, 1973, p. 13)
(2)   C. Fitz-Gibbon, R. Hazelwood, B. Tymms and J. McCabe, 'Performance indicators and the TVEI pilot.' *Evaluation and Research in Education*, 2, pp. 1–12.
(3)   See G. Claxton, *Classroom Learning* (Open University Course EP 228, Unit P2. Open University Press, Milton Keynes, 1988)
(4)   C. Dweck, 'Motivational processes affecting learning.' *American Psychologist*, 1986, 41, pp. 1040–1048. (pp. 1040–1041)
(5)   *Ibid.*, pp. 1042–1044.
(6)   J. Holt, *What Do I Do Monday? op. cit.*, p. 35.
(7)   G. Watson, *Conceptual Change: An Ecosystemic Perspective on Children's Beliefs about Inheritance* (PhD thesis, University of Surrey, 1986)
(8)   J. Nisbet and J. Shucksmith, *Learning Strategies* (Routledge & Kegan Paul, London, 1986, p. vii)
(9)   *Ibid.*, p. 7.
(10)   R. Pirsig, *Zen and the Art of Motorcycle Maintenance* (Bodley Head, London, 1974)
(11)   J. Holt, *How Children Fail*, Revised Edition (Penguin, Harmondsworth, 1984)
(12)   M. Lepper and D. Greene, *The Hidden Costs of Reward: New Perspectives on the Psychology of Human Motivation* (Lawrence Erlbaum Associates, Hillsdale NJ, 1978)
(13)   C. Dweck, *op. cit.*, p. 1045.
(14)   J. Nisbet and J. Shucksmith, *op. cit.*, p. 53.
(15)   R. White, *op. cit.*, p. 7.
(16)   'The shape of school timetables to come.' *The Independent*, 25 June 1987.
(17)   A. Einstein, *Ideas and Opinions* (Souvenir Press, London, 1973, p. 57)

Name Index

Adamson, C. 157
Anderson, L. 157
Armstrong, K. 32, 33
Attenborough, R. 157

Baker, K. 160
Ball, S. 132
Beckett, T. 157
Berne, E. 63
Bierce, A. 154
Bratby, J. 161
Burke, E. 1, 4

Dennison, G. 111
Dunham, J. 75, 203
Dweck, C. 177–9, 186, 190

Eavis, P. 160
Eccles, Lord 157
Edwardes, M. 157
Erhard, W. 114

Finniston, M. 157

Geldof, B. 11

Hall, P. 157
Harding, J. 130
Hargreaves, D. 16, 30, 168–9
Hart, D. 160
Hemingway, E. 5
Hemming, J. 166
Hepburn, K. 116
Hitler, A. 105

Holt, J. 31, 144, 163, 180, 185, 187
Huxley, A. 183

Isaacs, J. 157

Jacklin, T. 138
Jones, J. 27, 38, 65, 161

Kinnock, N. 157
Krishnamurti, J. 173

Lacey, C. 37
Lennon, J. 91
Lessing, D. 13
Loyola, I. 105

MacGregor, I. 157
Machiavelli, N. 10
Mann, P. 21
Maxwell Davies, P. 155
Menzies, I. 133, 135
Miller, J. 155

Nisbet, J. 185–7, 191

Pirsig, R. 186
Postman, N. 175

Robbins, A. 72

Shipman, M. 131
Shucksmith, J. 185–7, 191
Stenhouse, L. 151

Toffler, A. 108
Trelford, D. 157

Watts, J. 42

Weingartner, C. 175
Wragg, E. 108

Young, K. 158

Subject Index

ability 178–81, 192
acting 33
active tutorial work 40, 53
activists 40
affirmations 84, 190
agenda-setting 151
alarm calls 83, 189
alcoholism 79
A levels 161
anxiety 48, 134
appreciation 32
assertiveness training 146

Baker days 141

change agents 128, 131, 153
City Technology Colleges 22
classroom practice 8, 118
collaborative learning 184
communication 80–2, 154
conditions of service 18, 23, 89
counselling 82
CPVE 155
creativity 161
cynicism 4, 10–11, 38, 136–7

defensiveness 61–8
deprofessionalization 20
DES 158
dignity 169
double bind 46

Education for Capability 157
Education Network 14

Education Reform Act 7, 15, 17, 19,
    21–2, 146, 197
emotional resilience 180, 184, 189–90
empathy 190
equal opportunities 30

frustration 25, 27, 54, 103

GCSE 6, 18, 20, 23, 89, 155, 158–61,
    165–6
gestures 111, 115, 132
good learning 12, 175–88
governors 148, 156
gumption traps 186

headteachers 74, 146–50
HMI 10, 160

idealism 9, 30, 43, 100, 103–8
imagination 162, 183
implicit theories 36, 118–9, 139, 178,
    191
injunctions 57–61, 67, 70, 82–4, 89, 95,
    108, 112, 117, 126, 178–9, 190
in-service courses 67, 127, 130, 200
insight 95, 108, 119
intermediate education 198–200
intuition 162, 183
isolation 34, 67

learning 86–7
learning strategies 182, 184–5, 192
Local Education Authorities 14, 22–3,
    148, 156

locus of control 99, 181

management 151–2
Manifesto for Change 155, 159, 175
mastery-mode 177–80, 186, 190, 193
meditation 75
mental models 185
mentors 188–95, 200
micropolitics 132, 144–5
misgivings 123–7
modelling 192
monitoring 186–7

National Curriculum 1, 6, 18, 20–2, 159
nervous breakdown 63, 66
new teachers 36–7
noise 47
Nuffield science 3

opting out 6, 20, 22

peer support groups 82, 139–40
personal and social education 6, 24, 30, 40, 155, 162
personal philosophies 40, 52, 57, 99, 121, 154
professional development 26
profiling 167
psychologizing 133
psychosomatics 49, 69

rationalization 62
records of achievement 6, 24, 155, 167
reflection 108, 119, 123, 154
relaxation exercises 75, 190, 203–6
resistance to change 135
resources 130

external 53
personal 52
Royal Society of Arts 157

school ethos 73, 136–7
school policy 8, 147, 151–2
self-awareness 8, 187
self-esteem 58–61, 82, 112–4, 142, 172
self-image 96, 112–4, 126, 181
special educational needs 24, 53
stages of change 120–3
stances 170
status 38
stress 3, 5, 42–71, 141–2, 148, 165, 172, 189
 fuzzy stress 49, 101
 hard stress 49, 101
stressed institutions 131–8
student teachers 4–5, 14, 32, 35–6, 119, 145, 172
suicide 166
support 25, 138, 146
survival-mode 177–80, 186, 190, 193

teacher appraisal 6, 23, 25
teaching unions 7, 23, 40–1, 87
testing 6, 20–1, 89
transactional analysis 150
truancy 166
trust 191
TVEI 155, 160, 176

values 19, 46, 98–102, 133, 139
 base 98–102, 125, 180, 190
 face 98–102, 109, 125, 190
victim-blaming 64
vision 95, 100, 104, 107, 133, 152, 195
vocationalism 19